P9-BZV-679

HEROIC LIVES

BOOKS BY RAFAEL SABATINI

D
106
528

HEROIC LIVES

RICHARD I : SAINT FRANCIS OF ASSISI
JOAN OF ARC : SIR WALTER RALEGH
LORD NELSON : FLORENCE NIGHTINGALE

BY

RAFAEL SABATINI

BOSTON AND NEW YORK
HOUGHTON MIFFLIN COMPANY
1934

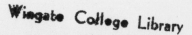
Wingate College Library

COPYRIGHT, 1934, BY RAFAEL SABATINI

ALL RIGHTS RESERVED INCLUDING THE RIGHT TO REPRODUCE
THIS BOOK OR PARTS THEREOF IN ANY FORM

PRINTED IN THE U.S.A.

CONTENTS

31394

HEROIC LIVES

I

LIONHEART

RICHARD THE FIRST

HEROIC LIVES

I

LIONHEART

INTO the chapel of the Abbey of Fontevrault, on a summer day of the year 1189, came a broad-shouldered young giant of two-and-thirty, in a long samite tunic worn over his chain mail and gripped to his loins by a long-tongued belt. He carried himself with a loose-limbed grace that advertised his unusual vigour. His small head lent him the appearance of a height beyond the six-feet-two that he actually measured. His features, with finely pencilled eyebrows and finely chiselled nose, were so delicate as to seem almost feminine. The short beard at his chin was red-gold, like his hair.

By a gesture arresting his attendants at the threshold, he went forward alone to the transept where a bier was flanked by burning tapers and guarded by four black-robed canons of the order of Saint Augustine.

Beside the bier he stood for a moment, gloomily considering the broad, sturdy body of his father supine there in the royal robes in which it had been arrayed. Presently he begged one of the canons to remove the cloth that covered the dead face. At sight of it, he is said to have shuddered. Then he sank to his knees, and so remained a little while, in prayer, be it for the repose of his father's soul, be it for forgiveness for the part he may have had in bringing that active, vigorous life to its sorrowful close. Of how great in the public estimation may have been this part is seen in the contemporary story that blood flowed from the dead king's nostrils from the moment of Richard's entering the chapel until he had taken his departure. It was a story born of the old northern superstition that a corpse will bleed in the presence of the murderer, and it was applied to him so as to condemn by implication his conduct.

Actually, however, Richard Cœur-de-Lion was no more guilty than his brothers. If, in addition to the King's bad health and the fever that burned him out, there was an immediate cause of death in the loss of the will to live resulting from a broken heart, it was John, the best-beloved of the King's sons who, rather than Richard, had provided this.

*   *   *   *

The numerous issue of that great prince, Henry Plante Geneste, Henry Curt Mantel, who ruled in England as Henry II, included four legitimate sons any one of whom might fittingly have borne the name of Absalom, just as Henry himself, from his fond paternal indulgence in the face of every provocation, might have borne the name of David.

It was this fondness, together with his mistrust of testamentary dispositions, which induced Henry, whilst still a young man in the middle thirties, and at a time when his sons, saving Henry, the eldest, were not yet in their teens, to divide amongst them his dominions. To Young Henry went the Duchy of Normandy, the Counties of Anjou and Maine and the crown of England; to Geoffrey, the second, went Brittany: whilst Richard, who was his mother's favourite, was invested with the dominions of Aquitaine and Poitou, which she had brought to the English crown. For John, the youngest and his father's predilect child—who, being left out of this distribution, came to be known as John Lackland—Henry had visions of establishing an Irish kingdom.

Thus was sown the seed which, fertilized by adventitious circumstances, was to produce the turbulence that distinguished his family.

It had been the King's intention to grant with the titles no more than the shadow of those dominions to his children. The substance he would retain for himself. As has been said, it was not in his views that he should take off his clothes until it was time for him to go to bed. The children came to think differently.

The disorders began when Young Henry was eighteen. He had been married, since the age of five, to Margaret, the daughter of Louis VII of France; and his crafty, treacherous father-in-law, with all to gain from setting son against father, so played upon his vanity and his ambition as to lead him to take up arms to enforce a demand for independence, be it in England, be it in Normandy.

Richard, who was sixteen years of age at the time, was brought into the quarrel by his mother, Eleanor of Aquitaine. She would employ him as an instrument to avenge the bitter grievance resulting in her from his father's many and even scandalous marital infidelities. The deep attachment which existed between mother and son, of which the future was to afford so many instances, permits us to suppose that it supplied now the dominant factor in Richard's share in this unfilial rebellion.

Geoffrey, too, was similarly prevailed upon to join hands with his brothers, and not until King Henry had defeated them in the field and placed their mother under arrest did they make submission to him, casting themselves at his feet. His paternal leniency forgave too readily, only to be abused.

Tumults between the brothers, or between the sons and the father, continue down to Young Henry's death of a fever in 1183. In an access of death-bed remorse, he had himself dragged from his couch and laid upon a bed of ashes on the floor, and in this posture of penitence he expired. He was only twenty-eight at the time, but the Dean of Saint Paul's opined that he had lived quite long enough.

By his death the turbulence of that family was diminished only to the extent proportionate with the removal of one of its refractory members. It was diminished further, three years later, by the death of Geoffrey, who, sly and subtle, has been named "the son of iniquity." He passed away mourned by none save the father whose life he had persistently troubled. If quarrels broke out again after that, Henry himself is not to be acquitted of the blame.

Alais, another daughter of Louis VII and sister of Philip Augustus, who now reigned in France, had long been contracted in marriage to Richard, and, as was usual in the circumstances, lived during the betrothal under the tutelage of Henry. This betrothal was protracted by Henry's reluctance to part with Alais, who had succeeded Rosamund Clifford—Fair Rosamund—in his affections. To this, since his heart was not engaged, Richard might shrug his broad shoulders, whilst taking the resolve that so far as he was concerned the marriage contract should remain unfulfilled. But when he was warned by Philip of France that Henry was proposing to promote the fortunes of his youngest and favourite son John at the expense of Richard's rights, by marrying him to Alais and placing him in possession of all the continental dominions save only Normandy, Richard revolted.

He was pacified by confirmation in his Duchy of Aquitaine, and to the truce that followed the news of the fall of Jerusalem may have contributed.

Aghast at the spectacle of the Holy Sepulchre and the True Cross in the hands of the Infidel, the princes of Christendom paused in their aggression towards one another, so as to unite in their duty to the Faith. Yet, after both Henry of England and Philip of France had taken the cross, war flamed out again between them, and Richard, mistrustful ever of his father's intentions concerning John, was found on the side of Philip.

The health of the great Henry, now in his fifty-sixth year, was giving way. In this, the final campaign of a life that had been spent campaigning, he was to taste at last the bitterness of defeat; and at Colombières he was constrained to accept the terms imposed by Philip. These included the surrender of Alais, so that she might marry Richard on his return from the Crusade to which he was now pledged; the recognition of Richard as King Henry's heir; and the remittance of all claim to allegiance from those of his subjects who had taken part with Richard in this quarrel.

Having bestowed upon his son the kiss of peace, and a curse at the same time, Henry was borne away to Chinon in a raging fever and crying shame on himself for a beaten king. With him went his loyal and affectionate natural son Geoffrey, sometime Bishop of Lincoln, who filled now the office of chancellor to his father.

At Chinon, on his bed of sickness, Henry called for the list of Richard's partisans, so that he might inform himself of the names of those whose allegiance he was pledged to remit. At the head of it stood the name of John, the cherished son for whose sake he had embroiled himself and suffered this defeat.

It is said that the great heart broke.

He turned, groaning, on his couch. "Now let all things go as they will," he is reported to have cried. "I care no more for myself, nor for anything in the world."

On the morrow he died.

* * * *

Whether in the spirit of remorse which had brought him to his knees beside his father's bier, or from unusual worldly wisdom, Richard at once received into favour those who had stood loyally by Henry, whilst with those who deserting the late King had come to range themselves under his own rebellious banner, he dealt so harshly as in some instances to strip them of their possessions.

He made, however, an exception in favour of his brother John. Possibly he may have chosen to perceive for John's unfilial conduct a justification akin to that which he took for himself, since to regard his brother's guilt lightly may have helped him to discount his own. So John was confirmed in the County of Mortain which he had received from his father and in the large estates which Henry had granted him in England. Indeed, Richard was to extend them after his coronation, by assigning to him all crown rights in Dorset, Somerset, Devon, and Cornwall, and creating him Earl of Gloucester. But mistrusting the loyalty he was so liberally engaging, Richard was careful to give him no share in the government or control of any stronghold.

It was to his devoted and spirited mother that this devoted son confided the care of his English interests. One of his first acts upon being installed at Rouen as Duke of Normandy, within a fortnight of his father's death, was the deliverance of Queen Eleanor from her duress at Winchester, thus ending a confinement which had lasted for sixteen years, and appointing her regent until he should come himself to take the reins of government.

He lost no time in doing this. No sooner was he installed as Duke of Normandy than he sought King Philip, to do homage to him as his suzerain for his French dominions. At this meeting these two princes who had taken the cross entered into a mutual engagement to set out together for the Holy Land in the following Lent.

We are told that Philip now advanced an old demand for the surrender of Gisors in the Norman Vexin. Decision was postponed. If, as is asserted, Richard compromised by giving an undertaking to marry the unfortunate Alais, he can hardly have done so in good faith. Not only were there obstacles of common decency to such a marriage, but Richard, romantic of disposition and a law unto himself, was not in such a matter to be ruled by the political considerations that normally obtain for princes. At the Court of Navarre, a year or so ago, when he was still Count of Poitiers, he had met and had been attracted by the Princess Berengaria, and he had decided to make her his wife, although it was a marriage that could bring him no political or territorial advantages.

A fortnight after his understanding with Philip, he embarked at Barfleur, landing at Portsmouth on the 13th August, and thence making a leisurely royal progress by way of Winchester, the old capital, through Salisbury and Marlborough, to London.

At Marlborough he paused for John's marriage, on the 29th August, to Isabel of Gloucester, who inherited from her father the estates of that great earldom of which the honour was now vested in John.

On Sunday the 3rd September, the tall young Duke of Normandy, with all the pomp and circumstance as dear to him as they had been odious to his father, came, under a silken canopy borne on lances by four Barons of the Cinque Ports, to Westminster Abbey to be hallowed and crowned.

He had been born at Oxford and suckled by an English nurse. Upon nothing more could he base a claim to be considered English. Born of an Angevin father and a Poitevin mother, he had not in his veins a single drop of English blood, and he could not speak a word of English. Nevertheless, he was joyously acclaimed as he passed to assume the crown of England.

For this there was no reason beyond such as might be supplied by the attractiveness of the man's personality. That he was viewed by his contemporaries in a heroic light is sufficiently attested by the sobriquet bestowed upon him. Only a popular idol could come to be known as Cœur-de-Lion. And the appellation carries in itself the explanation of this idolatry. He owed it to the prowess, the skill in arms, the dauntless courage that went so well with his stalwart good looks and long-limbed grace.

He was possessed in short of all the external attributes of a hero of romance, and the romantic elements in his history are to emphasize it. He is, emphatically, a hero in the Homeric sense. But for a hero according to the more modern view, there is something lacking; for he was concerned to serve no great ideal purely for its own sake. The nearest he comes to this is in taking up arms for the deliverance of the Holy Sepulchre. He pursued this saintly mission with a devotion that was unstinting, yet vitiated, from the point of view of pure heroism, by the equally present incentive of personal glory.

* * * *

The coronation-banquet followed in Westminster Hall; and whilst it was proceeding, the events of that great day were being closed by a massacre.

Under Henry II the Jews had prospered in England. Theirs was a prosperity which thriftless Christians have always made possible to the inherent thrift of that race. Largely they had flourished by money-lending, which brought in its train an odium ready to perceive in their religious persuasion a pretext for expression. Moreover, the crusading movement now afoot and supplying the chief topic of the day had let loose the evil spirit of religious persecution.

It was an unfortunate thing for the Jewish community that, to mark its appreciation of the favour enjoyed under Henry and in the hope of earning the like favour from his son, a deputation should have waited that day upon the new King at Westminster Hall with a handsome offering.

The ardent young Crusader had given orders that no Jew should be admitted either to the Abbey or the Hall. When the guards, on the strength of this order, would have denied admission to the deputation, its misguided members, persuaded that the gifts with which they were laden would earn condonation of the transgression, attempted to insist. Thereupon they were cast out with a violence that gave rise to the rumour that the King had abandoned the Jews to pillage. There followed an inhuman orgy of blood and fire which the Justiciar Glanville was impotent to stay, and Richard none too active in avenging.

* * * *

A bare four months was the extent of Richard's sojourn in England, and most of the time was employed in filling his military chest against the heavy expenses of the Crusade towards which his face was set.

Queen Eleanor, imperious and full of energy for all her sixty-seven years, had, immediately upon her deliverance, taken possession on her son's behalf of the royal treasure at Winchester. Of this and of other similar hoards, Richard, on his arrival, had caused inventories to be made. He provided further by so unrestricted a sale of honours, of offices, of crown rights and of dispensations from crusading vows, that they were justified who held that he regarded his English kingdom merely as a source of supplies.

Of those he left behind to govern in his absence, the chief were the lordly Hugh de Puiset, Bishop of Durham, who had purchased from Richard the Earldom of Northumberland, and the frail-bodied but vigorous-minded William Longchamp, who from a clerk in Richard's chancery had now been raised to the chancellorship, with the Bishopric of Ely. Between them these two shared the chief justiciarship, Puiset north of the Humber, Longchamp south of it, with his headquarters in the Tower of London.

Having made his dispositions by mid-December, Richard again crossed the Channel, and went to spend Christmas at Bures and to complete his preparations for the expedition to the Holy Land.

Already the departure of the crusading hosts had been long delayed by the quarrel between Henry and Philip. Now, at last, that England and France could proceed in amity to the fulfilment of their pledge, Germany, which had been waiting to act in concert with them, was also ready to face the long overland march to Asia. Word came that, with a following of a hundred and fifty thousand

men, Frederick Barbarossa had set out from Ratisbonne.
But the death of Isabel of Hainault, King Philip's Queen,
now occasioned a further postponement; and it was not
until the end of the following June that Richard took up at
Tours the pilgrim's scrip and staff that were the emblems
of his holy mission. A week later he was at Vézelai to meet
the brilliant French army under Philip, who had brought
the Oriflamme from Saint Denis. Here, in their glittering
encampment, the two kings renewed their pledges of alliance, to support each other in all undertakings, and equally
to share in all conquests and spoils of war.

Thence they marched to Lyons, and there temporarily
parted, Philip to cross the Alps to Genoa, Richard, at the
head of an army of eight thousand men, to proceed down
the Valley of the Rhone to Marseilles, where his fleet of a
hundred ships should have been waiting to embark his
troops. It had not arrived, however; and after some days
of waiting, Richard chartered what vessels were available,
some twenty galleys and half that number of large sailing
barges known as busses.

A week of pleasant, leisurely sailing in the August
weather brought him to Genoa and Philip. Then he continued down the Italian coast, sometimes by land, sometimes by water, at the rate of a score of miles a day. After
a long pause at Naples, he reached at last La Bagnara, on
the Straits of Messina, on the 22nd September. Here he
found his fleet awaiting him, and so he was able to make
his entrance into Messina with all the pomp and pageantry
in which his boyish heart delighted. Conspicuous in his
rich attire, on the prow of the foremost of his galleys, all
of which were gay with banners and decked along their
bulwarks with the shields of his knights, he sailed, to the
flourish of trumpets and the rolling of drums, into the

Wingate College Library

Sicilian harbour where Philip was already awaiting him,
and where he was received by the people with the
enthusiasm and homage which so brave a show commanded.

* * * *

The German Crusaders meanwhile, having marched
through the Greek Empire and Asia Minor, defeating the
Sultan of Iconium, had lost their leader in the early days
of June. Frederick Barbarossa had perished either by
drowning in the river Selef, or as a consequence of a chill
contracted in fording it. The remains of his army, under
the command of his son the Duke of Suabia, used up by
that long march, waited at Acre with the Crusaders of other
nations for the arrival of their French and English brethren. Without these it would be impossible to try conclu-
sions with the able, intrepid commander of the Saracens,
Salah-ed-Din, known to the Franks as Saladin. So they sat
down before the walls of Acre, which commanded the road
to Jerusalem and was the key to the Holy Land, and there,
whilst they waited, want, disease, and vice rapidly reduced
their numbers and their spirits. If they were not fruitlessly
to leave their bones in Palestine, the succour of their allies
must not long be delayed.

But delayed it was. In Sicily Richard found work to de-
tain him.

His sister Joan had married William II of Sicily, and had
been left a widow by him in the previous year. The crown
devolved upon King William's aunt, Constance, who was
married to Barbarossa's son Henry—now Henry VI of Germany. But Sicily, preferring a native prince, had crowned
Tancred of Lecce, an illegitimate sprig of the royal tree,

and because Joan upheld the German claim against him, Tancred had cast her into prison.

In the family interest, Richard felt himself called upon to interfere. He demanded, reasonably enough, the immediate deliverance of his sister, together with the return of her dower and personal property. Tancred complied promptly with the first part of the request. Since the second part was ignored, Richard proceeded to provide for his sister in the high-handed manner that was characteristic of him. He crossed over to the Sicilian mainland dominions, took possession there of the Castle of La Bagnara, and installed his sister in it. On his way back he occupied an island in the straits, expelled the monks from a convent there, and appropriated it as a storehouse for his troops.

These were not actions the Sicilians could condone. Already the strangers were far from popular in Messina. As if they conceived that, because they were pledged to a holy war, they had a heavy credit account of righteousness, against which they could afford to set a deal of license, the misconduct of the Crusaders everywhere was notoriously gross. In Messina the restraint imposed by Richard's edicts may have kept disorder within some bounds. But even so there was enough of it, and Richard's own action now supplied what might still be wanting to render exasperation active.

The King occupied a villa among the vineyards outside the walls of the city, with his army encamped about him in that suburb. Riding into the town to quell a disturbance, he found himself defied by a hostile mob, derided, and greeted with jeers on the subject of the tail which a southern belief attributed to every Englishman. The threatening aspect of the townsfolk was enough for Richard's never patient temper. He rode back to his quarters, to arm, whilst his trumpets were sounding the assembly, and after that the assault.

The gates of Messina were closed in haste, and the walls manned by their defenders. But Richard had been investing cities and carrying them by storm since the age of sixteen, and no time was wasted here. Whilst his main division made a direct frontal attack, he himself led a small party up to the heights to the west of the city, forced a postern, and smashed through to admit his army.

Messina was treated like any other city carried by assault. It was delivered over to all the horrors of a sack by the English Crusaders, and Richard, as a conqueror, hoisted his banners on the walls.

This last action moved the resentment of King Philip. During the affray he had stood neutral in the royal palace, where he had taken up his abode upon arrival. But now that the business was over, he remembered the terms of his treaty of Vézelai with Richard, under which he was entitled to share in all conquests and all spoils of war.

Discussions, protracted and none too cordial, ensued between the two kings, at the end of which Richard consented that the lilies of France should float beside the English lions, and that the city should be consigned to the care of the Hospitallers and Templars. He insisted, however, upon retaining hostages until he should have reached a settlement of the matter with Tancred.

Negotiations with the King of Sicily followed at once, destined to be far-reaching in their consequences, and singularly to shape the future destinies of Richard.

Tancred, perceiving what profit to his precariously held kingship he might derive from making a friend of the King of England, was so conciliatory in the conduct of these negotiations that they resulted in an alliance, consolidated by the betrothal of Tancred's daughter to Richard's nephew, Arthur of Brittany. Tancred accomplished this by the payment down of the imposing sums of twenty thousand gold ounces as a dowry for his daughter, and a further twenty thousand as a contribution to Richard's military chest.

* * * *

At the end of September, by when they might have sailed, the Crusaders accounted the season too far advanced. And so, whilst their German, Flemish, Danish, Genoese, and Pisan brethren were rotting before Acre with Guy de Lusignan, the King of Jerusalem, the English and the French settled down to winter in the pleasant climate of Sicily, possibly without suspicion of the extent of the plight in which their brother Crusaders found themselves.

Richard moved from his suburban villa and the encampment among the vineyards to a wooden castle which he ordered to be erected on the heights above Messina. There, entertaining not only his own knights, but the French King and his following with the prodigal splendour that was ever characteristic of him, the Christmas season was spent in gaiety, with tourneys, banquets, and spectacles of every description, Richard himself almost as pre-eminent among the troubadours as he was irresistible in the tiltyard.

Into this glittering scene of luxury came in February Queen Eleanor, indefatigable for all her seventy years, bringing with her that Princess Berengaria of Navarre whom Richard had chosen for his wife.

It was said of Berengaria by some that her charm lay in her character. *"Prudentior quam pulchrior,"* writes one;

whilst by others she is described as both beautiful and good: *"famosae pulchritudinis et prudentiae."*

Be this as it may, she was the woman of Richard's choice, and so definitely, that, again in the true romantic spirit, he did not even trouble to ask a dowry with his bride.

A few days only did the Queen-Mother remain in Sicily. Leaving Berengaria in the care of Richard's sister, the widowed Joan, until the nuptials should take place when Lent was out, Queen Eleanor set out for Touraine, charged by her son with matters touching the government of England. For part of her mission had been to bring him word of disturbances there between Longchamp and de Puiset on the one hand, and on the other between Longchamp and the crafty, treacherous John, whose hopes that his brother would never return from the Holy Land had grown into a conviction that made him impatient to wield the sovereign power. Queen Eleanor was to charge Walter of Coutances, the Archbishop of Rouen, and William Marshall, Earl of Pembroke, to take such order as might be necessary between the disputants.

Meanwhile, the relations between the Kings of England and France, which had lost something of their earlier cordiality by the dispute over the spoils of Messina, had been further seriously strained by the approach of Berengaria. In Philip's eyes this amounted on the part of Richard to a discarding of the mask he had worn in the matter of his betrothal to Alais. The scene between them will have been a stormy one; for the accusation of duplicity from Philip was met by Richard with scorn of the notion that he should seriously contemplate taking to wife a woman whom he was now prepared to prove, he said, had been his father's mistress.

A compromise was ultimately reached in the payment

by Richard of ten thousand silver marks for release from his contract.

The semblance of amity being thus restored, and as they were now in the springtime, Philip summoned Richard to the fulfilment of their mission in the Holy Land. But Richard was not yet ready. So Philip set out alone, ahead of him, on the 30th March, to arrive a fortnight later before Saint Jean d'Acre, and to be received there by the weary Crusaders engaged in the siege "with supreme joy, as if he were an angel come down from Heaven."

On Thursday of Holy Week, ten days after Philip's departure, Richard followed from Messina, his army conveyed in an imposing fleet of a hundred and fifty ships and fifty galleys, one of which, sumptuously furnished, was assigned to his sister and his future bride.

When two days out, they were scattered by a gale; and upon putting into Crete, on the 17th April, over a score of vessels were missing, among which was the one carrying Joan and Berengaria.

Not until the 6th May were Richard's anxieties allayed, when he came up with them in the harbour of Limasol on the island of Cyprus. His arrival was timely. There had been trouble with the Cypriots. In the storm, two vessels of the fleet had been wrecked on the island, and the survivors had been maltreated and cast into prison. A landing-party which had gone ashore to rescue them had brought them off by force of arms, after which the Crusaders had not dared to leave their ships.

For this outrage Richard now sent a demand for satisfaction to Isaac Comnenus, a Greek of Austrian kinship who called himself Emperor of Cyprus. The Emperor answered him with defiance and with the display of a force which he accounted sufficient to support it.

He did not know the man with whom he had to deal, or suspect how welcome at all times was battle to him.

Richard's trumpets awoke the echoes in the Cyprian caves. Under cover of a cloud of arrows, the Lionheart led a force ashore that swept the Emperor's army out of Limasol. This done, he took the town into his possession and comfortably established himself there with his following. Subsequently landing his horses, he completed the conquest by pursuing the no longer defiant Emperor into his capital of Nicosia.

But the end was not yet. Before it was reached, Isaac Comnenus and his Cypriots were to drain to the dregs the bitter cup that had been filled by their inhospitality to the shipwrecked Crusaders.

There was, however, a lull for them whilst Richard returned to his quarters in Limasol, and there, Lent being over, gave his mind to his nuptials with the gentle Berengaria. The royal marriage was celebrated with great pomp on the 12th May by the Archbishop of Bordeaux, after which they gave themselves up for a season to the festivities which such an occasion demanded.

These gaieties were brought to an end by the arrival in Cyprus of Guy de Lusignan, accompanied by his fire-eating brother Geoffrey, his brother-in-law Henfrid of Toron, the Prince of Antioch, the Count of Tripoli, and some other Syrian lords. They sought Richard with an appeal not of Christian against Infidel, but of Christian against Christian.

Guy de Lusignan had held the crown of Jerusalem by right of his wife Sybilla, the daughter of King Amaury. Upon her death at Acre in the previous October, the question had arisen whether the right to the crown should continue, nevertheless, vested in Guy, or whether it should pass to King Amaury's younger daughter Isabella, and so to her husband, Henfrid of Toron. But whilst the question was being considered, the ambitious, powerful, and unscrupulous Conrad, Marquis of Montferrat, perceived how to resolve it in his own favour. He had prevailed upon Isabella iniquitously to divorce Henfrid, and then to take him to husband. Thus Conrad had established a strong claim to the crown, and he possessed a powerful following to support him. This following had been enormously strengthened by the coming of Philip of France who had been induced to declare for him.

Richard graciously received these suppliants, cordially promised his support to Guy, and at once made ready to depart.

It occurred to him now, or it may have been suggested to him by these great lords of Palestine, that Cyprus, within a day's sail of Syria, would constitute a valuable outpost. Therefore, he set about giving the occupation into which he had been provoked the character of a permanent conquest, and he summoned Comnenus to a conference at Limasol.

The Grand Master of the Hospital, possibly moved by compassion for the unfortunate Emperor, counselled him to make humble submission lest worse should befall him.

On a mettlesome Spanish palfrey, with a richly inlaid and gilded saddle, Richard rode in splendour to the conference. He wore, we are told, a tunic of rose-coloured samite under a mantle spangled with silver crescents, a gold-embroidered scarlet cap on his red-gold head.

As imposing as he was urbane, he bent the reluctant Comnenus to his will. The Emperor of Cyprus did homage to him, agreed to pay an indemnity of thirty-five hundred silver marks, and to leave all his strongholds in the King's

hands as security for the fulfilment of the treaty. Upon that
the kiss of peace was exchanged.

But that night Comnenus slipped away, whereupon
Richard, assuming treachery, took up arms again, to hunt
him and to reduce the fortresses of the island. Not until
King Richard had occupied Nicosia and taken possession
of Comnenus' daughter, whom he found there, did the
Emperor acknowledge defeat and come forth, from the
monastery in which he had fortified himself, to make surrender. He cast himself upon Richard's mercy, with the
sole condition that he should not be put into irons. This
condition Richard granted, and he strictly kept his word
by loading the prisoner with chains that were made of
silver. In these Isaac Comnenus departed from Cyprus, to
end his days in a Syrian fortress, whilst his daughter went
in the care of Joan and Berengaria to Acre.

*   *   *   *

Cyprus having suffered an exhaustive pillage, and being
left in the charge of two of the King's officers, with an ade-
quate garrison, the fleet put to sea once more, and stood
away for the coast of Syria in the early days of June. Off
Beirut it came up with a large three-masted Turkish ship
on her way to Acre with reinforcements and munitions,
which was captured and sunk.

On the 8th June 1191—eighteen months after setting
out from England—Richard landed at last at Acre, to be
received with delirious enthusiasm by the weary besiegers,
who had been only partially relieved by the arrival, three
months earlier, of Philip of France. Not only was there the
considerable force that accompanied Richard to awaken
this enthusiasm; there was the renown of the leader himself, the Lionheart, Bellona's Bridegroom, the chivalrous

war-lord, whose prowess and whose deeds of arms were being sung by troubadours. At his coming weary hearts revived and confidence of victory was born anew.

That night the great Saladin, from his encampment on the heights of Mount Carmel, whence in his turn he had besieged the besiegers, beheld the bonfires in the Christian lines, lighted to celebrate the arrival of the Lionheart.

It was an arrival that certainly threatened to make matters serious for the defenders of Acre. For at once Richard entered into a vigorous co-operation with Philip to press the siege, and a persistent bombardment from mangonels and other petrarias prepared the way for the final assault.

Meanwhile, however, the rift between the two kings was steadily widening. The different sides they had taken in the matter of the kingship of Jerusalem might well result in placing them in opposite camps once the Holy City should be reconquered from the Saracen. And now, again, as in the case of Messina, Philip was claiming, on the strength of the treaty of Vézelai, the half of the fruits of the conquest of Cyprus. There was never a man more prodigally generous than Richard. But he who, whilst himself standing inactive, demands under the terms of a partnership the half of the proceeds of his partner's sole activities is not to be suffered equably for long.

These differences notwithstanding, the operations against Acre were vigorously pursued, and under the pressure of them, the garrison being worn out by two years of resistance, the Emirs Karakush and Mashtoub came finally to ask for terms of surrender.

On the 12th July, after protracted negotiations, the Moslems capitulated, agreeing to the surrender of the True Cross and of fifteen hundred prisoners and to the payment of two hundred thousand gold besants, the garrison, some twenty-five hundred strong, to be held as hostages for the fulfilment of these terms.

The Crusaders proceeded to occupy the city, whilst Saladin forced to acquiesce, remained observing them from his encampment on the eastern heights.

*   *   *   *

Besides the growing hostility of Philip of France, Richard already had to reckon with that of Duke Leopold of Austria, a kinsman of Isaac of Cyprus. To the provocation supplied by his Cyprian adventure he added now by ordering the flag to be pulled down which Leopold had hoisted above his quarters in Acre, deaf to the Duke's protests and indifferent to his indignation.

There were other, more important troubles demanding attention. The rival kings of Jerusalem were now pressing their claims, and they were to be quieted, at last, only by a compromise forced upon Conrad, under which Guy de Lusignan was to retain the crown for life, whereafter it should pass to the Marquis and Isabella and their issue.

No sooner was this settled than Philip, urging grounds of health, the conviction that the ultimate success of the Crusade was now impossible, and affairs of his own which were calling him back to France, announced the intention of returning home. This led to fresh trouble with the outspoken Richard, who reproached him with what he accounted a desertion. Then contemptuously bidding him go since he could not keep away from Paris, Richard bound him by a public oath to commit no breach of the peace against him in his absence.

But, although Philip departed, some ten thousand of his followers, the bulk of his forces, elected to remain, under the command of the Duke of Burgundy and Count Henry of Champagne.

On the 12th August, the time having come for fulfilment by the Saracens of the terms of surrender, the Christian envoys waited upon Saladin. The chivalrous and courtly Saracen leader received them graciously, and in joy mingled with awe they were permitted to behold the True Cross, mounted in gold and set with jewels. The money, they were informed, was in readiness. Saladin required, however, the immediate surrender of all the Saracen captives, against hostages for the payment of the indemnity; or, alternatively, that the Christians should give hostages for that ultimate liberation when the indemnity should be paid.

Richard would accept neither alternative; and having notified Saladin of this, he summoned him to a conference, whilst at the same time preparing to reopen hostilities.

Accounts of the dreadful thing that ensued are confused and contradictory.

Saladin did not answer the summons in person. Instead, he sent his envoys to inform the King that he was unable to carry out the treaty. Persuaded by this of the bad faith he was suspecting, Richard marched upon the Saracen camp. Saladin, construing this into a breach of the truce, massacred his Christian prisoners, and Richard retaliated by ordering the slaughter of the twenty-five hundred Saracen captives in his hands. Thus one version of the story. The other version has it that in this murderous business Richard's was the initiative, and Saladin's the retaliation.

But neither the chronicler of one version nor the chronicler of the other has any comment to offer upon an action which in those ruthless days, when human life was held of little value, was regarded as a normal military measure in the given circumstances.

The matter which had detained the crusading host in Acre, being thus barbarously concluded, preparations were made at once for the advance upon the Holy City.

The fortifications of Acre had been repaired and strengthened, and a garrison was left to hold that important base. There, too, Richard left his Queen and his sister when he set out at the head of thirty thousand Crusaders of all nations. It is in the course of this march on Jerusalem that he is signally revealed as something more than a terrific man of his hands, of a courage finding exultation in personal danger, and of a strength in his long, graceful limbs that enabled him to wield a battle-axe into the head of which twenty pounds of steel had been wrought. Whilst we behold in him all this, we discover also that he has developed in the course of his turbulent life gifts of generalship which were probably unequalled in his day.

His conduct is the more arresting and brilliant when we consider that he was opposed, in the great Saladin, to the most daring and skilful leader that Islam had yet produced and the mightiest Saracen army that had ever yet been seen, computed to number some three hundred thousand.

* * * *

Having decided to approach Jerusalem by way of Jaffa, Richard marched by the Roman road beside the sea that goes through Haifa and Caesarea. His fleet, sailing level with the troops, ensured their supplies through a country which could yield them none, since Saladin had laid it waste. He marched with the utmost leisure, so as to husband the strength of his army, content to advance no more than eight or nine miles a day, and this in the early morning hours, before the torrid August heat should become unbearable. On alternate days he marched not at all; but let the army rest. Being short of beasts of burden, it was necessary to employ half the infantry for porterage. In this, too, his provisions were of the soundest. The men alternated daily in that porterage duty, those whose turn it was to bear the tents and baggage, marching on the right, next to the sea, screened by the cavalry, which formed the middle line and by the infantry beyond it, on the left flank. Thus, those who acted as porters, whilst so labouring, were yet rested from the strain of combat; for the line was constantly harassed by Saracen skirmishers.

In this order of march, which at a moment's notice could become an order of battle, the long line plodded on by Haifa, Athlit and Caesarea, all of which had been dismantled, towards Arsûf and Jaffa, taking twenty days to cover eighty miles. And all the while, on their flank hovered bodies of Saracen horsemen to attack them, to discharge volleys of arrows into their ranks, and to retreat again when charged, so nimbly that in Christian eyes they seemed to move like swallows on their light, swift horses.

The temptation to give chase to these persistent assailants must have been almost irresistible. Yet Richard made his followers resist it. His shrewd military sense fully perceived the cunning strategy behind these irritating tactics.

Invisible in the folds of the hills to the east, whence these skirmishers emerged and into which they retreated again when the Crusaders turned on them, waited Saladin with his mighty host. Let him but goad them into breaking their line so as to push home a charge against one of his bodies of skirmishers, and he would fling his army into the gap and roll the Christians up.

Richard, fully aware of this danger, and rendered increasingly cautious by knowledge of the overwhelming odds with which he had to reckon, kept his infantry firm and level as a wall. They were reasonably protected from arrows by their gambesons, coats of quilted felt which descended to the knee; and as they trudged along many a man was to be seen marching with a half-dozen or more arrows sticking in his back. In return for their comparatively harmless shafts, the Saracens, lightly clad and without body armour, had to reckon with the deadly bolts from the crossbows of the Crusaders.

The Christian cavalry marched inside the line of infantry as if behind a rampart, from which it never issued save for those carefully restricted charges that drove off any party of the enemy that advanced too closely.

Thus in a solid, impregnable phalanx Richard's army plodded on, bearing in its midst a wagon surmounted by a wooden tower from which floated the lion banner of the King; and every evening, when they were encamped, a herald would come forth, and like the Mueddin, who in the Saracen camp invoked the help of Allah, thrice raise his voice to cry, "Aid us, Holy Sepulchre!" to which the Crusaders roared "Amen!"

Foiled by Richard's discipline in his every endeavour to lure the Christians from their iron formation, Saladin realized at last that something more was necessary if he were to prevent them from reaching Jaffa. The Crusaders were approaching the forest of Arsûf. For twelve miles their road would lie between this forest and the sea. That should enable him to bring his army under cover within striking distance.

Richard no less than Saladin perceived the opportunity the forest would supply. He warned his troops to be prepared, and still further tightened the discipline.

On the 5th September the Crusaders covered without
incident half of that distance which the forest flanked, and
they came to camp near the mouth of the Nahr-el-Falaik,
where a wide marsh to the east gave them shelter from assault.

There they rested on the 6th.

On the 7th they set out to cover the remaining six miles
to Arsûf.

The order of march was the same as usual, with the foot
and the crossbow men on the outer flank. But the army was
divided by Richard into several battles. In the van he
placed the Templars. After these, in three divisions, came
Richard's own followers: the Angevins and Bretons form-
ing the first; then the Poitevins under Guy de Lusignan;
and lastly the English and the Normans, and with these
the wagon of the standard. Next there were four divisions
of the French, whilst the Hospitallers brought up the rear.

They had emerged from their camp, and were south of
the protecting marsh when Saladin launched his attack.
Forth from the woods swarmed the Infidel host, in such
numbers that on the land between the forest and the road,
a space of some two miles, there was not, says the chronicler, a bare spot of earth visible. Black Soudanese, Bed-
ouins from the desert, and mounted Turkish bowmen
made up the front line of that fierce horde which broke
like a torrent upon the Christian flank. Behind these glit-
tered the Sultan's mailed Mamelukes and the contingents
of all the Syrian Emirs, before each of whom went his
musicians with trumpets, drums and cymbals to swell the
terrific din of howling voices. Above their serried ranks
floated the parti-coloured banners of the Emirs, and the
sunlight was dimmed by the dust cast up by their hoofs.

Saladin flung his main attack against the flank and rear

of Richard's hindmost division, with the clear intention of constraining it, in self-defence, to charge, so as to open the breach through which it was ever his hope to penetrate and break that hitherto impregnable line.

But Richard, perceiving the aim, perceived also the counter. So as to be sure of delivering it with effect, he must at all costs hold his forces steady, and continue, however slowly, the advance until his van should come to rest upon Arsûf, so that when it became his right wing it should be in no danger of envelopment. To this task he sternly addressed himself.

Vainly did the Grand Master of the Hospitallers, who bore the brunt of that attack upon the rear, beg Richard's leave to charge the assailants who now at close quarters were hammering upon his knights with scimitar and mace.

"It must be borne," was Richard's answer.

And so they continued to bear it, and the long line continued to crawl forward under the assault, the rearguard marching backwards now, so that they might face the pursuing squadrons and hold them in some measure of check with their crossbows.

Next to the rear, but in less degree, it was the middle of the line, composed of the French, which had to bear the pressure. The English and the Normans, and the Templars in the van, had comparatively little to sustain.

Richard, observant, ubiquitous, withheld his riposte until the conditions should be such as he hoped by endurance to create. Already Saladin, manifestly impatient, was himself among the skirmishers. Let that impatience but grow until the Sultan should commit the entire Saracen host to an engagement at close quarters all along the line, and then, God helping him, Richard would so deal with them, for all their numbers, that no Infidel army would be left.

The signal for that general engagement was to be six trumpet blasts. Until then, let the line continue its advance, maintaining its unbroken formation.

But more and more restive grew the Hospitallers under the punishment they were receiving; and at the eleventh hour, just as Arsûf was being reached, two of those knights could be restrained no longer to await the trumpet-blasts. The Marshal of the Order and the valiant Baldwin de Carron, calling upon Saint George and the Holy Sepulchre to aid them, wheeled their horses and charged out from behind the wall of infantry. Since they could not be left to hurl themselves alone upon the foe, the whole body of Hospitallers followed, unleashed at last in fury upon their tormentors.

It was the end of the march. The Crusaders halted, and along the flank rippled a spontaneous movement that converted it into a front. The French, perceiving what had happened, charged forth to support the Hospitallers. Another moment and the English and the Normans, the Poitevins and the Bretons, and, finally, the Hospitallers in the van, had similarly wheeled into the fray.

The general engagement had come, thus, some moments before Richard had desired it. It came too soon to enable him to deliver the exterminating blow upon which he had been calculating, but at least not too soon to result in a crushing defeat of Saladin's host. The very suddenness and cumulative character of the onset of an army, hitherto so passively defensive, startled and demoralized the enemy. And so impetuous was the charge of the Frankish knights that it tangled the Saracens into a mass that could neither fight nor run, helpless at the mercy of assailants who smashed them down in thousands.

The Infidel division that so long had harassed the rear

was cut off by the charge of the Hospitallers, driven down to the sea, and there exterminated.

Richard prudently stayed pursuit and re-formed his ranks. Saladin, having extricated his men, did the same, to receive two more charges from the Christians before he accounted the day lost beyond redemption.

The Saracens left upwards of seven thousand dead upon the field, among whom there were no fewer than thirty-two Emirs. Amongst the Crusaders who encamped undisturbed that night at Arsûf the loss had been of not more than seven hundred. Thus in the number of their dead they preserved the proportions in which the living had been opposed.

*   *   *   *

On the 10th September, two days after the glorious battle of Arsûf, the Crusaders were among the groves of Jaffa, Richard's great coast march magnificently accomplished.

They organized now for the inland march to Jerusalem, whilst the King sought, in pressing Saladin to negotiate for the surrender of the Holy Land, to take advantage of the weakness in which their defeat had left the Moslems.

Whatever may have contributed to thwart him in these aims, it is certain that the action of Conrad of Montferrat was the main factor. Simultaneously and treacherously the Marquis had opened negotiations with Saladin, offering to recover Acre for him in exchange for the lordships of Sidon and Beirut. It resulted directly from this that Richard was compelled to waste valuable time in a voyage to Acre, so as to bring Joan and Berengaria away from a place which might well become fraught with danger for them.

As a consequence the army did not move from Jaffa until the end of October; and it was not until the end of December, after intense suffering from the drenching rains, from scarcity of supplies, from consequent sickness, and from incessant skirmishing attacks, that it came to Beit Nuba, uplifted by the thought of being now within a day's march of the Holy City. To accomplish the aim with which they had come so far and endured so much, they had now but to go forward, for Saladin's army was in no case to oppose them. But again, as in the case of Conrad of Montferrat, though without his treachery, the self-interest of the Syrian Franks interposed. Much more concerned to retain the Crusaders in Palestine for the recovery of their own lordships than for the wresting of Jerusalem from the Infidel, they advanced plausible arguments against going farther. To occupy Jerusalem was easy. But to hold it, they must hold a line of communications with the coast, and for this they insisted that their force was insufficient.

These councils prevailing, to Richard's deep mortification, it was decided to fall back upon Ascalon, and thither, under rain and snow, the Crusaders now took their dejected way.

In Ascalon the first necessity was to repair the fortifications, which Saladin had dismantled; and to this, under Richard's directions, the Crusaders at once addressed themselves, knight and noble laying aside the sword and the mace to wield the pick and the trowel, and Richard himself bearing a hand in these labours of masonry. For the high stomach of Leopold of Austria, however, it proved too mean a task; whereupon Richard in anger completed the work he had begun at Acre when he tore down the banner of the too presumptuous Duke. With blows and insults he drove him and his following out of Ascalon.

He had trouble, too, and of no less mean an order with the Duke of Burgundy. To lend money imposes an obligation upon the lender more often than upon the borrower:

the obligation to lend again or incur resentment. The Duke had repeatedly drawn large sums from Richard for the pay of his men, which Richard with his open-handed lavishness had unquestioningly supplied. The Duke again applied to him. It was no longer possible to oblige him. Richard, who had been bearing almost the entire cost of the Crusade, was feeling the drain upon his resources, and was therefore constrained to refuse. Upon this the Duke, in dudgeon, went off with the bulk of his forces to Acre; and there, in venting his spite, entered into relations with Conrad of Montferrat and would have brought him into the city had not the Pisans who were there opposed it.

It was the lack of unity of action among the Franks, of which this is an instance, which eventually constrained Richard, in the spring, reluctantly to consent, in spite of the agreement which had earlier been reached, that Conrad of Montferrat should be accepted as King of Jerusalem.

No sooner was it done than the dissensions and tumults caused by the ambitions of the Marquis were settled once for all by his being stabbed to death in a street of Tyre by a member of the sect of the Assassins.

Richard's nephew, Count Henry of Champagne, who had remained with Cœur-de-Lion at Ascalon when the French took their departure, was now proposed as Conrad's successor to the crown of Jerusalem. It was a proposal that offered a solution to the existing difficulties, for Henry, being the nephew at once of the King of England and the King of France, could count upon the support of both nations. His right was to be consolidated by taking the already considerably married Isabella to wife, and once Richard's consent had been won no time was wasted. Actually within a week of the death of Conrad, his widow took Henry of Champagne for her third husband, whilst the dethroned Guy of Lusignan was consoled by Richard's bestowal upon him of the crown of Cyprus, which, if less consequential in title, was at the same time a less shadowy kingdom than that which he relinquished.

* * * *

News now reaching Richard may well have rendered him apprehensive lest, whilst pursuing conquests in Syria, he might not be in danger of losing his own dominions.

In England Longchamp and John were in arms against each other. By bribery and grants, John was building himself a party which presently recognized him as heir to the throne, in defiance of the nomination by Richard of his nephew, Arthur of Brittany, to whom the crown legitimately belonged.

Then Philip of France, unrestrained by his oath to keep the peace—from which on his way home he had actually sought, and been refused, absolution by the Pope—was intriguing with John for Richard's undoing, by offering him the hand of the unfortunate Alais, and with it his support in taking possession of Richard's continental dominion. John had been on the point of accepting the invitation when Queen Eleanor intervened, and, supported by Richard's envoy, Walter de Coutances, checked her treacherous son by the sternest threats uttered in the King's name.

These things awakened in Richard a natural anxiety to return, especially as he was now becoming persuaded that no ultimate definite success was likely to crown the labours upon which already he had lavished himself and his resources so unstintingly. Yielding, however, to the entreaties of his followers, he consented to make a last attempt to reach Jerusalem, and on the 11th June (1192) he brought his Crusaders once more to Beit Nuba.

There Richard paused, to await the reinforcements Henry of Champagne was bringing from Acre.

Whilst waiting, he performed a raid that greatly distressed Saladin.

He had received word of a powerful and rich caravan on its way from Egypt to Jerusalem. To intercept it he marched with five hundred horse and a thousand foot twenty miles in a night under the Syrian moon, lay quiet all day, and completed the journey—another fifteen miles—on the second night. At daybreak on the 23rd June he fell upon the caravan at the foot of the Hebron Hills.

The Saracens were in strength, for the attack was expected, and they had taken up a strong position on a slope, to beat off their assailants.

Richard divided his force into two battles, and charging at the head of the first cut right through the Saracen ranks. As these rallied from his tempestuous passage, and wheeled to take him in the rear, they were taken in the rear themselves by the second division under the Earl of Leicester. Utterly routed, they left in Christian hands a caravan of enormous value in gold, silver, precious stones, spices, tapestries, silks, arms and clothing, besides three thousand camels and as many horses.

It was also whilst at Beit Nuba that, in the course of a raid pushed as far as the Springs of Emmaus, Richard had the satisfaction of letting at least his eyes rest upon the Holy City, visible in the distance through the summer haze.

But Beit Nuba, now as before, was destined to be the limit of the Christian advance.

The sufferings from lack of water, and the constant attacks upon the long-drawn line of communications with

Jaffa, brought home to the leaders the insecurity of their position, and as vehemently now they urged retreat as formerly they had urged advance.

The King, who had brought them from Ascalon against his better judgment, yielded, and the retreat began.

On the 26th July, Richard was back in Acre, to learn there that, behind him, Saladin, taking advantage of that retreat, was laying siege to Jaffa. And so hard pressed was that siege that on the last day of the month the Saracens captured the city, driving the garrison into the citadel. At the end of their resources, the Christians asked for a truce until the following noon, with the condition that they would then surrender if not meanwhile relieved, the lives to be spared of those who could afford to ransom them, at the rate of ten besants for a man, five for a woman and three for a child.

But it was not in Richard's nature to stand idle at such a time. He was hastening south in his galleys, and during that night so fateful for the garrison of Jaffa, he came to anchor off the city.

Daybreak showed him a Moslem host drawn up upon the shore.

"If God will that we die with our brethren, perish the man who would hang back!" With that exclamation, he ordered the galleys to be rowed forward until they grounded. Then, leaping down into the water, he stood there shouldering a crossbow, in the use of which he was of exceptional skill, and picking off Saracens whilst his men stormed ashore.

The Moslem troops swarming before the citadel, which already they accounted doomed, suddenly beheld Saladin's flag cut down from the wall and the lion banner hoisted in its place. Whilst they stood dismayed, the despairing garrison, beholding this, too, took heart anew, and sallied forth to co-operate with Richard.

The Saracen was swept from the town and Saladin from his camp beyond it. And in that camp the Lionheart came to establish himself whilst the fortifications of Jaffa were being repaired.

There, some nights later, he was attacked by Saladin, who knew that he was far from being in strength. Fifty-five knights and two thousand foot—chiefly Genoese and Pisan bowmen from his galleys—made up his total force.

But he was warned in time, and, as he had already shown Saladin at Arsûf, he knew how to make the most of his resources. He was to prove it yet again, and even more signally.

He flung out his wings, so as to maintain communication with the city. The men of his main battle were ordered to kneel in line behind the cover of their semi-cylindrical shields, their spears grounded, the points levelled at the height of a horse's breast. Between every two spears, two crossbowmen were stationed, one behind the other, one to shoot, the other to load for him.

By this arrangement he was able to tear the ranks of the charging Saracens by volley upon volley. Five successive charges were made by these picked Mamelukes right up to that bristling wall of spears. It remained unbroken, the horsemen swerving aside each time, and riding off to reform. When the last of those onslaughts had ineffectively spent itself, Richard led forth his knights, to charge in their turn, although not more than fifteen of them were mounted.

The impetus of the Lionheart carried him into their midst, whence, smashing right and left with his formidable battle-axe, he hewed his way out again, and in the course of it by his irresistible prowess delivered not only himself, but also the Earl of Leicester and Ralph de Mauléon, who had been surrounded.

Whilst, according to Bohadin, the Saracen chronicler, Saladin was raging at this repulse, Richard rode up and down the line, challenging any Saracen knight to come forth and meet him. But neither Saladin nor any of his followers would venture to take up his challenge.

Upon that field of battle Saladin left seven hundred dead, whilst among the Crusaders, so sound had been Richard's order of battle, whilst many were wounded, only two were killed.

*   *   *   *

For a month thereafter Richard lay in Jaffa, sick of a fever, and glad of the snow and peaches sent him in the true spirit of chivalry by Saladin, with whom, meanwhile, he was negotiating peace through his representative, Hubert Walter, Bishop of Salisbury.

On the 2nd September terms were at last agreed. The Christians were to retain the coast towns from Jaffa to Tyre, with free access to the Holy Places. This engagement Saladin honourably kept. Bishop Walter, who led a party of pilgrims to the Holy City, was treated by the Sultan with every courtesy. Permission was accorded to Christian priests even to celebrate the Mass at the Holy Sepulchre, at Nazareth and at Bethlehem.

In this tame fashion ended an undertaking upon which Christendom had embarked with so much fervour and in which so much blood and treasure had been poured out. The only profit from it accrued to the Syrian Franks; and of all the princes who had engaged in that Third Crusade, the only one to emerge with glory, earned by stedfastness and high endeavour, was Richard the Lionheart.

* * * *

The state of King Richard's health dictating his removal to the better air of Haifa, it was not his to make the pilgrimage to the Holy City. It may well be, too, that he preferred to postpone his visit until he should enter Jerusalem as a conqueror; for certain it is—as he frankly warned Saladin—that he departed in the full intention of returning as soon as might be to renew the attempt.

On the 9th October, having been fifteen months in the Holy Land, he embarked at Acre to return. Berengaria and Joan, accompanied ever by the Cypriot Princess, had sailed a fortnight earlier, and after visiting Sicily had gone on to Rome, where for the present they remained. But Richard, buffeted by storms, was at sea until the 11th November, when he ran into Corfù. Thence he made his way up the Adriatic, encountering fresh gales and finally suffering shipwreck near Aquileia.

He was under no delusion as to the dangers that stood in the path of his return now that he was so far off his course. Whatever he might have left undone since sailing from Marseilles two years ago, certain it was that he had raised up a fine crop of powerful and dangerous enemies. His support of Tancred had incensed the Emperor Henry VI, who had been unsuccessful in arms to enforce his claim to the Sicilian throne; his conquest of Cyprus had aroused the indignation not only of the Greeks, but also of Comnenus' Austrian kinship; and with Austria the score against him was aggravated beyond calculation by his treatment of Duke Leopold and by his opposition to Conrad of Montferrat, whose murder he was maliciously accused of having procured.

If he were to win safely through the enemy territories which stood between home and the place where the storm had cast him up, the utmost prudence would be necessary.

He was attended by a Norman baron, Baldwin of Bethune, two chaplains, some Templars and servants, amongst whom was one William de L'Etang who spoke German, or the Saxon dialect to which in those days English was much akin. They disguised themselves, Richard assuming the garb of a merchant, and they took horse across Friuli. They numbered seventeen in all. Not few enough to escape attention; not numerous enough to deal with it when aroused.

In Count Mainhard of Goritz, a nephew of Conrad of Montferrat, Richard had a watchful enemy, who came down upon the party. Fourteen of them were captured. Of the three who escaped, Richard was one and L'Etang another. They took to the mountains, and for days were almost errant amongst them in the snow. What other hardships they may have endured, we do not know, but it would be about a month later when they came in an exhausted state to Vienna, and found shelter in a cottage of the suburbs.

Despite the vigilance of the vindictive Leopold, Richard might have come safely through but for the imprudence of L'Etang, who, being sent out to buy provisions, offered gold besants in payment. Followed, he unconsciously led the way to the cottage where his exhausted master lay, in no case to defend himself from those who came on Leopold's behalf to seize him.

So that he might atone for the insults offered to the Duke

in Palestine, Leopold sent him to his Castle of Dürrenstein on the Danube, reckless in his vindictiveness of the fact that by laying hands upon a Crusader he provoked the anathema of the Church. He was not permitted, however, to keep so rich a prize entirely in his own possession. His overlord, the Emperor, came down to claim the prisoner.

On the 14th February 1193, by when Richard had spent the better part of two months at Dürrenstein, an arrangement was made between Duke and Emperor to share King Richard's ransom, and this was fixed at one hundred thousand marks, or sixteen thousand pounds, an enormous sum, which in purchasing power would exceed some two millions of the present sterling currency. For the rest, the Emperor claimed, and the Duke agreed to give him, the custody of the royal captive.

*   *   *   *

The anxieties aroused in England by the complete disappearance of the King from the moment when he had left Acre were partially lightened at last in the spring of 1193 by the news of his captivity, news which came by way of France, as a result of the Emperor's communications with King Philip.

To John if not as good as would have been the news of Richard's death, at least it was the next best, and he took instant action to turn the situation to his own advantage. He crossed to France, and, although met by a refusal of the Norman barons to do homage to him as Richard's successor, he went in that capacity to do homage to King Philip, to offer to marry Alais, as Philip had earlier proposed to him, and to surrender the Norman Vexin which Philip coveted. Assured on these terms of Philip's support, he raised a body of mercenaries, and with these returned to England to disturb the peace hitherto maintained by Queen Eleanor and to claim the crown on the ground that King Richard was dead. But Walter de Coutances took arms against him. A truce was called, and it was agreed that during this, Queen Eleanor should retain Windsor Castle and John's other strongholds.

At the same time Philip was meeting with no better success in Normandy. His invasion of the Duchy was being resisted by the doughty Earl of Leicester, who was home by now from the Holy Land.

Meanwhile, it was not Blondel, the troubadour of the romances, who was wandering through Germany in search of his master. The Abbots of Broxley and Robertsbridge were the real and diligent heroes of that quest.

Although the Pope fulminated the Emperor and the Duke of Austria with excommunication for laying violent hands on a Crusader, they were not moved by it to relinquish their hold upon the royal prisoner, and presently he was arraigned before the Diet. The charges there preferred against him were of supporting the usurpation of Tancred in violation of the Emperor's rights to the Sicilian crown; of unlawfully dethroning the Emperor of Cyprus; and of insulting Leopold of Austria; to all of which they added the accusation that he had procured the murder of Conrad of Montferrat.

Whether the kiss of peace which he received from the Emperor Henry at the close of his defence was a sign that he had known how to justify himself, or merely an imperial way of expediting the business so that they might come to the ransom, is matter for conjecture. But the venal character of the Emperor suggests the answer.

In the meantime the figure at which his ransom was set was already known in England. The two questing abbots had come upon the captive King of Ochsenfurt in Bavaria. They had had an interview with him, and they had gone home to report upon it.

To provide now this ransom, the crown officers in England demanded a contribution of one fourth of all rents and movables from all classes, not excluding the clergy. Pride in their King had been aroused in the hearts of the English people by his knightly deeds in Palestine, deeds which on every hand and in almost every land were affording themes for troubadours and ballad-stringers, lending him an effulgence such as belonged to no other prince of his day. But despite this pride, and the consequently eager desire to ransom so gallant a sovereign, a tax which absorbed a quarter of men's incomes and movable possessions was not easily levied even although gold and jewels were freely given and Church plate melted down.

At last, however, by December, some seventy thousand marks had been collected, and this sum was paid over on account, with guarantees for the liquidation of the balance. Satisfied with these, the Emperor announced his intention of liberating the prisoner on the 17th January.

Philip and John, in dread of the wrath to come, now actively intrigued to prevent that deliverance. They offered the Emperor large sums as bribes to ignore his pledge and even a subsidy for every additional month that he should retain his hold of Richard. The mean-spirited Emperor was finding difficulty in resisting the temptation. When the 17th January arrived, he was still temporizing. To gain time he adjourned the Diet for a fortnight, and it is incalculable what course he might have taken in the end had not the Princes of Germany, with a sense of chivalry and honour of which their overlord was destitute, resolutely demanded Richard's release against the hostages surrendered for the completion of the payments.

*   *   *   *

Restored at last to his dearly purchased liberty after sixteen months of imprisonment, Richard landed at Sandwich on a day of middle March. He had been absent from England for four years and three months.

At Rochester he was met by Hubert Walter, the Archbishop of Canterbury. Thence he proceeded to London, where a welcome awaited him from his subjects, so joyously enthusiastic that it may well have reminded him of his reception on landing at Acre. He went in procession to Saint Paul's to render thanks, and for a week thereafter he remained in London. Then, taking up arms again, he rode north.

His brother John, when he perceived that Richard's enlargement was imminent, had beheld in this the frustration of all his hopes. From King Philip came a letter with the warning "The Devil is loose!" Rendered desperate and in panic lest Richard should do by him as he would certainly have done by Richard in the same circumstances, John had made a last wild throw for mastery before it should be too late. The rising which he engineered, abetted by Hugh of Nonant, the Bishop of Coventry, crumbled before the firm handling of the situation by Hubert Walter; and when Richard landed, the conflagration, which proved but a fire of straw, had been all but stamped to ashes. Nottingham alone still held out for John, but Richard's appearance in arms before it was sufficient to bring it to surrender.

Here, in Nottingham, the King held a Grand Council,

which was attended by his mother and Longchamp, the chancellor, who still continued to enjoy his master's confidence. The business was concerned with ways and means of raising money for the balance of the ransom and for the operations in Normandy which were rendered necessary by John's machinations with Philip and the latter's armed incursion into the territory.

Before this council John and his accomplice of Nonant were summoned to appear. But both of them were prudently across the Channel by then.

Coming south again, the King, to satisfy his subjects, went through a ceremony of recoronation at Winchester, so as to rehabilitate him in a status partially lost through bondage. Here again his mother was beside him, whilst Berengaria, the Queen of England who was never to stand on English soil, remained absent in Poitou with Joan. In this respect Richard himself was not in much better case. Four months he had spent in England when he assumed the crown; and of less than two months was this his second and last visit.

There was no rest for him. This man, who from the age of sixteen had been, almost without respite, engaged in warfare, was less Bellona's bridegroom than Bellona's slave. It was a fate imposed upon him as much by the times in which he lived as by the bad faith of those with whom his territorial possessions placed him in relations. At present the depredations by Philip of France, for which Richard largely had his brother to thank, were calling him urgently to the defence of his Norman possessions.

On the 12th May of that year 1194 he sailed again from Portsmouth, never to return, leaving England to be well and equitably governed for him by the upright Archbishop Hubert Walter. From this moment until his death, just five years later, his life is the restless life of the camp, spent in feats of arms, in sieges, in assaults, in erecting and demolishing fortifications, and the like. For the warfare of those days was almost entirely siege warfare. A pitched battle was comparatively rare. For the unfortunate populations of the cities over which princes wrangled, suffering at the hands now of one, now of the other, all the privations of investment and all the horrors attending capitulation, it was a time entirely of wretchedness.

On his way to carry a war of reconquest into the Norman Vexin which Philip had invaded, Richard was met at Bruis by John, who, terror-stricken, now that his redoubtable brother was taking the field, came in tears, laments, and self-abasement, seeking forgiveness. Richard was the least vindictive of men, yet, if his mother had not been present to intercede for her other offspring, or if Richard had been less devoted to her than he was, he might have been less amazingly lenient. For all the trouble that his brother had caused him, he was content to inflict no heavier punishment than to withhold from him the trust of any castle or land. They parted again, and, to settle some of that trouble, Richard marched on to Verneuil, the siege of which, however, was raised by Philip at the news of his approach. Thence he proceeded into Touraine, where Philip had also been busy. He prospered in arms as usual. Returning from the reduction of Lormes and Tours, he inflicted at Fréteval a severe defeat upon the King of France, and by the end of the summer there was not a rebel left standing in Richard's dominions.

There followed a truce, and, since Philip employed it in levying funds with which presently to resume the offensive, Richard perforce must do the like. But some considerable financial relief was afforded him at the end of the year by

the death of the Duke of Austria. Leopold had suffered a
fall in a tournament at Vienna, and his horse had fallen
with him, crushing one of his feet. The therapeutics of the
age could not prevent such an injury from becoming mortal. The terrors of death were magnified for Leopold by
the excommunication under which he still lay, and the
consequent prospect of an eternity of Hell fire. He must
make his peace with the Church; but the Church would
make no peace with him until he repaired, so far as still lay
in his power, the wrong he had done to the King of England. He procured the lifting of the curse by confessing
repentance of the unworthy part he had played, and he not
only remitted the balance of the ransom due from Richard
—which balance was to have been his own share of it—
but he sent him a letter, received from the Sheik of the
Assassins, and hitherto knavishly withheld, which entirely
acquitted Richard of the unwarranted charge of having
been concerned in the murder of Conrad of Montferrat.

* * * *

The truce between Richard and Philip, which was to
have endured for a year from November of 1194, came to
an abrupt end in the following July. Once more the kings
were in the field, and at Arques, in the course of the campaign that now opened, Richard suffered his only defeat
at the hands of Philip, a defeat which he was not long in
avenging.

Thus, raids and counter-raids, the repelling of assaults
upon his own dominions and the carrying of a war of reprisals into the dominions of his neighbour, make up the
history of Richard during those years, in which he constantly grows in strength and in knightly renown.

In 1197, he found himself hemmed about by enemies.

Brittany had formed an alliance with Philip, Aquitaine was in revolt, Toulouse in the south and Flanders in the north simultaneously made war upon him. Against them all he held his own, by his resources, his magnificent leadership, and his personal prowess gradually forcing all antagonists to their knees. It was in the course of this long-drawn campaign that Richard's bitter enemy, the Bishop of Beauvais, was taken in arms, and by Richard imprisoned in the Castle of Rouen. The raging prelate appealed to the Pope; and the Holy Father, whilst confessing that since the Bishop had been taken sword in hand the case was not one in which he could rightly exercise his pontifical authority, yet addressed to Richard a friendly letter of intercession. For answer, Richard wittily sent him the Bishop's blood-stained coat of mail, with a scroll attached to it bearing the following verse from the Old Testament: "This have we found. Know now whether it be thy son's coat or no."

Pope Celestine is said to have replied: "No. It is the coat of a son of Mars. Let Mars deliver him." And awaiting that supernatural deliverance Richard left the warlike prelate in his dungeon.

It was Celestine's successor, the great Innocent III, who at the end of 1198 intervened to enforce a permanent peace between the warring kings.

Pope Innocent had set his heart upon the organization of a fourth Crusade, and in this he sought to enlist both England and France. As a preliminary he despatched the Cardinal of Capua to Normandy, with instructions to compel the two kings, at need by threats of an interdict, to sign, if not a permanent peace, at least a five years' truce.

The Cardinal's mission wore the appearance of prospering, and already the twain were orally pledged to the truce, when Richard's attention was drawn aside by a paltry matter of treasure-trove in the Limousin. As suzerain he claimed the treasure which had been unearthed there. Because the Viscount of Limoges would not part with more than half of it, Richard impetuously marched into the Limousin, and when the Castle of Chaluz closed its gates to him, he sat down to besiege it. The garrison offered to surrender with the honours of war. But Richard, incensed by the resistance, demanded a surrender at discretion. So the siege went on.

On the afternoon of March the 26th, whilst Richard, without any armour beyond his headpiece, and careless of taking cover behind the square shield placed for the purpose, stood watching the siege operations, he was struck between the left shoulder and the neck by a bolt from a crossbow. He went off without great concern to his quarters; but, in the attempt to draw out the bolt, the shaft came away, leaving the iron head in the wound, so that it had to be cut out. It is said that Richard was impatiently negligent of the precautions enjoined by his physician. Be that as it may, mortification set in, and the King realized that this comparatively trifling wound, taken in a matter utterly unworthy of his attention, was to give him his death.

In haste he sent for his mother. The old Queen—now seventy-four years of age—was at Fontevrault at the time, and she came promptly to his bedside. He made his dispositions; named the worthless John as his successor, possibly under his mother's influence; left a legacy to the poor; and chivalrously bethought him to give orders that the man who had shot the bolt that had slain him should not suffer for it. He made his peace with God, received Extreme Unction, and at sunset on Tuesday the 6th April of 1199, the Lion heart ceased to beat. He was in his forty-second year.

In obedience to his last wishes that heart, said to be unusually large, was enclosed in a golden casket and taken to Rouen, whilst his body went to Fontevrault, to lie at the feet of the father upon whom he had looked his last in the chapel of that abbey.

It is not too well said of him that "he was the creation and impersonation of his age." In honour and loyalty he was much above his age. A quick, passionate man, he was yet without vindictiveness, or meanness of any kind. Generous in the word's every sense, staunch, just, and winning, he knew how to command service and affection. It is testimonial enough to his worth that he could deserve the love of such men as Hubert Walter and the saintly Hugh of Lincoln.

To the chivalry of his own and subsequent days he was a model and an inspiration. He lives on in the popular imagination because of his truly regal quality, which is the knightly quality *in excelsis*. It is this which gives him his place among the heroes.

II
THE BRIDEGROOM OF POVERTY
Saint Francis of Assisi

II

THE BRIDEGROOM OF POVERTY

HE WOULD be the bridegroom of Poverty. He would take the Lady Poverty to wife.

That was the sum of his reply to the banter of the revellers who had elected him their president.

He had accepted this frivolous presidency as belonging to him by right of a custom established in the days before his first absence from his native Assisi. But the pride and eagerness with which once he had filled the office of Master of the Revels, receiving his election to it as a proper tribute to his worldly gifts, were absent now.

Wealthy and prodigally open-handed, encouraged to spend by an indulgent and worldly father, splendid in his dress and his appointments, and more splendid still in the equipment of his spirit, magnetically dominant, and of a natural and exuberant joyousness which was never to quit him in life, it was inevitable that the pleasure-seeking, wealthy, and patrician youth of Assisi should have chosen this Francesco Bernardone for their leader.

At first, in the days of his adolescence, it is possible that the restlessness which is the spur of ever-questing genius may have found an outlet in these riotous pursuits. But impossible, even without the events that went to shape his destiny, that he could have derived from them any enduring satisfaction.

First to interrupt his life of sterile gaiety had come the call of patriotism. Assisi was in danger. The dawn of the thirteenth century was in Italy the season of the first revolt against feudalism. Assisi, writhing under the heel of patrician oppressors, followed the example of other Italian states, elected consuls and rose in arms against her rapacious masters. Having demolished the great fortress from which the forces of the Duke of Spoleto had dominated them, they dealt similarly with the palaces of the nobles. After this, so as to render themselves secure, they girt the city with fortified walls, and then proceeded to destroy the feudal strongholds of the countryside.

The feudal lords, unable alone to confront the storm, appealed to Perugia for assistance, offering allegiance to the Perugian consuls. Perugia, confident of her strength, more tolerant in her communal spirit, and perceiving clear advantages to be reaped, took up arms to procure redress for those who placed themselves under her protection.

To defend the homeland every Assisian who was not of the feudal party flocked to the lion standard of the city, and went down into the valley, to meet the Perugian host on the banks of the grey Tiber. Near the Bridge of San Giovanni the Assisians suffered a heavy defeat, and Francesco Bernardone was among the captives who went in bondage to Perugia. Even then the joyousness of his nature rose superior to the afflictions of the situation; and the troubadour he was at heart sought by jest and song to uplift his companions in misfortune. We gather this from the chronicled reproof of one of them, who cried out upon him that "it was like a madman to rejoice when they were in duress."

For a year that captivity endured, and then, peace being made between Assisi and Perugia, Francis and his companions were sent home.

He came back, a youth of twenty, or twenty-one at most, to the luxurious, pleasure-loving life that he had quitted.

But it is possible that in his brief military experience he had known an exaltation which he was anxious to recapture. It is possible that, confusing cause and effect, he conceived this exaltation to spring from the martial pursuit itself rather than from its worthy object: the defence of the homeland and the readiness to sacrifice himself in that high endeavour. Hence he may have imagined that in a soldier's life and in the pursuit of glory, the energies seething within him would satisfy their needs.

That famous condottiero, Walter of Brienne, was raising troops at the time for the defence of the Pope against the Emperor. Here Francis perceived a great cause to serve and a great captain to follow.

His worldly father cordially approved him. Thus would the gold of that wealthy merchant, Pietro Bernardone, be spent to the magnification of his family and name; for it was by the career of arms that men came to knighthood and nobility. His wealth would serve to remove initial obstacles and gild the ultimate achievement.

So Francis joined a company that Count Gentile of Assisi was assembling, and magnificently mounted and accoutred he rode out of the city, the most splendid in that splendid band. He was destined to ride in it no farther than a couple of leagues. That night, at Spoleto, where they lay, he was taken ill; and on the morrow, having become worse, and being unfit to travel, he was left behind. Consumed with fever he lay there for some days, and they were days that were big with Fate.

* * * *

Thomas of Celano, who was to become one of his followers, and, later, his biographer Saint Bonaventura, proceeding in the spirit of their time, choose the easy road of miraculous intervention to explain the far-reaching change now wrought in him. They begin by telling us of his despair at this frustration of his hopes of military glory, at this dissipation of the bright vision that had drawn him on, and of the consequent despondency into which he fell. But no such frustration actually existed. Once he had recovered his strength, there was nothing to prevent his following and making his way to Walter de Brienne's camp. He was well-provided with the means to do so, and one who later, in the service of the Lord, was to journey barefoot and penniless into distant lands, can have thought little of travelling a few leagues into Apulia well-mounted and equipped.

"One night as he slept," says Saint Bonaventura, "the Lord spoke to him with the voice of a friend."

We are meant to take the statement literally. Without doing this, we may yet accept it as entirely true. For inspiration is surely the voice of Divinity speaking within us; and the inspiration which was to bear fruit a little later may well have come to Francis in those hours of physical prostration, a state not uncommonly attended by a peculiar clarity of vision and a penetrating acuteness in the perception of values.

It is to what he thus perceived, and not to any physical obstacles, that we should assign the fact that when he was sufficiently recovered, he did not resume the road to Apulia, but turned back and rode home to his native Assisi.

In those weary days at the inn at Spoleto, alone with his thoughts, he had come to see not merely the vanity of military pursuits, but how fundamentally antithetical they were to the spirit that must ever have been very ardent in him. The career he had contemplated, viewed now at close quarters, dispassionately, was a career of strife; and strife was the fruit of hatred. He had been about to dedicate himself to a service that violated the cardinal tenet laid down by the Redeemer, that knocked away the very corner-stone upon which Christianity is built.

A mind travelling as far as this, would next seek the cause of all the strife and hatred that troubled the world and thwarted the establishment of that Kingdom of Love which the Saviour had preached. He did not need to seek far or long. He found it to lie in acquisitiveness, in the greed of possessions, in the fierce competition for wealth, the *auri sacra fames* of Horace. This was the evil, dominant passion that set men at one another's throats, that drove nation to war with nation, class with class. It was in his sight, then, like a leprosy that had fallen on the world. And it was all-pervading. It rendered princes false to their trusts, it moved feudal lords to inhumanity towards their vassals. The very Church had not escaped the taint, but, amassing wealth, had put on pomp and had grown so patrician and worldly that it was losing its power over the souls of men, its hold for good upon the people. The poor and lowly could look to-day for little sustenance from the great baronial institutions into which the monastic orders had built themselves up from their humble beginnings. The spiritual power which monasticism had once possessed had in the great wealthy abbeys been largely replaced by feudal power.

Upon a mental soil rendered fertile by such reflections fell, we must suppose, a recollection of the Saviour's words to the rich man: "If thou wilt be perfect, go and sell that thou hast, and give to the poor, and thou shalt have treasure in Heaven; and come and follow Me."

He perceived, as he certainly can never until then have perceived, the force of that injunction. He perceived the ignobility, the degradation of all labour that has for sole object the acquisition of wealth, that is creative of nothing that will enrich men spiritually or bring them to raise their eyes above sordid levels.

The injunction took root in his soul the more readily, since he was by nature as piteous and loving as he was joyous. The quest of pleasure, the self-indulgence in which he had been reared, had never stifled the rich charity that was inherent in him. To succour the sick, the afflicted, and the needy had ever been one of his readiest impulses, and it was carried to such lengths that where Saint Martin merely divided his cloak with a beggar, Francis had been known to strip off his fine clothes that he might bestow them upon a poor man-at-arms who had asked an alms of him one day in the streets of Assisi.

* * * *

Of some such tenor, whilst lying sick at Spoleto, must have been the reflections construed by his biographers as divine revelation. This they may well have been, if not quite in the sense implied. So that to deny the miracle may be to fall more gravely into error than to affirm it.

They were reflections which stifled in him all aspirations to military glory. They brought him to realize that in no service but the service of humanity—which is the true service of God—would he find contentment and satisfy the longings of his soul.

Not yet perceiving the means to be employed, he came back to Assisi to his father's home and warehouse, to resume his part in the thriving cloth trade his father drove.

His old companions will have hailed with joy the return of one whose radiant presence had been so sorely missed. They crowned him once more with garlands, set the wand of the master of the revels in his hand, and announced themselves the subjects of his festive will.

From habit he suffered them to have their way with him. But his heart was no longer in these vapid revelries, and his lean, narrow countenance, with its dark, liquid eyes, must have betrayed his heart.

Wrapped in abstraction, pensive to the point of gloom, he presided at a banquet, and when thereafter, late at night, they trooped singing forth to disturb a sleeping town, lighting with flambeaux their hilarious way through the narrow streets, Francis, hitherto their leader, was to-night a laggard. He fell behind. Missing him, the revellers retraced their steps, and came upon him lost in reverie.

By bantering questions they sought the cause of this change in him. They discovered it in the obvious assumption that he was love-lorn, and they fell to rallying him with the advice that he should take a wife.

Then, at last, under their jests, the thought in his bosom blossomed forth.

"Yes. You say well. It is time I were wed. My bride is chosen. She is my Lady Poverty."

They conceived that they had at last aroused him, awakened in him the dormant humour, and that he was meeting jest with jest. For they must suppose that he jested, however obscure the jest might be to them.

Very soon the sequel was to show how profoundly he was in earnest.

* * * *

The nuptials did not follow immediately upon that declaration of betrothal.

For some little time yet Francis was to continue in his duties as a merchant, until he should clearly perceive how to fulfil the vocation he had discovered in himself. Nor, at close quarters with its practice, can it, for one reared in

luxury, have been easy to follow in the footsteps of Him
"Who was despised and rejected of men." Luxury breeds
fastidiousness; and this fastidiousness found much that was
repugnant standing in the path he sought to tread.

A year or so must have passed over his head whilst in this
state, between attraction and repulsion, for it was not until
1204 that he took at last a decisive step.

In that year he made a pilgrimage to Rome. He sought
inspiration at the tomb of Saint Peter, set in that great
basilica for the foundation of which tradition held that the
Emperor Constantine had dug the first spadeful of earth.
As an act of humility, and in honour of the Twelve Apostles,
the Christian Emperor had himself carried thence twelve
baskets of that Vatican soil, hallowed by the blood of mar-
tyrs; for the site was that of Nero's circus.

Having knelt in prayer before the sepulchre of the Prince
of the Apostles, amid other pilgrims from every quarter of
the earth, Francis came forth onto the cathedral steps, and
stood considering there the multitude of beggars, ragged
and crippled, who sought to arouse by their laments the
charity of the faithful.

Here he perceived at last the opportunity to celebrate his
nuptials with my Lady Poverty to whom a year ago he had
announced himself betrothed.

It is too much to assert—as is asserted of what he now
did—that he sought to experience in himself the destitution of these mendicants, to bear upon his own soul the
burden of their misery. Circumstanced as he was, with
wealth at his command, no such experience could yet be his.
The poignancy of destitution is not to be felt by assuming
the outward forms of it. Rather, when we see him putting
off his pilgrim's cloak, so that he may don the filthy rags of
one of these unfortunates, so that he may stand, bowl in

hand, among that piteous, whining crew, we are to perceive no more and no less than an act of self-abasement, a protest against the inhibiting fastidiousness that had troubled him, a deliberate trampling underfoot of the pride by which he had been trammelled.

It is related that he begged in the French tongue, and whilst not important, it may well be true, for it was a language that he must have used as freely as Italian. It was the language learnt at the knee of his mother, who was a native of Provence.

The pursuit of his prosperous trade took the elder Bernardone far afield, travelling in a sort of state with his wagons of merchandise and his armed escort, bearing to the fairs of other countries, and particularly of France, the beautiful scarlet cloths that were woven in Assisi. On one of these journeys Bernardone had married his wife Pica. Whilst he was absent on another, his first child had been born, and he had named him Francesco—the Frenchman—in commemoration of that circumstance, and perhaps, too, in honour of his mother. This very name may have been to Francis a further incentive to employ the French tongue as we know that he so often did. It is asserted that he composed his songs in it. But the only one that has come down to us—the Lauds of the Creatures—is in Italian.

This act of voluntary mendicancy upon the steps of Saint Peter's, this symbolization of his union with poverty, of his self-dedication to the service of the poor, seems to have constituted his first step in mysticism, which is a merging of one's own with the divine essences, an ecstatic apprehension of the divine nature, reached intuitively and by none of the ordinary channels of ratiocination.

It was an experience that so definitely set its mark upon him that when he came back to Assisi, the change that hitherto had been working in him gradually was now so pronounced that it could no longer escape notice. This, and the immediate fruits it bore, came to sour his relations with his father. Ready enough to supply him with money to be lavishly spent upon social aggrandizement, Pietro Bernardone grew angry to see his wealth bestowed upon the indigent. In his worldly eyes this was an insane, a wanton squandering of his substance. These differences between himself and his father added to the travail in the soul of Francis.

It was in these days that, according to Saint Bonaventura, he was given an experience that carried him a long way farther upon that journey the first step of which was taken when he stood in rags on the cathedral steps. It was an experience that completed his self-conquest and the subjugation of the lingering remains of a fastidiousness that still stood between himself and the perfect humility that he sought.

He was riding alone one day in the plain of Assisi when he met a leper. The horrible disease of leprosy, which was so abruptly and so inexplicably to disappear from Europe in the dawn of the sixteenth century, was very prevalent still in the thirteenth. Familiarity, however, diminished none of the dread and loathing it inspired. A leper met outside any of the lazarets in which they were segregated and neglected was shunned in horror. And in horror Francis was now urged to ride on, until, suddenly remembering that who would be a soldier of Christ must first conquer himself, he drew rein and dismounted. Perhaps it was to expiate the momentary uncharitable feeling of repugnance that he now not merely filled with money, but actually stooped to kiss, the hand which this poor unclean wretch extended.

The emotional act yielded him at once its almost inevitable emotional fruits. Inspired by a sweetness of charity that approached to ecstasy, there was born in him on the spot the desire to bear to others in similar affliction the amazed, uplifting comfort he had brought to this poor fellow, and to work in future in the lazar houses, in an endeavour to lighten the terrible burden of these among God's most piteous creatures.

Yielding to this saintly impulse, he made it a habit to go down to the leper settlement beyond Rivo Torto, and administer such charity as he could to the poor wretches huddled there. To give them sympathy and spiritual consolation as well as to relieve their material necessities. Of the moral effect of this upon himself, he tells us in his testament:

> See in what manner the Lord gave it to me, Brother Francis, to begin to do penance; when I lived in sin it was very loathsome to me to look upon lepers; but the Lord himself led me amongst them, and I abode with them a while. And when I left them that which had seemed to me loathsome was turned to sweetness in my soul and body.

* * * *

From this time onwards, it becomes more and more his custom to roam alone over the countryside, passionately seeking in solitude and meditation an outlet for the ardour within him, guidance as to the nature of the service to which he feels so strongly called.

In the course of these wanderings he came on an autumn day, as the vines were turning red, to the little Church of San Damiano, situated on a little hillock that was grey-green with olive trees.

He contemplated with sorrow the decay and ruin into which indifference was suffering the little church to fall.

He entered. The place was empty. He went down upon his knees before the altar, above which a Byzantine crucifix was suspended, and in the utter stillness of the place he sank into an absorption of prayer which may well have produced that deadening of consciousness which attends all really intense concentration.

Whilst in this state it seemed to him that the crucified figure spoke aloud.

"Francis, seest thou not that my House is being destroyed? Go, then, and repair it for me."

It was an echo, booming out of his subconsciousness, of the very thought that had engrossed his conscious contemplation. Aroused by that illusion of sound, convinced that an audible physical voice had addressed him, he was penetrated by awe. He could suppose only that this voice was—as well it may have been, whilst still a projection of his subconsciousness—the voice of God. He could assume only that the command touched upon the subject of his thoughts, never suspecting that those thoughts might have given shape to the command. The House that was being destroyed must, of course, be the house whose decay he had so sorrowfully contemplated, this Church of San Damiano. Nothing remained but to address himself at once to providing for its repair.

He sought the poor priest who had charge of the place, and gave him money for oil, to the end that an altar lamp should always be kept burning before that altar whence the heavenly voice had addressed him. Then he went his ways, to consider the provision of means for fulfilling the task imposed upon him.

The elder Bernardone was absent at the time. Had he been present, it is certain that he would never have furnished money to be so unprofitably squandered. His absence, however, supplied the opportunity. Francis took from the warehouse some bales of cloth, and with these rode ten miles to the Umbrian market-town of Foligno, where he offered them for sale. Having sold them, he sold also his horse and its furniture, and he returned on foot to Assisi, going, however, no farther than San Damiano.

To the old priest there he offered not only the money which the sale had realized, but also himself, having by now taken the resolve to quit the world and devote himself entirely to the service of God, to which he accounted himself summoned.

At first the priest supposed it an ill-considered jest on the part of this young man, whom formerly he had known merely for a pleasure-seeker and a reveller. Even when at last persuaded of his earnestness, and whilst ready enough to shelter Francis and to accept the service which he offered, yet he could not bring himself to touch the money, being aware of the source of it and shrewdly fearful of the wrath of Pietro Bernardone. Since the priest would not receive it into his hands, Francis cast the purse into the church, and there let it lie.

The merchant, returning home, missed his son and probably also the bales of cloth. Inquiries eliciting that the young man was at San Damiano, thither the angry father went in quest of him, and summoned him to return home. Francis fled at first before the paternal wrath; then, taking heart, he confronted it, and met the order by a firm refusal, from which neither entreaties nor threats could move him. No earthly power should turn him now from the service which he had embraced. But what restitution could be made, he made. To pacify his angry parent, he delivered up the money produced by the sale he had effected at Foligno.

Bernardone went off in dudgeon, and appealed to the

consuls to constrain his son to obedience. The consuls summoned Francis to appear before them. But Francis, setting up as a plea the religious life which he had entered, and which in his view constituted him a cleric, declined to recognize their authority over him. Thereupon the outraged father addressed his appeals to the ecclesiastical authorities, and Francis received an order to wait upon the Bishop of Assisi and answer the plaints his father laid against him.

Bowing to this, Francis went up the hill from San Damiano, and took his way to the episcopal palace.

There, in the audience chamber, crowded with citizens, among whom there were some of those who only a few months ago had been the young man's fellow-revellers and who now supposed him mad, Bishop Guido sat in judgment. There the indignant father appeared as plaintiff, to demand of this undutiful son either obedience or renunciation of his heritage.

There was in Francis no hesitation over that choice. At once he made abdication of his rights, and so as to symbolize its completeness, he stripped off his clothes, notwithstanding that it was winter-time by now, and cast them at his father's feet, addressing him, says Saint Bonaventura, with a marvellous fervour.

"Until this hour I have called you my father upon earth. Henceforth I turn confidently to my Father who is in Heaven, in whose hands I have set all my treasure, all my trust and all my hope."

Touched by the fervour with which he perceived the young man to be inspired, the Bishop came down from his throne to embrace him, and to cover his nakedness with the episcopal mantle.

Thereafter, in an old cloak from one of the Bishop's servants, the gift of which he accepted with the joyous gratitude proper to the Bridegroom of Poverty, he departed the place, leaving the spectators stricken with awe and wonder to behold one who had been known for pleasure-loving and worldly so signally penetrated by a spirit of holiness and renunciation.

* * * *

Wrapped in that mean cloak, to protect him against the wintry weather, Francis set out for Gubbio, some twenty miles to the north, over the hills, to seek assistance from a friend who dwelt there. The identity of the friend does not transpire, nor why Francis should have preferred to go so far afield when surely there must have been friends nearer home who would have come to his assistance.

On the road he was set upon by robbers, and stripped of his poor cloak. At nightfall he stood in his shirt at the gates of a monastery, begging shelter. This shelter he was given, and with it some poor and scanty food. To earn the one and the other he was set to do scullion work in the kitchen. Clothing of any kind was refused him.

It may well be that his destiny led him to this convent, so that in the grudging charity extended to him, he should realize at first hand how little remained in monasteries of that Christian spirit first responsible for their institution. It may have led him to realize how the people came to be left without spiritual sustenance or guidance; how ossified religion had become, confined to ritual observances and to theological exegesis, to the utter neglect of the practical application of its principles. It may be that it was by reflections of this kind, prompted by this bitter experience, that he ultimately came to perceive the work that was to be done, and to attach a deeper, fuller meaning to the command imposed upon him at San Damiano.

He came at last to Gubbio, and from his friend there readily obtained the little that he craved: a grey tunic with a leather belt, a pair of shoes and a staff. Thence he went to his charitable work among the lepers at Pareti, and then, at last, back to San Damiano to undertake those repairs with which he believed himself divinely entrusted.

Difficulties, however, are now far greater than before, for he commanded no means whatever. He will beg them. To this end he goes once more up into the rosy city of Assisi, which rises by terraces in the shadow of Mount Subasio. This time his mendicancy is no mere act of self-abasement. It is a reality. In performing it he despises the shame of the act for the love of "Him who was poor and lowly of heart." Yet all that he begged at present was stone. He begged it so passionately that his fervour awakened fervour. Not only were the stones forthcoming, but willing hands to assist him, too, in his pious work. Labouring with a vigour that seemed amazing in so slight a man, he completed at last the rescue of that little temple from decay. When it was repaired and sound once more, Francis turned his attention to other neighbouring churches, which, neglected, stood in similar need: first to that of Saint Peter, just outside the walls of Assisi to the west; then to that of Santa Maria della Porziuncula, down among the cornfields of the valley, some three miles away. Both these churches were the property of the great Benedictine Monastery on Mount Subasio, whose abbot could but look on in approval at this pious work of restoration.

Whilst Francis was engaged on these labours, he continued to share the home of the priest of San Damiano. But once the work was finished, he departed thence and went to dwell alone near Santa Maria della Porziuncula— called also Santa Maria degli Angeli—the humblest of the

three churches, but one that was to become very dear to him
in the future.

He supported himself by begging his bread in the streets
of Assisi, "for the love of Him who was born poor and did
most poorly live in the world, remained naked and poor
upon the cross, and was buried in another's sepulchre."

*   *   *   *

It was upon the Feast of Saint Matthew, the 24th February, of the year 1209, at Mass in the Church of the Porziuncula, that he heard in the gospel of the day—the Gospel
according to Saint Matthew—a command imposed upon
himself, which was at once an explanation and an amplification of the earlier command received at San Damiano:

"Wherever ye go, preach, saying: 'The Kingdom of
Heaven is at hand.' Heal the sick, cleanse the lepers, cast
out devils. Freely ye have received, freely give. Provide
neither silver nor gold nor brass in your purses, neither
scrip, nor two coats, nor shoes, nor staff, for the labourer is
worthy of his hire."

From the moment that he perceived in this gospel a message addressed to himself, he discovered a new and fuller
meaning in the words that he believed had been spoken to
him at San Damiano. He had interpreted the message in too
literal and narrow a sense. The House of the Lord that he
had been bidden to repair was not merely, as he had supposed, that little Church of San Damiano, but Christianity
itself, which, in prey to heresy and indifference and ministered by worldlings, was falling into ruin. In the command
that he conceived imposed upon him by the Gospel according to Saint Matthew he saw not only the real task awaiting
him, but also the particular manner in which he should
fulfil it.

His obedience was immediate and literal. He cast away his staff, his scrip, his purse, and his shoes, and so went forth on the apostolate with which he believed that he was charged.

As little Brother Francis, Christ's Poor Man, he would henceforth continue to beg his bread, but, in return, nourish the starved souls of the people by recalling them to the service of God and humanity.

He was twenty-seven years of age.

He was greeted at first in his native Assisi with mockery and insult. Scorned as a madman, he was derided, pelted with filth, even beaten, all of which he bore as so many favours bestowed upon him.

He preached a simple gospel of love that could be understood by all, and presently, before the inspired fervour of his words, supported by the example of humility, charity, and self-denial which his life was become, mockery was gradually silenced, and the Assisians came in ever-increasing numbers to listen to his message. Passionately sincere in his plea that men should give up ill-gotten gains, renounce all enmities and prevail by gentleness and love, he bewildered his audiences by no exegitical subtleties, propounded no doctrines. He spoke to them in their own simple language of simple things which they could understand and which were concerned with their own simple lives. He stripped Christianity naked of all the theology in which it was swaddled, lost, and stifling, and held it up to them in its pure irresistible loveliness.

Little by little the people came to discover in his words that spiritual nourishment for which all men crave, but which there had been practically no one to dispense to them. He touched the hearts and awakened the souls of his audiences. A people brutalized by ignorance or corrupted by false culture, a people who knew not where to seek happiness save in the will-o'-the-wisp of pleasure, were made to realize the joys that may irradiate lives lived for others, the peace and tranquillity that may so be won.

Amongst those who came frequently to hear him there was one, wealthy, noble, and still young, Bernard of Quintavalle, who was early convinced that here was no lunatic, but a man of holy and inspired sanity. So profoundly did he realize it that he was impelled to associate himself with Francis.

He invited him to supper, and thereafter opened his heart to him; announced himself so touched by the words and example of Francis that he had taken the resolve to distribute his possessions and join him in the apostolate he had assumed.

Having invited Bernard to consider well the hardships and difficulties that would be present, Francis conducted him early next morning to hear Mass in the Church of Saint Nicholas. On the way thither, whether spontaneously or by prearrangement with Francis, they were joined by another who had been similarly stirred, one Peter of Catania, a canon of the Cathedral Church of San Rufino and a doctor of laws.

At the end of the Mass, Francis led them both up to the altar, opened the missal, and read aloud to them the answer of Jesus to the rich young man who questioned Him: "If thou wilt be perfect, go and sell that thou hast, and give to the poor, and thou shalt have treasure in Heaven; and come follow Me."

Next he read the words from the Gospel of Saint Matthew in which he had heard his own vocation announced to him.

To these he added the passage: "Then said Jesus unto

his disciples: If any man will come after me, let him deny himself, and take up his cross and follow me. For whosoever will save his life shall lose it, and whosoever will lose his life for my sake shall find it. For what is a man profited if he shall gain the whole world and lose his own soul?"

"My brothers," he said to them, "this is our life and our rule, and that of all who may join us. Go, then, and do as you have heard."

In this simple fashion, on that spring morning of April 1209, on the altar-steps of the Church of Saint Nicholas, among those three, was founded the great Franciscan Order and the Rule enunciated by which it should be governed.

* * * *

In the same simple manner as the Order came into existence was its first home found for it. As soon as Bernard and Peter had distributed their possessions, they went with Francis to the Porziuncula, barefoot and clad in the coarse ashen-coloured tunic which Francis had adopted, and there they built themselves with boughs and reeds the hut that was the first monastery of the Order.

A week later they were joined by yet a third neophyte, a youth named Egidio, than whom no man was to prove himself more faithful to the Franciscan ideal, of whom Francis was later to say, in one of those poetical allusions in which he expressed himself: "Egidio is one of the paladins of my Round Table."

Since it was not the contemplative life of the anchorite concerned only with the salvation of his own soul that Francis desired for himself and his brethren, but the active mission of bearing to their fellow-men a gospel of peace and joy and compassion for moral ugliness, they did not long remain at the Porziuncula. Dividing their forces, Bernard and Peter went south into Emilia, whilst Francis and Egidio, going in the opposite direction, sought the March of Ancona.

They lived not only on the bread received as alms, but also on the bread they earned by the labour of their hands, toiling when they could with the peasants in the fields. They took no thought for the morrow. On their pious journey they slept where they might, like other homeless outcasts, in caves, under haystacks, in the porches of churches, or wherever else they could find shelter. Their only guide was the injunction Francis had laid upon them: "Cast thy care upon the Lord, and He shall nourish thee."

To those who asked them who they were and whence they came, they answered: "We are penitents, natives of the city of Assisi."

Going barefoot, thinly clad in their poor grey tunics with a girdle of hemp, they attracted attention and drew not a little insult upon themselves, especially in cities.

They were mocked, despised, abused, ill-treated, all of which they bore with an uncomplaining, unprotesting patience that disarmed their assailants.

But if many were moved to treat them as vagrants and madmen, many more were brought to consider their voluntary poverty with wonder, and out of regard for it to listen to their message. Recruits joined them, slowly at first, but in ever-increasing numbers, so that by the end of the first year, Francis was compelled seriously to consider the situation which was arising. In a measure, as their spreading fame earned them consideration and rendered them immune from the attacks of the ribald, they found themselves confronted by a much graver hostility; that of the clergy. It was a hostility not entirely without justification when it is remembered that these Poor Men of Assisi had no authority or ordination for assuming a task that belonged to ecclesiastics. They found themselves viewed with mistrust and perhaps suspected of adding, like the Poor Men of Lyons, one more to the heretical groups that were already distracting the Church.

As a result, not so that he might escape persecution, but so that this great movement which he had set on foot for the awakening of consciences should not be stifled, Francis now perceived the need to draw up the Rule of his Order, and submit it to the Pope for his approbation and sanction.

This he expounded to his companions assembled at the Porziuncula, which remained their headquarters, and where, to accommodate them, further huts had been built in the grove about the little chapel.

To accompany him upon that journey to Rome he chose eleven of his followers, so that with himself they made up a company of twelve, the number of the first Apostles. Some biographers hold that there were twelve besides Francis. But this implies something too alien to his profoundly humble spirit to be acceptable. Whilst seeking in all things to make of his life an imitation of that of Jesus, he would have shrunk from any step that would have identified him, however remotely, with the Saviour.

Foremost among those who accompanied him were Bernard of Quintavalle, Peter of Catania, and Egidio, and it was Bernard who was chosen as their guide and director.

They went on foot, joyously, singing as they tramped like the joculatores Domini—the jongleurs and troubadours of the Lord—Francis was to name them.

*   *   *   *

In Rome they had the good fortune to find the Bishop of Assisi, that same Guido who had sat in judgment when

Bernardone brought his plaint against his son. The Bishop took them under his protection, spoke for them and presented them to Giovanni Colonna, Cardinal of San Paolo, who professed himself ready to employ his influence on their behalf. Before employing it, he questioned them closely and searchingly upon their aims; and this not once, but several times. He represented to them that the life they had chosen was unendurably harsh, and he sought to prevail upon them to be content to gratify their monastic vocation by entering one of the orders already in existence. Against this, however, Francis stood humbly firm.

Perceiving that they were not to be moved from their purpose, and having satisfied himself that heresy formed no part of their impulse, Cardinal Colonna consented to present them to the Pope.

Innocent III, still young—in his fiftieth year, and the twelfth of his pontificate—a stern pope, clear of intellect, indomitable of will, a great jurist, and one of the most imposing figures in history, had done much to suppress ecclesiastical disorder, to drive the money-changers from the temple. But even for such a will and such energy as his the task was proving immensely difficult. The harm had gone almost too far before he took the reins. Through the laxity and greed of the clergy, the Church had lost her grip of humanity. Heresy was besetting her on every side; and the Albigenses, the Manichæans, and the Cathars, the most prominent and dangerous of them all, were daily increasing in power and influence.

Enthroned in majesty, Christ's Vicar listened carefully to the petition of this man who strove to make of his life an imitation of Christ's. He considered attentively the slight figure, barefoot, in its despicable tunic, the unhandsome olive-tinted countenance, bearded, ill-kempt, with heavy black eyebrows over dark, gentle eyes; and the Holy Father was not to suspect that here stood one who, seeming nothing, yet counted for more in the world than did he, whose iron hand had brought the princes of the earth into subjection.

The fervour animating Francis left the Pope in no doubt. He said so. But, like Cardinal Colonna, he raised the objection that the life of these men was too harsh. If he were to approve the Rule that governed them, he would be imposing it upon those who would come after them, and who might well find its fulfilment beyond their strength. Still, he would consider; he would take counsel with the College. Upon that he affectionately dismissed them.

A consistory followed, in which it is to be gathered that feeling ran strongly against the Penitents of Assisi, for it was asked what innovation, what new doctrine was this with which the College was assailed? How could it be possible for anyone to live without temporal possessions?

These scornful questions were silenced by the Cardinal of San Paolo.

"But if we hold that to observe gospel perfection and make profession of it is an irrational and impossible innovation, are we not convicted of blasphemy against the Author of the gospel?"

That gave the questioners pause, whilst upon the acute mind of Innocent III it made a profound impression. None was better aware than he of the extent to which the great possessions of ecclesiastics raised obstacles to reform, and rendered the Church vulnerable to the powerful attacks of the Albigenses and the Cathars and the rest. The propounders of those heresies, too, preached a communistic doctrine of poverty, and it was by this that they won their ever-increasing adherents.

Since, and for reasons obvious to this clear-sighted man, the banner of poverty was one to which the poor, who composed, when all is said, the great mass of humanity, would inevitably flock, let it at least be borne by men in whose simple teaching there was no heresy destructive of the existing hierarchy.

Thus, in sanctioning the Penitents of Assisi, Innocent perceived, and perceived shrewdly and truly, that he might be raising a powerful bulwark against the forces that were threatening to overthrow the Church and engulf Christianity. At least it was worth an experiment.

Therefore, when Francis and his brethren came again before him, he received them with affection and announced to them that he would authorize their missions subject to their obtaining the local consent of the ordinaries in every instance.

"Go, my brethren," was his dismissal of them, "and may God be with you. Preach penitence to all according as the Lord may deign to inspire you. Then, when the Almighty shall have made you increase and advance, you will refer to us. We will grant what you ask, and we may then with greater security grant you even more than you ask."

He required them, as in the case of the other orders, to elect a superior, to whom the ecclesiastical authorities could address themselves at need, and he directed that they should receive the diaconal tonsure. Thus, whilst the sanction accorded them was no more than oral, and, therefore, to be regarded as little more than probationary, yet the seal of the Church was placed upon them.

Dismissed with the apostolic blessing, they went to render thanks at the tomb of Saint Peter. Then they quitted Rome, fortified and enheartened by the consciousness of the authority with which they were invested. There was a new ardour now in their preaching in the villages and townships through which they passed on their homeward journey, and they prefaced their sermons with the announcement of the authority they had received from the Holy Father.

Of Francis it might be said that he preached as the lark sings, simply, directly, and joyously, from the heart of him to the hearts of the multitudes that now flocked to listen. He was no doctrinaire, as has been said. He had discovered no new Heaven or new way to the old one. Where the clerics of the time, like the Epicureans of old, seemed to put God outside the world, aloof and remote in His celestial abode, Francis brought Him into the world, into every man's heart, and pointed to His benign self-revelation in all humanity and all nature. The simple words in which he preached the simple ideals upon which Christianity is founded were touched with the fire of his poetic, mystic spirit.

We have of him a precious pen-portrait by one Thomas of Spalato, who when a student at Bologna heard him preach there on the Feast of the Assumption of 1220. And for all that ten years lie between that date and the time of Francis' return from Rome, yet there is no reason to suppose that the description will not apply as fittingly to one date as the other.

> . . . I saw Saint Francis preaching on the piazza of the lesser palace before almost every man in the city. The theme of his discourse was of Angels, Men, and Demons. He spoke on all these subjects with so much wisdom and eloquence that many learned men who were present were filled with admiration at the words of so plain a man. Yet he had not the manner of a preacher. His ways were rather those of conversation. The subject of his discourse bore especially upon the abolition of enmities and the necessity of peaceful alliances. His apparel was poor, his person in no respect imposing, his face not at all handsome. But God gave such

great efficacy to his words that he brought back to peace and harmony many nobles whose wild fury had not even stopped short of shedding blood. So great a devotion was felt for him that men and women flocked after him, and they esteemed themselves happy who succeeded in touching the hem of his garment.

Whilst he extolled the virtues of poverty, whilst he perceived in poverty deliverance from all those anxieties that debase existence, yet it must not be understood that he preached poverty to the world as a necessary preliminary step to salvation. The injunction, "Go give to the poor," was, like that of celibacy, only for those who proposed to embrace the religious life. It was the corner-stone of the Rule he had drawn up for the men who were to share his apostolate, so that thus they might emancipate themselves from worldly cares, escape from the gilded cage which prevents the soul of man from soaring into spiritual regions.

From the Legend of the Three Companions we learn that he admonished the brethren that they should judge no man, nor despise such as live delicately and go clad in gay and sumptuous raiment. He reminded them that God could justify these, and that they helped good men to works of repentance by providing them with the things the body needs. The joyousness that was ever in him and that he inculcated into his followers was rooted in tolerance. Whilst embracing poverty for love of and in imitation of "Him who was poor and despised of men," yet he neither preached nor practised a sour asceticism, but rather warned his followers against fasts and the mortifying of the flesh that enfeeble the body, thereby rendering it unequal alike to the physical labours by which it was to earn its meat and to the spiritual labours to which its life was dedicate.

"The sinner can fast, he can pray, weep, and mortify his

flesh. But one thing he cannot do: he cannot be faithful to God."

There was in Francis no puritanical moroseness or pietistic gloom. He did not whine his way through life. Mirth and joy were with him religious duties. "It becomes not," he says, "the servant of the Lord to show sadness and a woeful countenance before his brother or anyone else."

In his relations with women we find him pure and simple and direct, with that profound purity of soul which is under no necessity of setting restraints upon the flesh as the only means of ensuring that it, too, shall remain pure. The chastity—which, with humility and obedience, made up the three cardinal principles of the Rule—imposed no extravagant necessity of shunning women, or of keeping his eyes upon the ground when they were addressed. He was as frank, direct, and loving with them as he was with men and with all created things, animate and inanimate. All creation was to him a great brotherhood, and so he addressed it in his Lauds of the Creatures: Brother Sun, Sister Moon, Brother Fire, Sister Water. The flowers and the birds were similarly his brethren, and his poor, patient body that so long had borne the burden of his soul, he addressed on that account as Brother Ass.

*   *   *   *

In the Umbrian Plain, at the foot of the hill up the flank of which Assisi rises, at a distance of an hour's walk from the city, on the edge of a mountain torrent that here has lost its fury, stood the abandoned and decaying leper-house of Rivo Torto. It was situated midway between San Damiano and the Porziuncula, and within easy reach of these two spots so dear to Francis, and so intimately associated with the beginnings of his apostolate.

It was here, in this ruin, on their return from Rome, that the brethren now established themselves, and it was from here that they went forth upon their missions to the neighbouring townships. Their steadily increasing numbers soon crowded these narrow quarters; they were inundated when the torrent came down in flood; and they were at times forced to subsist on roots and berries; yet they bore their hardships not only stoutly, but with actual joy, their hearts uplifted by the abundant evidences of the great fruitfulness of their labours.

The papal sanction with which they came invested procured Francis on his return to Assisi an almost triumphant reception. Such was the eagerness to hear him preach that the Church of Saint George, which was now thrown open to him by the clergy that so lately had regarded him askance, proved inadequate to house the crowd, and the Cathedral of San Rufino was placed at his disposal.

Quietly conversational in manner, as we know, disdaining the rhetorical and casuistical arts that had rendered pulpit utterances unintelligible to the masses, he denounced the horrors of war, the sins of the populace, the abuses and rapacity of the great; and he showed how all these evils afflicting the world sprang from the lack of that love which should unite all mankind into one great brotherhood. By his ardour, his sincerity, his divine tenderness, he succeeded in arousing in his hearers an enthusiasm for good.

Nor were his activities now confined to preaching and to the care of lepers. Strong in the papal approbation he had received, rendered by it more sure of himself and of the sanctity of his mission, Francis intervened in civil affairs and in the politics of Assisi which were in a deplorable condition. Ever since the subjugatory peace which had been forced upon the people by Perugian intervention on behalf of the patricians, unrest had been smouldering, to betray itself in occasional vivid outbursts. Liberties were accorded grudgingly to the malcontents, and only under pressure of fear. The state of things between the *minores* and the *majores,* as the people and the patricians were respectively termed, was little better than an armed truce, a hotbed of mutual hatred, poisoning existence.

Francis applied himself, and employed the influence he had won, to repair this evil. And so effectively did he go to work with both parties that he brought them eventually to compromises mutually satisfactory. A treaty was signed on the 9th November 1210 embodying the terms to be observed by the factions hitherto opposed. This treaty, known as the *pace civile,* still exists. It provides against any alliances other than by common accord, and binds both parties to do all which may be necessary for the honour, safety, and advantage of the Commune of Assisi. From this resulted an era of peace and tranquillity for the city, the credit for which belongs entirely to Francis' benevolent and pacificatory influence.

It was at about this time, and not altogether unconnected with this, that the Order was at last given a name by which it was to be celebrated down the centuries.

One day, at Rivo Torto, a brother was reading aloud the Rule. He was interrupted by Francis at the words: "In whatever houses the brothers may serve or labour, let them be not chamberlains, or cellarmen, or stewards . . . but let them be underlings, subject to all who are in the house."

The term in the Rule, as in fact, for underlings was *minores*. Perceiving its applicability to their Order, which was still nameless, Francis seized upon it, and announced to them that henceforth they should be known as *Fratres Minores,* or Friars Minor.

*   *   *   *

By the following spring (1211) the growth of the Order found the brethren overcrowded at Rivo Torto. The inconvenience of this was relieved by the Abbot of the Benedictines of Mount Subasio, whose friendly disposition had earlier been earned by the repairs Francis had carried out on the two churches that were the property of the monastery. He granted them in perpetuity the Church of the Porziuncula, and no grant could have been more welcome to Francis than that of this little temple which his own hands had laboured to restore and beside which he had built his first hut.

The friars set to work in the forest that surrounded the Porziuncula, and rapidly built themselves huts of wattles, plastered with mud, and rudely thatched. A quick-set hedge was planted to enclose the space they appropriated, and thus came into being the first convent of the Friars Minor, which for ten years was to be the headquarters of the Order.

Yearly, in fee for the gift, Francis offered the Benedictines of Mount Subasio a netful of fish and a measure of oil.

When abiding here in the intervals of their missionary work, the brethren laboured to earn their bread. Mendicancy, for its own sake, as an act of humility, and because necessary to men who were permitted by their Rule to carry nothing, was adopted only on their missionary journeys, when they might well be considered to earn, by their spiritual labours, the food they received as alms.

At the Porziuncula, those who were skilled in a handicraft continued to exercise it; those who were not, could learn one; or else they hired themselves out to labour in the fields, to plough and sow, to hew wood, draw water, harvest the corn, to gather the olives and at vintage time the grapes, to crush the oil or tread the wine. To sustain themselves they sold their products or took wages for their toil, but always in food, and never in money, which they were forbidden to touch.

They cultivated, too, the land which they had cleared in their enclosure, and Francis insisted that this cultivation should not be entirely concerned with edible things. Some portion was to be set apart for their sisters the flowers.

Here they led a life of industry, mirth, and love, and hither to join them came men from every walk of life: men noble and wealthy, like Brothers Angelo and Rufino; simple peasants, like Brother Juniper and Brother John; and a few clerics, like Brother Silvestre, the first priest to join the Order, and Brother Leo, who became the secretary and confessor of Francis, and who, to the end of his long life, when schism had come to split the Order, remained stoutly true to the original ideal.

* * * *

And now came the founding of the Second Order, so that women, too, might live according to the Rule and share and complement the work the brethren were doing.

The event was not sought or contemplated by Francis. Perhaps it was not even desired by him until the occasion presented itself.

Mention has just been made of Brother Rufino among the companions of Francis. He was connected with the noble house of Scefi, who were Counts of Sassorosso. His conversion and perhaps his talk of Francis may first have aroused his cousin Clare's interest in the friar. She was still very young—born in 1194, she would be not more than seventeen—when first she went to hear Francis, during Lent, in the Cathedral of Assisi. She had been reared in the ways of devotion by a fervently devout mother, who had made a pilgrimage to Jerusalem, and she was given to charitable works in Assisi among the poor and the afflicted.

To hear Francis preach proved to her, as it had proved to so many others, to be infected with his zeal for good, and to desire to devote her life to its promotion, casting aside the vanities of the world. She consulted a widowed cousin, Bona Guelfucci. Through her, and possibly also through her cousin Rufino, she obtained an interview with Francis. She cast herself at his feet and divulged the aspirations he had aroused in her to follow in his ways.

His acceptance of her does not appear to have been immediate. It hardly could have been, for no highway to the gratification of her pious wish stood open. But at last his consent was won, and Palm Sunday of 1212 was the day appointed for her consecration.

On that day, at Mass, in the Cathedral, she appeared for the last time in the raiment of her rank. She was very beautiful, we are told, tall and golden; and she came to the Cathedral sheathed in scarlet, her head-dress of white lawn, and a jewelled girdle at her waist.

That night, in the Porziuncula, she shed for ever these splendours.

She had slipped out of her father's palace after nightfall, and made her way to the Palazzo Guelfucci, where Bona and some other ladies waited to accompany her.

They set out on foot through the clear spring night, and made their way down to the plain and the grove which enshrined the Porziuncula.

Loud, joyous chanting greeted them as they approached, and through the trees to meet them, bearing lighted candles, came Francis and a band of his brethren.

She knelt before the altar of the little chapel, on the spot where Francis himself had been inspired to his vocation, and there Francis, a simple deacon, usurping powers which belong to a bishop, received her vows, shore away her golden hair, covered her with the penitential veil, and replaced the brave scarlet gown by the mean frock of the Order, the jewelled girdle by a hempen rope.

This done, he conducted her that same night to the house of the Benedictine nuns at San Paolo on the Chiuso.

Thither next day came storming Count Favorino Scefi, her father, prepared to carry her away by main force. But before her resoluteness his anger left him, his intention melted away.

Perhaps the scene was too disturbing to the Benedictine sisters, and they foresaw and feared repetitions of it, or perhaps there were other reasons for her removal; but removed she was within a week or two to the Convent of Sant' Angelo in Panso. There she was joined by her sister Agnes, a child of fourteen, and there we have a repetition of the stormy scene with their father, exasperated to see his children thus deserting him.

He prevailed, however, with Agnes no better than with Clare, and this notwithstanding the violence to which he is said to have subjected her. Strong in her determination, she brought him to understand that he might slay her, but that he could not break the sacred tie in which she considered herself bound.

That sojourn with the Benedictines proved no more than a temporary arrangement for the sisters. It lasted only until Francis could dispose that, with other women whom he knew were now waiting to join them, they could live as they desired, according to the Rule by which the friars were governed.

It was again the Benedictine Abbot of Mount Subasio who came to his assistance, ceding to him this time the Church of San Damiano, where first Francis had received the injunction to repair the House of the Lord.

By Francis Clare was given the Rule, in the same simplicity as that which was observed by the brethren, but excluding the obligation of missionary work. The necessities of life were to be supplied to them by the friars, and the Poor Ladies—as they were first called—were to earn them by nursing the sick received at San Damiano for the purpose, by spinning and weaving and making altar-cloths and vestments, and in other ways that might be to the glory of God and the benefit of the Order.

Thus arose the Second Order, later to be known as that of the Poor Clares. It came into being as automatically as the First Order, without any calculation on the part of Francis, who at the outset, in laying down his precepts had no thought to do more than present a way of life to be followed by the faithful in the world at large.

* * * *

Very soon the Porziuncula became as inadequate to accommodate the ever-increasing brotherhood as Rivo Torto had become a little while before. The necessity arose to establish further quarters; and since the Order was not only increasing but spreading, new convents began to be set up in other parts of Italy. For their regulation it became necessary to convoke chapters, and these meetings were held at the Porziuncula, which thus continued to be the headquarters of the Order. They were convoked twice yearly, at Whitsuntide and at Michaelmas, when additions to, or modifications of the Rule were determined, in a measure as the widening and changing circumstances required, but never varying in the fundamental Rule of poverty.

Thence Francis—"being in the midst of them," says Thomas of Celano, who must have joined the Order at about this time, "as a true well-spring from which each might drink the living water of life"—would dismiss them with his blessing upon their missionary work, reminding them that as they proclaimed peace, so they should carry it in their hearts.

Whilst his brethren pursued in ever-widening circles the evangelizing of Italy, Francis himself was now moved to carry his message still farther afield. He set out to gratify a very natural desire to see the Holy Land and at the same time to preach the gospel to the Saracens, persuaded that if they heard it in the simplicity in which he presented it they would be won to Christianity. Unfortunately, the vessel that bore him was wrecked on the Dalmatian coast, whence he had no early opportunity of resuming the voyage. He returned, therefore, to Italy landing at Ancona. But the intention to carry the gospel to the Saracen remained unimpaired, and in the following year he renewed the attempt, and set out for Morocco. Again he was thwarted. He got no farther than Spain. There he was taken ill, and as a consequence constrained once more to return, and yet again to postpone a mission upon which his heart was set.

* * * *

In the summer of the year 1216 died not only the great Pope Innocent III, who had sanctioned the Order, but also the Cardinal of San Paolo, to whose intervention this was in a measure due, and who had thereafter remained the recognized protector of the Brothers Minor.

To succeed him in this, Cardinal Ugolino Conti, the Bishop of Ostia (later to occupy the throne of Saint Peter as Gregory IX) now came forward. He was another prelate who had lent Francis his support in those early days in Rome, and his protection now was gratefully accepted.

He took an early opportunity of visiting the Porziuncula, and we gather how deeply impressed he was by the simplicity in which he found the brethren living, from a comment chronicled by Thomas of Celano: "Alas for us who to live at all require so much that is superfluous."

It is asserted that so powerfully was this great Prince of the Church attracted by the saintly simplicity and joyousness in which the Order lived that he at one time actually consulted Francis as to whether he should join it.

Meanwhile, in the Papacy Innocent III was succeeded by Cencio di Savelli, who reigned as Honorius III, and who at once took up the preaching of the Crusade which had been engaging his predecessor when death overtook him. The matter was one that closely concerned an order which, like that of the Friars Minor, had made missionary work its particular function, and at the Pentecostal Chapter of 1217, which was attended by Cardinal Ugolino, one of the chief decisions taken was that a number of friars should accompany the Crusaders. These being chosen, they were given for their leader Elias of Cortona, a brother destined to great celebrity in the Order.

At the same time other missions were organized, and in view of the wide diffusion which the Franciscans had

reached, ministers-provincial were officially appointed to
rule the various provinces of the Order established in Italy
and abroad.

Francis himself now proposed to undertake a mission to
France. He contemplated with natural joy this visit to a
country in which his mother had been born and whose
language he had spoken from the cradle. He must have
yielded with pain to the well-founded dissuasions of Cardinal Ugolino. The Cardinal represented that it was not in
the interests of the Order that Francis should be absent
from Italy just then. The Friars Minor, he pointed out,
did not lack for enemies in the Roman Curia. Ugolino
himself, and others who shared his views, would continue
to defend the Order from all attacks, but only on the
condition that Francis should remain at hand.

Francis protested. "It would be shame for me to send
my brethren afar, whilst I remain idly here, sharing none
of the tribulations they must confront."

"Why, then, have you sent your brethren so far away,"
asked the Cardinal, "exposing them to starvation and
danger?"

"Do you think," he was answered with warmth, "that
God raised up the friars for the sake of this country alone?
They have been raised up for the arousing and the salvation of all men, and they shall win souls not only in the
countries of those who believe, but also in the very midst
of the infidels."

Whilst bowing to this, Ugolino still insisted that for
the reasons urged Francis should remain, and another
brother be sent in his stead. To this Francis submitted.

Set-backs to the ever-widening spread of the movement
were few. Missions to Germany and Hungary failed for

lack of foresight. The brethren sent spoke no German or Hungarian. And the mission to Spain failed because of the bigotry and intolerance always present in countries where religions are mixed. The Jewish and Moslem population of Spain rendered the Spaniards acutely jealous of the integrity of their faith and fiercely apprehensive of heretical assaults upon it, of which of late there had been many from within. These Franciscan lay preachers, usurping clerical functions, came promptly under suspicion of heresy, and to escape persecution they crossed the border into Portugal, where they were well received.

The hostility of some of the members of the Sacred College, which had concerned Ugolino, was more serious, because destined ultimately profoundly to affect the Order, although perhaps far less disastrously than some have supposed. With these prelates, too, the hostility was based on resentment that a lay order which, from such small beginnings, was rapidly spreading over the face of the earth, should usurp functions that properly belonged to the priesthood, and this upon no more than a verbal, and more or less probationary, sanction. To an increase of this sanction by any bulls that should bring the Order into bondage, or that should confer privileges upon it with one hand, whilst, by a complication of its Rule, robbing it with the other of its pristine simplicity, Francis was sternly opposed.

Not even upon the ground of expediency would he yield the point when it was pressed by Ugolino and even by some of the friars who conceived that they saw the reasonableness of the Cardinal's recommendations.

When these pointed out to Francis that often bishops would not permit them to preach and compelled them to stand idle for days, and that surely it were better to obtain from the Pope a privilege that would remove these barriers, we have the reply that sums up his attitude in the matter:

"I would first convert the prelates by humility and respect. When they have seen us respectful and humble towards them, they will themselves beg us to preach to the people. As for me, I ask of God no privilege, unless it be that I have none. Let us be full of respect for all men, and convert them, as our Rule ordains, more by our example than our words."

After this, as a means of stifling clerical opposition, Ugolino could think of nothing better than to bring Francis to preach before the Pope. Thus the Holy Father might satisfy himself that in the friar's message there was no taint of heresy such as was being implied. Whatever Francis may have felt, he could not refuse. But for so grave an occasion he could not trust, as he usually did, to inspiration, could not confine himself to the simple improvisations which hitherto had so well succeeded.

The story runs that he wrote out and committed to memory his sermon, but that, face to face with the Pontiff and the Sacred College, his memory betrayed him, and he forgot every word of it. He took refuge in a frank confession of this, and then passed on to speak extempore, gathering his inspiration as usual from the needs of the time and of the Church. He spoke with the candour, fervour, and simplicity which had won him his followers and had made him, as his present audience well knew, the greatest moral force in the world of his day.

The Sacred College was convinced and conquered. But not on that account was it pacified. The desire to harness to the Church the great power which had its source in this Poor Man of Assisi was as natural, comprehensible, and even laudable, as was the desire of Francis to remain free and unharnessed. Only thus did he feel that he could continue securely to build upon the simple foundations he had laid down, and whose very simplicity contained the whole secret of their power.

At the Whitsuntide Chapter of 1218 there was an outburst from him in repudiation of these attempts to affiliate the friars to one of the established orders, an attempt of which Ugolino had made himself the mouthpiece and towards which some of the friars were leaning.

"My brothers, my brothers, the Lord called me Himself, by a simple, humble road, and showed me in truth this way of life for myself and for those who will follow me. Therefore do not speak to me of any other Rule, be it Saint Benedict's, Saint Augustine's, or Saint Bernard's, or of any other manner of life save that which has been shown to me by the Lord in His mercy."

Domingo de Guzman of Calahorra, the ardent founder of the Dominican Order, an order of preachers, whose mission was to combat heresy and who, still with this mission, are later on to be found presiding over the Inquisition, was present at this chapter, and was so profoundly moved by what he there heard and beheld that he decided to take these Minors for a model for his own order. He would, had Francis been willing, have amalgamated the two orders into one. They had met in Rome during Francis' last visit there, and Dominic had proposed this fusion, encouraged by the Curia which would have placed them both where it had already placed the very willing Dominic under the rules of the Augustines. Francis, however, for the reason that he now stated so warmly to the chapter, had not been attracted by the proposal.

It remained, however, that the failures of the German, Hungarian, and Spanish missions, and the measure of persecution by which the last had been attended, supplied Ugolino with arguments so unanswerable that Francis was constrained to submit at least to a slight departure from his ideals and to accept from the Pope Letters Apostolic by which the missionaries should in future be protected.

For some of the friars, however, this was not enough, nor did it seem enough for Ugolino, the official protector of the Order. In their view the simple Rule that had sufficed for the few early followers of Francis was inadequate to govern the vast organization which had come into existence and was still spreading. Francis, however, had meanwhile set out for the Holy Land, able at last to gratify his consuming desire to visit it, and nothing could be done until his return.

He had sailed, accompanied by Peter of Cattani and several friars, from Ancona with the Crusaders, on the 24th June 1219, and he was in the Christian camp before Damietta, commanded by John of Brienne, brother of that Walter of Brienne under whom, so many years before, Francis had set out to embrace the career of arms.

The moral condition of the Christian army so moved his indignation that he foretold the defeat which in his view it deserved. When the event followed, in the Saracen victory of the 29th August, he came suddenly into unsought repute as a prophet, and found men willing now to listen to him and take to heart his words.

Neophytes of every nationality flocked to him there, and the Benedictines of the Black Mountain in the neighbourhood of Antioch surrendered their property and joined the friars in a body.

With the Sultan, to whom he went to preach the gospel, and by whom he was received, he was less successful. Yet far more successful than was to have been expected, all things considered, in that the Sultan not merely heard him with deference, but testified to the impression Francis made upon him by according him and his companions liberty to visit the Holy Sepulchre and to go freely whithersoever else they listed. Probably there is no higher testimonial than this to the magnetism and winning powers of the Poor Man of Assisi's saintly personality.

He wandered in the Holy Land for the best part of a year, of which there is practically no record. He returned in the late summer of 1220, and landed at Venice with Peter of Cattani, Elias of Cortona, and Cæsar of Spyer. This last was a comparative newcomer in the Order, but destined to play a brilliant part in its history by the work he did to establish it in Germany. He had been won by Elias of Cortona at a time when, fired by ideals not dissimilar from those of Francis, he might have founded an order of his own, or else have ended badly in an attempt to do so. In the ranks of the Friars Minor he discovered all that he needed to satisfy his own reforming longings, and he threw himself passionately into the work.

With these and other companions Francis was back in Assisi and at the Porziuncula for the Michaelmas Chapter of the year 1220.

He was greeted there with news of the martyrdom suffered in Morocco by five of the brethren who had gone on a mission to the Saracen. Many more of these brethren were to seal their fidelity with their blood and suffer martyrdom in their attempts to carry the Gospel of Christ to the infidel of many lands. But these were the first. News of their death had been received in Lisbon, and had been transmitted thence by the minister-general of the Portuguese province.

Deeply grieved though Francis must be, yet his grief was irradiated by consciousness of the glory of that end.

With tears running down his lean, swarthy cheeks, he exclaimed: "Behold our first-born! Those whom above all others we may claim as our true brethren."

On his way to Assisi he had spent some time with Ugolino at Bologna, and it was there that he was compelled to stifle reluctance and consider the necessity urged by the Cardinal for a wider constitution than that which hitherto had governed them.

In yielding to necessity, and departing from an ideal which had proved itself capable of such glorious realization, he must have suffered keenly. Possibly this was partly responsible for his resignation of the office of minister-general, which he had held ever since Innocent III had pointed out the necessity for a responsible head of the Order. Another reason will have been supplied by the state of his health. He had come back from the Holy Land an ailing man, suffering from an affection of the liver. But the chief reason of all will have been his natural humility and the consciousness that wide government and matters of organization such as were now demanded did not lie within his functions.

To succeed him his choice fell upon Peter of Cattani, who being a doctor of laws and a man of great mental energy seemed to him to possess the qualities necessary for that office, which now became so onerous. Francis himself was to draw up the new and more elaborate Rule required for an order that was now brought fully under the ægis of the Church. For the Church had spoken definitely with the voice of Honorius III, and herself had imposed a law where hitherto Francis had been the only lawgiver. By the bull *Cum secundum* a novitate was imposed, as in other orders, whereas until now Francis had required no probationary period for those who offered to enrol themselves under his banner.

At that Michaelmas meeting of the chapter, Francis communicated to the brethren the text of this bull, together with the other matters which were to be incorporated in the new Rule he was to prepare. This done, he tendered his abdication in the words preserved for us by Thomas of Celano, who was present: "From this hour I am dead to you. But behold here Peter of Cattani whom I and you shall obey." And prostrating himself before the new minister-general, he promised him obedience and submission.

The friars [Celano goes on to relate] could not restrain their lamentations when they saw themselves thus becoming orphans. But Francis arose, and clasping his hands, with eyes raised to Heaven said: "Lord, I return to thee this family which Thou didst commit to me. Now, as thou knowest, most sweet Lord, I no longer have strength or ability to continue to care for them. I commit them therefore to the ministers. May they be responsible before Thee at the day of judgment if any brother perish through their neglect, ill example or harsh correction."

It was natural that the brethren should not suffer the abdication to be as absolute as he would have made it. He was their spiritual father. They were his spiritual children. Whilst he lived nothing could dissolve such a bond. Into whatever hands he might depute the legislative functions of the brotherhood, none but he who had called it into being could be regarded as its head. This view seems likewise to have been the view taken by the Church, for during his lifetime those entrusted with the administration were usually known merely as vicars-general.

* * * *

Peter of Cattani held the office for a half-year. He died in the following March, and was succeeded by Elias of Cortona, elected at the following Pentecostal Chapter, which has come to be known as the Chapter of the Mats; this from the screens or mats woven of willow, used in the construction of the huts, in which were accommodated the five thousand friars who, according to Saint Bonaventura, were in attendance.

It is not known at what date Elias of Cortona entered the Order. Pronounced by contemporaries one of the brightest intellects of his age, he was a man of humble origin, who had been a schoolmaster at Assisi, whilst also working at the trade of a mattress-maker, and afterwards a notary at Bologna. Had he entered the ranks of the regular clergy he might by his gifts and his character have become a great Prince of the Church. In the ranks of the Friars Minor, those qualities in this masterful, ambitious, self-willed man, make him largely responsible for the differences that afterwards divided the Order.

It was Elias who presided at this chapter of Whitsun of 1221. The concerns were the appointment of the mission to Germany under Cæsar of Spyer, and the foundation of the Tertiaries.

This Third Order was to be composed of those who, remaining in the world with their families and pursuing their ordinary avocations, were yet to rule their lives by evangelical ideals, to practise brotherly love, to comfort the afflicted, sustain the weak and the ailing, and support the poor, to exclude avarice and hatred, and to avoid all debasing interests.

The foundation by Francis, twelve years after the commencement of his apostolate, of this Tertiary Order is so curiously supererogative that the will of the Church, rather than that of Francis himself, is to be assumed in it. Actually such an order as this was the order that he had originally set out to establish, all that originally he had preached before ever he can have suspected that the apostolate he undertook was to grow into the vast organization it had become by 1221. From his point of view, then, all that happened was that those who had hearkened to his preaching and that of his companions, and who had been moved by it to conduct their lives upon his tenets, were now formally recognized as constituting a third order of this great army of salvation that was enrolled.

It remains, however, that by this establishment of the Tertiaries the Order received an impetus destined to have an incalculable effect upon European civilization. It resulted in a drawing together of all classes of society, leading to a better mutual understanding and collaboration amongst them. In this we may see the social, as distinct from the spiritual, value to the world of the apostolate of the Poor Man of Assisi.

* * * *

From this time onward, strengthened ecclesiastically by definite pontifical support, and laically by the creation of the Tertiaries, the growth of the Order assumes proportions transcending all that had gone before. Huts and caves can no longer suffice as headquarters for the branches of this great organization. Houses have become an absolute necessity; and in the possession of these is lost the founder's cardinal principle that they should possess nothing. Solid headquarters of this nature seem to demand, as an inevitable corollary, churches of their own in which the faithful may come to hear the friars. And so, little by little, they lose their itinerant character. This brotherhood, in its origins merely ancillary to the clergy, content to preach the gospel at street-corners and in the market-place, is gradually imperceptibly becoming a clergy in itself. Gathering impetus, this movement, this acquiring and building of churches, proceeds at such a rate that before another twenty years have passed we are to hear the outcry that secular churches are becoming useless and may soon close their doors since their congregations have been drawn away by the Friars Minor.

Long before then, however, Sister Death will have come to claim her little Brother Francis, and so he was spared the sighs he must perhaps have bestowed upon the passing of the destitution and homelessness upon which he had founded so mighty an edifice.

One of the last transforming measures he resisted was that bishops should be appointed from the ranks of his brethren. Cardinal Ugolino had proposed it, with the best intentions, believing that the Church would benefit from this leaven. But Francis had repelled the suggestion vehemently, reminding the Cardinal that when he gave his brethren the name of Minores it was not so that they might become Majores.

Yet in the time to follow, the coarse livery of poverty was to be exchanged by some for the purple, and from the ranks of the Friars Minor, four men—one of whom was the great Sixtus—were to climb as high as the throne of Saint Peter.

*   *   *   *

It may well be, as has been said, that a reason for his abdication additional to the character of the labours which the office of minister-general must from that time entail, lay in the fact that, although not yet forty years of age, Francis was already conscious of the failing health and strength of a body which he had not spared—that poor, patient Brother Ass.

From the time of his abdication he goes more and more into retreat. The last chapter which he attended was that of Whitsuntide of 1224, when, amongst other transactions, was the appointment of the first mission to England.

On this we refer to the chronicle of Thomas of Eccleston, *De Adventu Minorum in Angliam,* which tells us that three months later—on Monday, the 12th September of 1224—the mission, composed of nine minorites, landed at Dover. They were a priest, a deacon, two sub-deacons, and five lay brothers. They established foundations in Canterbury, London, Oxford, and elsewhere, and so well did the Order thrive on English soil that by 1250 there were fifty friaries and over twelve hundred friars in England. In their ranks, among many men of mark, we find in those early days Roger Bacon and Bishop Robert Grossetête.

At the time that those friars were landing in England, Francis was in retreat at La Verna, a rocky mountain in the Casentino, at the head of the Valley of the Arno, where he had gone to keep the Lent of Saint Michael. Ten years before, this mountain had been bestowed upon Francis, as a place of retreat for himself and his brethren, by Count Orlando of Chiusi, who had a castle there. The occasion to take advantage of the gift occurred at last, and thither Francis repaired, accompanied by Rufino, Angelo, and Leo—the Three Companions of the Legend—and Masseo, who was charged with the direction of the party.

Francis was very weak by then, and on the second day of the journey his strength gave out, so that they were constrained to borrow an ass on which he might reach his goal. The sense of impending death was already upon him. Thomas of Celano relates that on that first night at La Verna Francis spoke of this to his companions, told them that he had come there to prepare himself for his end, and begged them that during the Lent he was about to keep they should secure him from intrusion in the little hut of boughs that had been made for him. There he was to be left alone to his contemplations, save that each day Brother Leo should bring him what he would require.

*   *   *   *

There is a legend which tells us that, when Francis preached before the Sultan, that Malek Kamel, who was known throughout the East as the Perfect Prince, he was invited to support his arguments by the performance of a miracle. He answered that if Malek would command a great fire to be built, he would go into it together with the Sultan's Mohammedan priests, so that it might be seen which faith was to be held the more certain and holy.

But this was not the sort of miracle the Sultan required; for, as he is reported frankly to have confessed, he did not believe that he could induce his priests to play their part in it.

The story, which forms the subject of one of Giotto's illustrations of the life of Saint Francis, seems calculated to hold up to scorn a mind which could not be penetrated by unsupported truth, and which required to witness a portentous violation of the laws of nature before it could bring itself to believe. So blind are we to shortcomings of our own even when they are identical with those which we decry in our neighbour! For the Sultan's case was very much that of the mediæval Christian.

There is a curiously parallel story told of Charles VIII of France during his invasion of Italy, some three hundred years later. Coming to Florence at a time when Savonarola had acquired there a great reputation for saintliness, the French King asked him to perform "just a little miracle." This for his edification, and, no doubt, entertainment. Whilst ludicrous, the request is perhaps less ludicrous than it appears to us. To work marvels, to give sight to the blind, to cast out devils, to cleanse lepers, to raise the dead, had become in the popular mind so much the attribute of saintship, that to establish a man's sanctity it was almost necessary to show that he had performed at least some of these portents.

Francis, canonized already in his lifetime by the popular voice, could not escape this necessity. It was not enough that he should have performed the great natural miracle—using the word in the sense of marvellous achievement—that he had performed. It was necessary that supernatural operations should be attributed to him; therefore attributed they were, some in his lifetime, more after his death, and many of these posthumous in their alleged performance.

Some of his miracles are miracles merely because the people concerned chose so to regard them. Thus we have seen how his foretelling the defeat of the Christian army before Damietta was accounted a miraculous prophecy, whereas in fact it was no more than an intelligent deduction. On one occasion, we see an article that had been in contact with him placed in contact with a woman who was in difficult labour, whereupon she was instantly and easily delivered.

Other miracles are less due to a natural course of things. Thus, Thomas of Celano relates how on one occasion he washed the offensive body of a disgruntled leper, whose mind seems to have been equally offensive, with the result that the leper's sores were miraculously healed.

Miracles in this class we may treat as Francis himself would have treated them had the report of them been brought to his notice. A miraculous flavour has been given to the episode known as the Sermon to the Birds, which it is related in the Legend of the Three Companions that Francis preached to an assembly of birds at Bevagna.

> Little birds, my sisters [the sermon runs], much do you owe to God, your Creator, and always and in every place should you sing his praises. For He it was made you free to fly about hither and thither; and He has given you two-fold and threefold raiment. Likewise, He preserved your seed in the ark of Noah, so that your kind might not die from the earth. Also should you be grateful for the air which He has given you for your kingdom. Moreover, ye sow not, neither do ye reap; and God feeds you, and gives you the rivers and the springs for your drink, and the hills and the valleys for your refuge, and the high trees wherein to build your nests; and since you cannot sew or spin, He clothes you and your little ones. Thus your Creator loveth you much since He hath given you so many good things; and, therefore, my little sisters, give heed ye be not ungrateful, and ever strive to sing the praises of God.

And Brother Masseo, who is the narrator, says that at these words all the birds began to open their beaks, to stretch their necks and spread their wings, and reverently incline their heads to the ground.

It is a story, we are told, that Francis himself was fond of relating, and it may be received in part, at least, as an allegory—for it is not without application to humanity—

and at the same time an expression of his attitude towards the birds of the air, and indeed, towards all created things, his love of which is constantly being disclosed.

There remains, however, one miracle, which looms so largely in his life that it is not to be dismissed with the rest. It is that stupendously miraculous manifestation upon his own body which is recorded in every picture and in every image of him.

The event took place, we are told, during this retreat at La Verna, and the following is the account of it given by the Three Companions:

> On a morning about two years before his death, and close upon the Feast of the Exaltation of the Cross, whilst he prayed on the side of the mountain that is called La Verna, there appeared to him a seraph having six wings, and bearing between the wings the form of a most beautiful man crucified, his hands and feet stretched out after the manner of a cross, thus most evidently setting forth the image of the Lord Jesus. With two wings he veiled his head, with two the remainder of his body, and two were spread forth to fly. And when the vision was now past, a wondrous flame of love abode in his heart, but yet more wondrously there were found upon his flesh marks of the Stigmata of our Lord Jesus Christ.

This mystery, of course, has been the subject of a deal of controversy. It has been denounced as a pious fraud perpetrated by Elias of Cortona, who published it in a letter written on the morrow of the death of Francis. The assertion of the Three Companions that Francis concealed the stigmata until his death, "not being minded to make public the sacred mystery of the Lord," has been employed in support of that contention. Discrepancies have been pointed out in the descriptions of the stigmata. Sometimes they are described as wounds, open and bleeding, and sometimes, so far as the hands and feet are concerned, as black fleshly excrescences having the form of nails. On the hands the heads of the nails are sometimes placed in the palms, sometimes—as presented in the statue of Saint Francis by Andrea della Robbia—on the back of the hands, the points being in the palms, and as if clinched by a hammer. This is odd only if we are to regard the stigmata as supernaturally bestowed.

At the time of the vision, Francis had been fasting, praying, and contemplating for a month. His health was reduced and he was losing his sight. All this, experience tells us, would contribute to his attaining a state of mystical exaltation. It has often been observed that the psychic forces in a man are given freer scope in a measure as the physical trammels upon them are slackened by a low vitality. In such a state of exaltation the human spirit may travel a long way along that dark road towards the unknown ultimate extent of its control of matter.

That the vision of the seraph was a subjective vision none could venture to reject in explanation of it. Just as the voice speaking to Francis from the crucifix in San Damiano would be a subjective voice giving tongue to the pious thoughts upon which he was dwelling, so this vision may have been a subjective representation of the theme of his contemplations at this time. The date itself creates a coincidence to support the theory. "It was nigh unto the Feast of the Elevation of the Cross." Would not the Passion, then, be an insistent subject in his thoughts?

To accept as subjective a vision is one thing. So to accept an accompanying material manifestation is quite another. But what we are told took place here is not so much a materialization as a modification of matter in the

body of the subject; and however indisposed the material-
ist may be to accept this as a subjective possibility, he will
not in the present state of knowledge deny it without
presumption.

*   *   *   *

At the end of that September, Francis left La Verna,
taking a leave of it in the course of which he said that he
would never see it again.

Reduced in health, and almost blind as he was, he was
found too weak to walk. Saint Bonaventura attributes this
to the nails in his feet; but that cannot be other than
conjecture, just as it is his conjecture that Francis was
carried. Actually he rode a horse that was lent by Count
Orlando.

Great as for years now had been the enthusiasm which
his appearances everywhere excited, never before had it
reached the heights of that with which he was now greeted
in the townships through which he passed. Everywhere
crowds surrounded him, asking his blessing, pressing forward to kiss the hem of his mean gown.

It was during this journey that the supposed miracle of
the woman in labour occurred. Francis had paused at a
hermitage on Mount Casale, determined to spend a few
days there, to rest and recuperate, and he sent back the
horse to Count Orlando. As the brothers who were leading it came to the village where the afflicted woman lay,
rumour ran that Francis was approaching. Full of faith in
the powers of the Poor Man of Assisi, the hopes of the
woman's husband were raised, to sink again when he
found only the friars who had been the saint's companions. Nevertheless, he did not despair. Borrowing the
bridle which the saintly hands had held, he bore it to his

wife, so that, by herself holding it, she might be miraculously delivered.

This incident, in itself of no great significance, is yet of enormous historical value for the clear notion it conveys of the light in which Francis was then regarded.

In spite of failing health, he continued for a time his evangelizing work, accompanied now by Elias of Cortona. But soon his infirmities and his increasing blindness compelled him to yield. He was taken to San Damiano and given into the care of Clare, now the Abbess of the Poor Ladies established there.

A cell of reeds was made for him in the monastery garden, amid the perfume of roses and carnations and sweet-smelling herbs that Clare cultivated, and there, in the tender care of his spiritual daughter he abode for a month, during the half of which his blindness was so complete that he could not distinguish between light and darkness.

Yet it was here and in these circumstances that he composed his Lauds of the Creatures, the only one of the many songs this Troubadour of the Lord is said to have made which has come down to us. It is sometimes called the Canticle of the Sun, from the opening strophe, which may thus be rendered:

> Praised be Thou, my Lord, with all Thy creatures,
> Especially Messer Brother Sun,
> Who brings us the day and the light,
> Who is beautiful and radiant with great splendour,
> Significant, Most High, of Thee.

After a month thus spent at San Damiano, he yielded to the representations of Brother Elias that he should accept the urgent invitation of Cardinal Ugolino and go to

Rieti. There the Pontifical Court now lay, and in its train there were physicians who might bring him relief.

He went, and he was housed in the Bishop's palace and given over to those who practised medicine. They desired, after the failure of other experiments, to have recourse to cautery, hoping that by drawing a white-hot rod across his brow they might relieve the congestion to which they attributed his eye-trouble. When they approached him with this glowing iron, he made the sign of the cross over it, and uttered a prayer in the following characteristic form:

> Brother Fire, noble and lovely among all the creatures, be gentle unto me in this hour. Always have I loved thee, and shall love thee, for love of Him that made thee. So I entreat the Creator who made us both that He may temper thy heat so that I may endure it.

It is not to be supposed that the treatment brought him relief. His condition became rather worse. Then, no doubt under the *vis medicatrix naturae,* an improvement followed, and no sooner was he aware of it than he again attempted to resume his work.

Some months later we find him at Siena, where hæmorrhages so reduced him that the brothers, fearful that the end might overtake him at any moment, sent for Elias. He came in haste. When he arrived, the immediate danger was over, but the end could not be far off, and since Francis desired, before it came, to behold once more his beloved Assisi, he begged to be taken back to the Porziuncula. In this last desire, however, he was thwarted by the Assisians, who flocked out to meet him and insisted, in view of his condition, that he should be taken to the Bishop's palace,

where he would be properly housed and properly attended.

There he lingered for some time, tended by those four
dearest amongst his companions, Masseo, Leo, Rufino,
and Angelo, labouring for the Order to the end, by in-
junctions to these and to other friars who came to visit him
and by letters to the ministers.

At last in September of the year 1226 he learnt from a
doctor that his condition was beyond hope. The prospect
of release filled him with such joy that he at once composed and sang an additional strophe to his Lauds of the
Creatures:

> Praise to Thee, my Lord, for our sister, Corporeal Death,
> From whom no living man may escape.
> Woe to them who come to die in mortal sin.
> Happy they who find themselves in Thy most holy will,
> For to them the second death can do no hurt.

As he lay there now, he constantly lifted up his voice to
sing those Lauds of the Creatures, in which he would beg
Brothers Leo and Angelo to join him, or to continue when
his own strength failed him.

The sound of it seems to have scandalized the Bishop.
This was no way for a man to meet his end. To go to his
Maker with songs upon his lips seemed an appalling thing.
The Bishop spoke of it to Elias, and Elias must so far have
agreed with him that he came to remonstrate with Francis
for singing aloud these songs of joy upon his death-bed.

But Francis patiently begged that he might be left in
his own way to rejoice in the Lord.

When the end was imminent, they yielded to his desire
that he should go to die in the Porziuncula, and there he
went to meet death, according to Thomas of Celano, still
singing.

It was in these last days at the Porziuncula that he drew up his testament. It is partly retrospective, sketching the stages by which he came to take up his apostolate, partly an amplification of and an insistence upon the Rule which he had left to the Order. Most significant perhaps is the passage: "I interdict absolutely by obedience all the brothers, clerics or laymen, to introduce glosses in the Rule or in this testament under pretext of explaining it."

His dearest friars were about him, and amongst them that Bernard of Quintavalle who had been the first to join him, like himself casting off all earthly possessions.

When at sunset on Saturday the 3rd October of 1226 his sweet soul went out quietly in a sigh, immediately, the legend runs, a flight of larks that had gathered on the thatch broke into an exultation of song.

*   *   *   *

He could fall asleep in peace, for his great work was done. It would not be undone, no matter what schisms should come to divide the Order, no matter that for a time there should even be open strife between those who elected strictly to observe the rule of poverty and those who preferred to disregard it and to build themselves up into a powerful ecclesiastical institution, their monument the stupendous basilica that to-day dominates Assisi.

He had revived the reality of Christianity by rendering it practical once more and he had saved it from the dangers in which it stood. By drawing together men of every class in the bond of that practical Christianity, he had broken the shackles of feudalism that bound and galled humanity, and had rendered possible a spiritual progress that completely changed the face of civilization.

Nor does it really matter whether or not after his death the stigmata were discovered on his body, as Elias of Cortona reported to the friars and the world. What is not to be doubted is that he bore them on his soul.

III
JOAN THE MAID

III

JOAN THE MAID

In 1429, the Hundred-Years War appeared to be coming to an end, as, indeed, it was, but not in the manner of which the appearances justified the assumption.

The Kingdom of France had virtually ceased to exist. The royal house of Valois had been steadily declining ever since Edward III of England, as the grandson of Philippe le Bel, had laid claims to this heritage. Victorious in 1346 at Crécy, in 1355 at Poitiers, and finally, and signally, under Henry V at Agincourt in 1415, the English remained masters of Guyenne and Normandy.

In 1417, Charles, Duke of Touraine, the third son of the imbecile Charles VI, became Dauphin and Regent. He was aged fourteen, a puppet in the hands of factions, and he lost Picardy, Champagne, the Ile de France, and Paris itself. Driven into Poitou, he there committed the frenzied blunder of permitting the assassination of Jean Sans Peur, Duke of Burgundy. By this deed he lost his last supporters; and by the treaty of Troyes his mother surrendered the Kingdom to England, and gave Henry V (who married Charles's sister Catherine) the titles of regent and heir to the crown of France.

With the resources left him, his Armagnacs and the foreign mercenaries (Scots and Lombards) in his pay, the Dauphin made a last stand against this disinheritance, and was beaten at Crévant in 1423 and at Verneuil in 1424.

By these victories the English immeasurably increased their reputation for invincibility, and their own faith in it, acquired at Agincourt. Masters of all the north, with their flanks assured by treaties of neutrality with the Duchies of Brittany and Anjou, the Duke of Bedford, Regent of France for his young nephew Henry VI, resolved to carry the war south, and in the summer of 1428 the Earl of Salisbury began the siege to Orléans, which was the key to the lands beyond the Loire.

Killed by a cannon-shot, fired it is said by a child who, wandering idly along the ramparts at dinner-time, mischievously touched off a gun, Salisbury was succeeded in the command by Sir William Glansdale. Later came Talbot and Suffolk, and then the siege began in earnest. The English erected forts and threw up earthworks. On the left bank of the Loire, opposite the city, eight hundred of them occupied the bridge-head fortress, known as the Tourelles, and the half-ruined convent of the Augustins which they converted into a fort. On the right bank, some four thousand were distributed between a fort set up on the ruins of the Church of Saint Laurent and another opposite the Bannier Gate. Bastions were built to link the forts.

Orléans was garrisoned by twelve to fifteen hundred men and could arm another five thousand from among the inhabitants. It was commanded for the Duke of Orléans, then languishing in an English prison, by his brother the young Bastard of Orléans, commonly, but wrongly, called Dunois by writers describing these events. He was not created Count of Dunois until ten years later.

So that the siege might be pressed with greater energy, Sir John Fastolfe was despatched from Paris with twenty-five hundred men and a convoy of victuals. The Dauphin, informed of this, sent some three or four thousand men under the Count of Clermont to intercept him, whilst those experienced Gascon captains, La Hire and Xaintrailles, went out from Orléans with fifteen hundred men for the same purpose.

On the 24th February 1429, the men of Orléans met the convoy as it was filing out of Rouvroy Saint Denis, and they would at once have attacked it but that the orders from Clermont were to do nothing until he arrived. By the time this happened, Fastolfe had entrenched himself within a barricade of his wagons. Thence he beat off the attack when it came, and safely convoyed his victuals to the besiegers, all but some barrels of herrings which, being burst by cannon shot, strewed the ground with their contents. From this detail the affray was known as the Day of Herrings.

That reinforcement of the English reduced Orléans to despair. There was no help to be expected from the Dauphin, whose thoughts by now were of seeking refuge in Scotland or in Spain. And so, rather than allow the Duchy to fall into the hands of the English, the Duke of Burgundy was invited to take under his charge the heritage of his cousin the Duke of Orléans. Burgundy was willing enough, and consulted his brother-in-law the Duke of Bedford. Bedford lacked tact. He had not, he said, chewed the meat so that Burgundy might swallow it. Burgundy, offended, withdrew, which diminished the strength of the besiegers by some twelve hundred men.

The English, however, were not perturbed. They erected yet another fort on the right bank at Saint Jean le Blanc, and continued to press the siege. The Orléannais, encouraged by the Burgundian withdrawal, persevered in their resistance. They would have persevered with even stouter hearts had they known that assistance of an extraordinary nature was approaching in the person of Joan the Maid.

*   *   *   *

Whether we take of Joan of Arc the realistic view of Anatole France, or the idealistic view of writers such as Andrew Lang, the Maid remains equally a portent.

One famous biographer has asserted that her knowledge of the art of war was the amazement of the great captains of her time. But there is no evidence whatever in her achievements to support the assertion, whilst there is some very definite evidence to contradict it. It was not the art, but the artlessness of her victories that was the amazement of the captains of her day. For this is what lends them their miraculous quality, a fact unperceived by a biographer who insists upon every apocryphal miracle legend records of her, but misses the one great miracle of her career.

She was born in 1412 at Domrémy, a village in the valley of the Meuse. A brook divided the village, placing half of it in Champagne, which was France, and the other half in Lorraine. In this latter half stood the house of the peasant Jacques d'Arc and his wife Isabel. There were five children, three boys and two girls, and the elder of these girls, Joan, was from her earliest years a model of piety and industry. She took pride in her spinning and sewing, and she was diligent in housewifery. At need she would lend a hand out of doors with the plough or the cart, and sometimes she would act as deputy for her father when it was his turn to herd the village flock. Her piety was accounted excessive, and it is in this that we discover the reason for those supernatural experiences to which she began to be subject at the age of thirteen.

The first of them was a voice that spoke to her one

noontide, as she sat in her father's garden. It frightened her until she realized that it was the voice of an angel, whom presently she beheld clearly, the Archangel Michael. After that he continued to appear to her, and he spoke to her of the distress of France. His appearances were succeeded later by those of Saint Catherine and Saint Margaret, sent, as Saint Michael had foretold, to guide Joan's life and to bring her God's commands.

They announced themselves to her by name, she says. But in this they did no more than confirm her recognition of them, since their features, raiment, and the crowns upon their heads corresponded with those of their images with which she was familiar. For not only Saint Catherine and Saint Margaret, but also Saint Michael, were objects of particular veneration in the Valley of the Meuse. Saint Catherine was the patron saint of the neighbouring village of Maxey, and Joan had frequented the church there for a time, when that of Domrémy had been burnt down. Of Saint Margaret a statue still exists which in Joan's time stood in the Church of Domrémy; and the Church of Moncel, near Domrémy, was dedicated to Saint Michael.

It will seem, then, that the saints appearing to her were precisely those who would have touched her imagination, whose history she knew, and of whose physical aspect (as represented by the images she had contemplated) her consciousness carried the impression.

When she heard them speak of the distress of France, she heard something with which she was already acquainted, something that had been borne in upon her not only by the tales that circulated in the countryside, but by disquieting personal experiences of the brigandage devastating the land. She had known the alarms created by the reported approach of Burgundian troops. Once all the cattle had been conveyed, for safety from these raiders, to the river island opposite to Domrémy. On another occasion of similar panic when all the inhabitants of the village had decamped, she had fled to Neufchâteau in Lorraine for safety.

Of the warfare that distressed the land she had witnessed simulacra in the frequent encounters which took place between the mobilized youth of Domrémy, which was stoutly Armagnac, and that of Maxey, across the Meuse, which was Burgundian. Pitched battles were fought between these groups of children, make-believe combats in which all was not make-believe, for feeling ran high, blood was shed, and rancour fomented.

Thus, what she hears in the voices of her saints is the voice of her own inner consciousness, clothed in the impressions she has received expressing the pity and indignation they have evoked.

In noble natures pity and indignation are emotions that inevitably arouse the desire to solace and to punish.

As if further to stimulate and give practical expression to these inclinations so natural in her, there are two legends or prophecies current in the countryside. One is that France, lost by a woman, will be regained by a woman. She would know that the woman by whom France had been lost was Isabeau de Bavière, the Queen of Charles VI. The other prophecy is that out of the Bois Chesnu, according to some, from the borders of Lorraine, according to others, will come a maid who will perform marvels for her country.

This sombre oak forest, the Bois Chesnu, crowned the heights of a slope above the flowering banks of the river. Between the two stood a great beech tree, known as the Ladies' Tree. These "ladies" were the fairies with whom popular half-beliefs inhabited the spot. There was here, too, a spring accredited with healing properties. In summer-time people came to eat and drink in the shade of this tree, and to drink the water of this spring. Children danced and played about one and the other, and wove garlands of flowers which they hung upon the branches as offerings to the fairies. All this one day is to be of sinister importance.

There, to the beech tree and the fountain, Joan would often go alone, to sit and meditate; and frequently on such occasions her voices would speak to her. As time went on, it seemed to her that these voices, the expressions of her own subconscious heroic desire, were urging her to go to France.

The growth of the idea that she was the maid of the prophecy, the maid from the Bois Chesnu, from the borders of Lorraine, and of the clear and firm belief that a command was being objectively imposed upon her, may thus be traced.

To some extent, it follows that Joan was an ecstatic, for it was in the ecstasies into which she was plunged by a contemplation in which pious and heroic thoughts were mingled that her voices and visions came to her. But neither in her person nor her actions does she even remotely suggest the mystic. She was a well-grown, strong-limbed girl, toughened by a healthy country life and the avocations it procured her. From evidence adduced at the Rahabilitation Trial we gather definitely that she was without that quality termed in modern jargon sex-appeal, and hence we may assume that her body was such that the male attire which she came to wear did not lay stress upon her sex; in short, that she was of a boyish shape.

Presently, and no doubt whilst subconsciously she is

considering ways and means to gratify the growing desire
to devote herself to the service of France, her voices tell
her to seek Robert of Baudricourt, who is Captain of Vaucouleurs, nine miles away. The Captain she is told will
supply an escort for her into France.

At first, because she mistrusts herself, she resists the
command, and pleads with her voices that she is but a
poor ignorant country girl, knowing nothing of arms or
war. In the end, however, she bows to what she believes to
be the will of God.

To accomplish her design, she goes on a visit to her uncle
Durand Luxart at Burey-le-Petit, near Vaucouleurs. At the
end of a week she informs him of her intention. She is to
go to France, seek the Dauphin, and contrive that he be
crowned. She herself is the maid who is "to raise France
up again."

Luxart yields, and conducts her to Vaucouleurs. We are
in May of 1428 by now, approaching the Feast of the Ascension, and Joan is sixteen years of age.

Baudricourt is an accessible man. He receives Joan in
his castle at Vaucouleurs.

"I come," she tells him, "on the part of my Lord, who
wishes the Dauphin to be made King, as he will be in
despite of his enemies; and I myself will lead him to his
consecration."

In scornful amazement the Captain of Vaucouleurs con-
siders this strong-limbed peasant girl in her red petticoat.

"And who may be this Lord of yours?"

"The King of Heaven."

Baudricourt turns to her uncle. "You would be well advised to slap her soundly, and take her back to her father,"
he says, and so dismisses them.

Her father must have had wind of the adventure, for it is

recorded that he declared to his other children: "If I thought such a thing could happen, I would say to you, drown her; and if you didn't, I'ld drown her, myself."

It may have been so as to turn her from these dreams that an attempt was now made to marry her to a young man of Toul, in Lorraine, twenty miles away; and a formal betrothal, amounting to a contract, must have been made on her behalf. But she will be no party to it, and when she refuses to fulfil it, the young man of Toul summons her to appear before the authorities. She duly appears and by her answers confounds him, which does not surprise us when later we discover what power as an advocate she derives from her simple directness. There is no self-consciousness in the make-up of Joan; no inhibitions trammel her. She is frank and downright, and full of common-sense; and her utterances at need are not without a spice of rough wit, which, after all, is only the sublimation of common-sense.

In spite of opposition, she induces her uncle yet again to take her to Baudricourt. Once more the Captain is harshly contemptuous and advises her to get back to her cows. She remains serene under the rebuff, and stays on for three weeks at Vaucouleurs, at the house of a wheelwright named Le Royer. She works in his house, discharging domestic duties, and spends a great deal of time in prayer at Notre Dame de Vaucouleurs, sometimes remaining for long hours upon her knees before the statue of the Virgin in the underground chapel there.

She was now openly announcing that she was under a command from her Lord, the King of Heaven, to seek the Dauphin. Betide what may she must be with him before Lent even if to reach him she is to wear away her legs to the knees.

She becomes the talk of the town, and Baudricourt is moved by this to come and see her. He questions her. He has brought the curé with him, as an expert in spiritual matters. She satisfies the priest more easily than the Captain. Baudricourt is not disposed to be impressed by prophecies, and it does not move him to be told of the prophecy about the maid from the Bois Chesnu.

But if the Captain does not yet believe in her, the people do, and it results from this that in the end two men-at-arms, Jean de Metz and Bertrand de Poulengy, offer to conduct her to the Dauphin at their own charges. In view of this, Baudricourt finally shrugs his shoulders, and bids her "Go, and betide what may."

To the two who have offered to escort her, four more are added, and Joan sets out. She rides a horse provided by her uncle, and is clothed in male garments, justaucorps and hose, her dark hair cut at the nape of the neck, *en rond,* porringer-fashion as the term runs. She wears a tunic to the knees, long boots with spurs, hauberk, and chaperon.

They start on their journey south on the first Sunday in Lent, the 13th February of 1429, a few days before the Battle of the Herrings was fought. They cross the Loire at Gien, and come to Saint Catherine of Fierbois, where Joan hears three Masses in one day. Here occurs a mysterious matter about a sword which her voices tell her is buried behind the altar. It is dug up, the rust is furbished from it, and it is delivered to her, together with two beautiful scabbards, one of red velvet and one of cloth of gold. Despite the holiness attributed to the weapon, if the rest of the tale is true, it cannot have been a very good sword, for it broke over the back of a harlot when Joan, using the flat of the blade, was driving a regiment of these camp-followers out of the lines. The Dauphin, when he heard of it, uttered one of the few sensible remarks of his life. "She would have done better," he said, "to have taken a stick."

It was from Saint Catherine of Fierbois that Joan dictated a letter to the Dauphin (she could neither read nor write herself), in which she begged permission to come to him at Chinon, telling him that she has travelled a hundred and fifty leagues for the purpose, and that she comes to inform him of several things for his good. As an earnest of her mission she promises to pick him out at sight from amongst his courtiers.

That she should have come unscathed through a country infested with enemies seems in itself a miracle, and Charles consents to receive her. Although in the last stage of distress for money, and although the fall of Orléans will consummate his ruin, yet he is idling here at Chinon, living softly with his favourites, of whom the chief, La Trémouille, does not mean to relinquish his ascendancy.

Joan is suffered to come, but not immediately to see the Dauphin. Obstacles are placed in her way. First she must submit to searching questions from members of the court, who suspect her of being mad when she says that she is sent by God. The priests are consulted, and they interview her. Whilst reserving their opinions, they see no harm in her being received by the Dauphin, and so, at last, she is introduced by the Count of Vendôme.

The future Charles VII possesses none of the attributes that imagination associates with kingly rank. Probably no one in the Grand Logis, where he received her, looked less like a king than this spindle-shanked, bulbous-nosed son of an imbecile father and a wanton mother. And it is said that to test her he was careful to wear no insignia of his rank. Nevertheless, she went straight to him, and fell on her knees.

"Gentle King, God has sent me to succour you."

"I am not the King," he protested, and pointed to a courtier standing near him. "This is the King."

She shook her head. "In God's name," she said, which was her usual form of emphatic affirmation, "you are the King."

After this she seems to have come quickly to the point, asking for men to go with her to raise the siege of Orléans.

It sounded like an answer to his desponding hopes. But what faith could he attach to it, however confident her tone? On the other hand, being in a state to clutch at straws, he hesitated to reject her. Frank, simple, and natural of speech and manner, and with an utter absence of self-consciousness even in the presence of these great and noble personages, she assumed a tone of authority. Her easy self-possession was perceived in her greeting to the young Duke of Alençon, who had been taken prisoner by the English at Verneuil, and had lately been ruinously ransomed from that captivity.

"Be very welcome," she greeted him. "The more there are gathered together of the blood royal, the better."

And on the morrow, after Mass, she addressed the Dauphin much in the same tone. "Place your kingdom in the hands of the King of Heaven, and the King of Heaven will do by you as by your forebears, re-establishing you in all your ancient estate."

Whilst the extraordinary matter of her proffered assistance was under consideration, she was lodged in the Tower of Coudray, the innermost of the three fortresses composing the Castle of Chinon, and she was placed in the care of the wife of the Lieutenant of the Castle. Clerical messengers were despatched to Domrémy to inform themselves secretly of her antecedents; and in the meantime at Chinon she was kept under observation by ecclesiastics who came daily to talk with her and question her. Thus time dragged on until one day she addressed herself more definitely to Charles.

"Gentle Dauphin, God has taken pity on you, on your kingdom and your people, for Saint Louis and Charlemagne are on their knees to Him on your behalf. I will give you, may it please you, a sign which will prove to you that you are to believe me." And upon this, she startled him by the revelation of a secret which he believed to lie between God and himself.

"What it was that she said to him," writes Alain Chartier, "no one ever knew. But he became as radiant with joy as if at a revelation by the Holy Ghost."

Some pretend to have overheard her words, and that they were: "I tell you in the name of my Lord that you are the true heir of France and the son of the King."

There would seem to be no startling revelation in this until it is understood that Charles was troubled by doubts of his own legitimacy, doubts that might well trouble the son of Isabeau of Bavière. Chastellain, a Burgundian historian, has said that Charles had been disowned by his father as a bastard.

If this is correct, then it is easy to understand the effect of those words. To simple minds nothing appears so true as that which they wish to believe.

Whatever it may have been that she said to him, Charles made an end of indecisive delays. He took Joan to Poitiers, where his parliament sat and where there were a few members of the University of Paris. To be a member of that University in the fifteenth century was to rank among the intellectually elect, the few really enlightened men of this world. The faculty of theology of that University was composed of all who might be counted as the most eminent theologians of Christendom. It included men of all nations and of all religious orders in its embrace, and constituted the highest court on earth on all matters appertaining to the faith.

Politically at this time the University was in the main on the side of the English. Only a few of its members had remained faithful to Charles, and these had repaired to Poitiers as much to express that fidelity as to shelter themselves from the hostility their politics must excite in Paris.

Regnault de Chartres, Archbishop of Rheims and Chancellor of France, was entrusted by Charles with the investigation of Joan's claims. He took advantage of the presence of these learned doctors from the University, to enlist their assistance as well as that of some available bishops, the Bishop of Castres, who was Charles's confessor and afterwards Bishop of Senlis, and the Bishops of Maguelonne and Poitiers.

This considerable ecclesiastical body addressed itself to a rigorous examination of the Maid. There were conferences and lengthy arguments. Some of the latter survive, and we may read the shrewd yet simple candour of her answers.

One of the professors of divinity said to her on one of these occasions: "If it is God's will to drive the English out of France, that should suffice without men-at-arms."

"Help yourself," was her answer, "and God will help you. Men must battle. God will confer the victory."

A flash of her rough humour displays itself in a reply to Brother Seguin, another doctor of divinity, a sour but honest Dominican who spoke with the broad accent of the Limousin, to inquire in what language her voices addressed her.

"In a better one than yours," said she.

The good doctor is himself the chronicler of this. Per-haps stung a little by that gibe at his accent, he rejoined: "God forbids that we should believe without some sign which compels it."

"In God's name!" she cried. "I didn't come to Poitiers to give signs. Lead me to Orléans, and I'll show you a sign of why I have been sent."

This inquiry into her revelations and into her faith lasts for three weeks. At the same time she is kept under the closest observation as to her ways of life. Gradually she brings them to believe in the sincerity of her inspiration. Gradually they come to see in her, as she sees in herself, the Maid of the Prophecy.

Six weeks after her first coming to Chinon, the divines announce that after strict inquiry they discover in her only "good, humility, purity, piety, honesty, and simplicity." And they opine that to reject her in these circumstances would be to render themselves unworthy of God's aid.

Finally a jury of matrons is empanelled. The Queen of Sicily (the Dauphin's mother-in-law) and my Ladies of Gaucourt and Trèves, composing it, testify to Joan's vir-ginity; and the virgolatrous belief being universally held, that Satan can have no commerce with the pure soul of a virgin, the last doubt is set at rest.

The question of her male garments, later to assume, with another group of divines, such enormous importance, seems here scarcely to have arisen. The general view probably agreed with that of the Archbishop of Embrun, who, after the relief of Orléans, wrote to the Dauphin: "It is more decent to do these things in male attire since they are to be done in association with men."

Charles hesitated no longer. He assigned to her a military household, with Jean d'Aulon, for her esquire, at its head, Louis de Contes for her page, and Jean Pasquerel, an Augustinian monk, for almoner, besides her two brothers who had come from Domrémy to join her, the two men-at-arms who had ridden with her from Vaucouleurs, several grooms and two heralds.

The Dauphin supplied her with an entire suit of armour, and she procured a standard made of linen and fringed with silk, on which was figured an image of God holding the globe of the earth in his hand, flanked on each side by an angel bearing a fleur-de-lys, with the legend *Jhesus Maria* painted above.

* * * *

The blockade of Orléans had by now become so tight that only small parties could contrive to slip through the lines and bear some relief in the shape of victuals to the besieged. To the forts already described, the English had added those of Saint Loup (on the 10th March) and Saint Jean le Blanc (on the 20th April).

When it was decided finally to accept Joan's services, a great convoy was prepared at Blois under the Duke of Alençon; and this circumstance may have helped the decision. Associated with Alençon in this projected enterprise were the Marshal de Broussac and the Lord of Laval —that Gilles de Rais who afterwards was to become the original of Bluebeard and to end so infamously, but now young and chivalrous—and those two valiant Gascon adventurers Poton de Xaintrailles and Étienne de Vignolles, known as La Hire. This La Hire was by now a hard-bitten man of forty, much addicted to coarse soldiers' oaths, whose well-known prayer before going into action was: "O God, I pray that you will this day do unto La Hire as La Hire would do unto you if La Hire were God and you were La Hire." He became deeply attached to the Maid, and is said, such was his reverence for her, to have allowed her to cure him of his habit of blasphemy.

The force assembled was for those days a very considerable one, numbering some five thousand men. Before they attempted to engage the enemy, Joan sought by a letter to avoid bloodshed. Addressed to the King of England, to the Duke of Bedford, and to his lieutenants, William de la Pole, Suffolk, Talbot, and Scales, it summoned them to render to the Maid, sent hither by God, the King of Heaven, the keys of all the fair cities taken and violated in France. She exhorted them, in the name of God, to depart into their own country, warning them that if they did not they would shortly receive a visit from the Maid to their great hurt.

It was a long letter, but actually it said no more than that, being taken up with repetitions more natural to the spoken than to the written word, an indication this of the ingenuous manner in which Joan dictated it. It was despatched on the Tuesday of Holy Week (the 22nd of March).

Not only did the English scorn to answer it, but, in contempt of all the usages of war, the herald who bore it was held as a prisoner.

* * * *

To the strains of the *Veni Creator Spiritu* the army set out from Blois on the 28th April, for Orléans.

Joan would have proceeded by the shortest road, marching straight on the city along the right bank of the Loire on which it stands. This would have entailed running the gauntlet of the strongest of the English siege works. But the Maid, utterly sincere in her conviction that she was an instrument of God, could not attach importance to obstacles or conceive of any opposition to her banner.

The captains, however, would not agree to plans based upon nothing more than a spiritual assurance. Practical men, they could not imagine that the English would suffer the passage of a convoy of victuals, which would be extremely welcome to themselves. It was resolved, therefore, to proceed along the left bank, placing the river between themselves and the strongest of the English positions, until beyond Orléans, when they would cross and double back upon the city. In this way, going wide of the siege works south of the Loire, they drew up abreast of the Island of Bourdon, ten miles above Orléans, a convenient place for embarcation. Boats, however, could reach them only from Orléans, and whilst the besieged were informed of the approach of the convoy, and anxious in their extremity to receive it, they were baffled at present by a contrary wind.

The Bastard of Orléans, who had come out with a few followers to meet Alençon, joined him here.

Joan, who was realizing by now how the captains had deceived her, in greeting that gallant young leader asked him if it was by his advice that the convoy had been brought along the south bank, instead of driving straight through Talbot and the English. When he had admitted that it was by his advice and by that of others of greater knowledge, she reproached them for their lack of faith and for setting their wisdom above that of God.

Their state of check, however, did not last long. The wind veered, and the boats were able to come from Orléans. They sufficed to convey the victuals, the corn, and the cattle; but not the army. Nor was it possible to build a bridge of boats in the present swollen state of the river.

But now that its convoying errand was accomplished, the army could contemplate with comparative equanimity a return to Blois, so as to cross the river, and then approach Orléans along the northern bank.

As for Joan, however, it was decided that she should go on to Orléans with the Bastard. Word of her coming, and of the mission on which she came, had run ahead of her, and she was eagerly awaited in a city that had almost abandoned hope.

So she embarked with the Bastard and with two hundred men-at-arms in boats following those that carried the victuals. Keeping close to the left bank, so as to avoid the English fire, they effected a landing at dusk to the east of Orléans, at a point guarded by the enemy in the fort of Saint Loup. The landing, however, was successfully covered by a sally from the city, which kept the English in check.

It was eight o'clock at night when Joan entered Orléans. She was armed from head to foot, mounted on a white horse, and rode at the head of a troop, the Bastard at her side, and her standard borne before her.

Progress was slow through the great press of people that flocked to behold, by the light of their torches, and where possible to touch, this Maid whom they were told was filled with divine virtue.

Joan and her following rode first to the church, to return thanks for this safe arrival. After that, accompanied by her brothers, the two men-at-arms from Vaucouleurs, and the remainder of her military household, she repaired to the house of Jacques Boucher, the treasurer of the Duke of Orléans, where she was lodged.

Her presence sufficed to infuse a new spirit into the people, a trustful eagerness to engage these English whose prowess had come to be so highly rated that latterly the necessary odds upon which to oppose them had been reckoned at not less than four to one. This eagerness matched her own, which urged that the besiegers should be attacked on the very next day. The Bastard, however, with soldierly prudence, insisted upon a postponement of operations until the troops from Blois should have arrived.

In the meantime she sent a second summons to the English, in the course of which she claimed the return of the envoy previously despatched. And lest her present messenger should share the same fate, the Bastard sent them a threat to put to death some of his English prisoners unless they observed the inviolability due to a herald.

Although the only reply she had from the English were defiant insults, she made yet another attempt to prevail by peaceful means.

She rode out onto the bridge, to the Belle-Croix bastion of the Orléannais, and thence summoned Sir William Glansdale to surrender with the honours of war.

Sir William answered her with taunts, addressing her as strumpet and cowherd, and threatening to burn her when he took her. His offensive epithets drew tears to her eyes, but from her lips an assurance that Sir William would be departing soon for all his confidence.

It was not until Wednesday the 4th May that the awaited troops arrived; and they might not have arrived then had not the Bastard himself ridden over to Blois to make sure that there should be no change of plan. The Maid, accompanied by La Hire and a troop, rode out to meet the reinforcements as they approached. With her banner unfurled, she placed herself at the head of this little army, which then advanced past the English bastions, singing hymns as if in procession. The enemy, probably stricken by amazement, offered no interference.

Thus reinforced, and their courage reawakened by faith in the Maid, the Orléannais now took the initiative. From being besiegers, the English began to find themselves in the position of besieged, and they discovered that reinforcements would now be necessary to them, too, if they were to prevail against this new spirit in their opponents.

Word comes that Fastolfe, approaching with men and victuals, is already at Janville. Thereupon the Bastard decides without further delay to attack the fort of Saint Loup, commanding the river and situated on the road to Burgundy. He not only takes the decision and makes his arrangements without telling the Maid, but he actually sets out without her; and the noisy excitement in Orléans over the adventure, awakening her early in the morning, is her first intimation of what is afoot.

She upbraids her page for having allowed her to sleep on at such a time, calls for her arms, her horse, her standard, and, followed by her esquire d'Aulon and a few attendants, she departs by the Burgundy Gate at an indignant gallop to follow the Bastard. On her way she passes the wounded who are being carried back from the assault, and the sight of them, this first contact with the grim actualities of warfare, affects her deeply. "I never could see French blood," she is to say much later, "without feeling the hair rising on my head."

She pushes through the foremost ranks of the assailants, and reaches the edge of the ditch. There in the forefront of battle, amid the smoke and dust of the combat, she plants her standard, and adds her fresh young voice to the general uproar, shouting encouragement to the assaulting Frenchmen.

Saint Loup, strongly fortified, is well held by its three hundred defenders. But the attack is of such unusual grimness that it begins to look as if it must prevail. In alarm, English troops from other bastions attempt to come to the rescue, only to be driven back again and yet again by the force which the Bastard holds in reserve for precisely this. And so in the end Saint Loup is carried by storm, its defenders killed or captured, its stores and ammunition appropriated, and the place finally set on fire and destroyed.

This first success, although small in itself, is of enormous moral importance. Belief in the divine virtue in the Maid is consolidated. She is acclaimed, praised, and thanked, until she threatens to depart unless the Orléannais, remembering that God is the real author of this victory, address their thanks to Him. At the same time she ventures upon an assertion in which they perceive a prophecy, that within five days the last Englishman will have departed from before Orléans.

The morrow being Ascension Day is kept holy and Joan seizes the opportunity to send yet another summons to the enemy.

"To you, men of England, who have no right in this Kingdom of France, the King of Heaven orders you by me to quit your bastions and depart to your own country, otherwise you shall have from me such a rousing that it will remain a perpetual memory. This I write to you for the third and last time, and I shall not write to you again. *Jhesus Maria*—Jeanne la Pucelle."

She adds a postscriptum to the effect that this letter, which is shot into the English camp round the shaft of an arrow, "would be sent in a more honourable way had they not retained her herald."

Once again insult is the only answer, and once again she is reduced to tears to hear herself called the harlot of the Armagnacs. But these tears have no source in weakness. Her eagerness for battle is unabated. And she will have no half-measures. She urges an attack against the fort of Saint Laurent, which is the very heart of the English siege works.

The experienced Bastard, however, again does not see eye to eye with her. He prefers to make a beginning by clearing the bridge-head, reducing the fortress of the Tourelles. To achieve this he plans a simulated attack on the northern positions, so as to draw thither the main body of the English forces. He works out the details with his captains without consulting Joan, and when she learns of it, she is indignant, not only that they should deliberate without her, but that they should be planning an attack against any but the cardinal English position. In her conviction of divine support, she is justified of her indignation; for these half-measures imply a lack of trust in God. The Bastard, however, pacifies her and convinces her that the attack on the Tourelles is a sound preliminary.

To reach the Tourelles, it is necessary first to reduce the fort of the Augustins which the English have set up ahead of it upon the bridge itself. Whilst a party of French cross the river at an island above, so as to make a flank attack, Joan herself leads the troops which advance directly upon the Augustins.

An English sally, to repel the onslaught, is already thrusting back the French when Joan rallies them, and then, summoning them to follow her standard, leads them right up to the palisades. The impetus bears them on. The place is carried, and set on fire; the survivors are driven back into the shelter of the Tourelles, and the French prepare for the investment of this. But as the hour is late, the assault is postponed until the morrow.

At six o'clock on the following morning operations are resumed, and the Bastard, with Gilles de Rais, Greville, La Hire, Xaintrailles, and some other knights, engage in the attack.

The English, fighting now for their very lives, since there is no further strong place in their rear to which they can retreat, offer a desperate resistance under the leadership of that Sir William Glansdale who had called the Maid a strumpet. Assault after assault is hurled back with dreadful slaughter, and but for the enheartening presence of the Maid, French valour must have withered under the punishment it received. Fully exposed, on the very edge of the ditch she stands, her banner aloft, calling to them: "On! On! Do not doubt! The place is yours!"

Early in the afternoon, she jumps down into the ditch, and plants a ladder against the wall. She is beginning to scale it when she is struck by an arbalest-bolt between the shoulder and the neck.

As she falls, her courage momentarily falters, and she gives way to tears. Strong hands lift her up and carry her out of danger, and then she herself plucks the bolt from the wound, which is dressed for her with a compress of olive oil.

The event is beginning to sow a superstitious dismay in the French, and they are proposing to retire, when Joan, with no further thought for her wound, urges them in God's name to stand firm. Let them pause to rest and refresh themselves, and then recommence.

"Now," she admonishes them after that respite, "return to the attack, in God's name, and the Tourelles will be taken. The English no longer have strength to defend it."

The attack is resumed. At the height of it, Joan, now sufficiently recovered, mounts her horse, seizes her standard, and rides forward once more to encourage them.

When the English again behold her whom they had seen carried off and whom they believed dead, the remnant of their capacity for resistance is paralyzed. Towards evening, at last, the French enter the place, and discover how terrible has been the slaughter there. Sir William Glansdale himself is amongst the dead. The few still alive are made prisoners.

The French, and Joan with them, remain all night in the Tourelles, lest the English from Saint Laurent should attempt to recover this important position.

Nothing, however, is attempted, and next morning Joan, her reputation still further enhanced, rides back into Orléans, once more to be acclaimed as a returning conqueror and deliverer. She disarms, and when her wound has been re-dressed, she goes to rest whilst the bells are ringing to celebrate the victory.

In view of the losses suffered, the weakening of the siege works by the capture of the Tourelles which introduces a measure of precariousness into the entire position, and also perhaps because of a manifestation among his followers of the first symptoms of that superstitious dread of the Maid of which more is to be heard, Talbot, for all his stout heart, takes the bitter resolve to raise the siege, abandoning the prey which a week ago had seemed all but within his grasp.

On Sunday morning he marshals the remains of his army, and, lest the retreat should invite pursuit and degenerate into a rout, he makes a show of drawing up his men for an engagement.

The French come forth from Orléans to deliver battle. Joan is with them, and they look to her to give the signal to fall on. But she will not give it. It is Sunday, and if the English have come out of their fortifications with the object of retiring, in God's name let them go.

Thus she admonishes the Orléannais before ordering an altar to be set up, at which Mass is celebrated in the open before the entire army.

After this, the English retire in good order, and are suffered to depart unhindered. They have set fire to some of their forts. But they leave behind them a considerable store of victuals, of arms and ammunition as well as their wounded.

* * * *

The Maid had given the sign demanded of her.

By her inspiration, Orléans, besieged for seven months, had been delivered within a week of her appearance there.

That this was proof that she had been sent by Heaven to the assistance of the French was agreed by all. The voices proclaiming it include that of the learned Jean Gerson, once Chancellor at the University of Paris, who in theological matters was regarded as the greatest light of his century. "Let that party whose cause is righteous," he writes, "beware of rendering useless by incredulity or ingratitude the divine lesson so miraculously manifested."

Her work in Orléans accomplished, the Maid now rode back to Blois, and thence on to Tours, whither the Dauphin had hastened from Chinon to do her honour. At the meeting he approached her bareheaded and embraced her. As a mark of his high appreciation, he granted her for arms the lilies of France flanking a drawn sword supporting a crown, and this became the blazon of her family.

The first step having been successfully taken, she urged now the second one, the coronation, whereafter Charles could undertake the reconquest of his kingdom with all the force and authority of a consecrated king.

He took counsel with his favourites, and found opposition. Against the design they urged the dangers of crossing a country held in great force by English and Burgundians, and the imprudence of going north to Rheims whilst leaving the English in their rear on the Loire. For after retreating from Orléans the enemy had occupied Beaugency; and Talbot was now at Meung, and Suffolk at Jargeau. The Bastard, wishing to profit by the spirit which Joan had left behind her in Orléans, had already made an attempt upon the latter stronghold, but had been compelled to retreat.

Perceiving that there was some ground for these strategic objections, Joan proposed to remove them by at once proceeding to expugn the enemy from the strongholds in the south.

An army was assembled of those who had returned from Orléans, and it was placed under the command of the Duke of Alençon. Joan was to accompany him, and, such by now was the faith in her, that he received orders to do nothing save on her advice.

They set out from Tours on the 6th of June, the Bastard, Gilles de Rais, and Gaucourt being of the company, and they marched upon Jargeau. They passed through Orléans, where Joan was received with incredible scenes of enthusiasm, and eight thousand strong they invested Jargeau, defended by Suffolk. Bedford, learning what was afoot, despatched Fastolfe from Paris with five thousand men, and others were being armed to follow. The news of these hostile reinforcements were not without effect upon the French, amongst whom there were still many who retained the old fear of the English. Some desertions resulted. But in the main, Joan's simple, unpretentious confidence sufficed to uphold the courage of her followers.

Jargeau being vainly summoned to surrender, a night was spent in preparation for the attack, and the following morning showed the French batteries in position. At nine o'clock Joan ordered the trumpets to sound, having decided to make the assault at once notwithstanding that the day was Sunday. She gave the word to Alençon: "En avant, beau duc!"

For four hours the battle raged without intermission about the walls of Jargeau. Then, so as to give a fresh impetus to the besiegers, Joan and Alençon jumped down into the ditch. The Maid, standard in hand, began to scale a ladder planted there, when she was struck by a stone that broke her helmet and hurled her down. But she was instantly on her feet again, crying: "Up! Up! My friends. Our Lord has doomed the English. Courage, and they are ours!"

Stimulated by her unconquerable faith and courage, they stormed the walls, gained the ramparts, and drove the English back.

In Suffolk's personal defeat there is an interesting instance of the usages of chivalry. Hard pressed by an esquire of Auvergne, Guillaume Regnault, and feeling his strength spent, he called to his adversary:

"Are you a gentleman?"

"Yes."

"Are you a knight?"

"No."

"Then receive the accolade from me." And Suffolk knighted him on the spot, so that without derogation he might surrender to him.

On the following Wednesday the Maid's army set out for Meung, and made a lively attack on the bridge which the English had strongly fortified. These fortifications seized and occupied, the city was left for the present, and the army moved on Beaugency, so as to obtain command there, too, of the crossing of the Loire.

Here the English fell back from the town, and shut themselves up in the castle, which the French invested on the Thursday.

* * * *

Richemont, the Constable of France, as a result of the intrigues against him of the favourite La Trémouille, was living retired and in a sort of exile in his lordship of Parthenay, chafing at his enforced inaction. He would have taken part in the advance on Orléans had he been permitted, and when he heard of it he had gone so far as to arm at his own charges four hundred lances and eight hundred archers, and set out. At Loudon, however, an order from the Dauphin commanded him to retire under pain of being attacked. He obeyed. But learning now that the campaign was being renewed, he could restrain himself no longer; he crossed the river at Amboise to march like the others on Beaugency.

Alençon, under definite orders from the Dauphin, declared that if Richemont came, he himself would have no choice but to depart. This meant that, as a result of a court intrigue which had its source in a worthless man's jealousies, Beaugency would be left in the hands of Talbot, and much of what already had been achieved would be wasted. The Maid intervened. The great influence into which she had come, and the orders which Alençon had received to do nothing save upon her advice, supplied the necessary powers; and when Richemont had made oath loyally to serve the Dauphin, Alençon consented with the others to sponsor his reconciliation. It is possible that in this her sound common-sense was assisted by the approach of Fastolfe. Sir John, unable to reach Jargeau in time, was hastening now to the point where he was most needed.

To meet him, the French departed from before Beaugency, and they came up with him midway towards Meung. Here, six thousand strong, they occupied an eminence, whilst Fastolfe in the plain below dismounted his men to receive the attack. In front of their line the English planted, as their custom was, a row of pointed staves to make a palisade, and thus they waited.

As the French did not come down to assail the position, Fastolfe sent a herald to challenge them to combat.

"Go and find yourselves lodgings for to-day," he was answered. "It is too late to engage. To-morrow, please God and Our Lady, we shall hope to see you at closer quarters."

Having sent that answer, the French returned to Beaugency. In view of this, the English fell back on Meung, and spent the night in bombarding the position on the bridge which was held by a French force. Fastolfe's aim was to clear it, so that by crossing he might from the other bank reach the Castle of Beaugency, and either enter to strengthen the defence, or bring out its garrison to swell his own force for an attack.

He was, however, forestalled. For whilst he was busy endeavouring to win a passage at Meung, the Maid's army was just as busy taking possession of Beaugency.

The defenders of Beaugency, like those of Jargeau, were the remains of that army which had suffered defeat already from the Maid at Orléans. Her presence under their walls had in itself been sufficiently intimidating. When her forces were swelled by those of Richemont, the English spirits were still further lowered. If they rose again for a moment when they saw her marching away to meet Fastolfe's army, they fell again, and fell to their nadir, when they beheld her returning upon the following morning. They were left to assume that Fastolfe had either been beaten or had fled, and utterly discouraged they were glad to surrender with the honours of war.

Fastolfe had the dismal news of it at Meung, and very shortly afterwards he beheld the vanguard of the French who were returning to take up the challenge he had issued yesterday. Immediately he began a retreat, and continued it as far as Patray. Here, as the French were overtaking him, Talbot, who was now with him, drew up the army, and dismounted five hundred archers in the hope of repeating the achievement of Crécy.

But at Crécy there had been no demoralizing fear of a Maid before whose standard it began to seem that nothing could successfully stand.

The impetuous La Hire, commanding the van, fell upon the English, and was amongst them, already throwing them into confusion, when the main body of the French came up. Alençon had hesitated to attack, seeing the strength of the enemy's numbers and position, until the Maid, with characteristic insistence, had swept away his hesitations.

"Though they be suspended from the clouds, you must engage them. My voices tell me they will all be ours."

The result was a complete rout of the English, with some two thousand slain and some two hundred prisoners taken, amongst whom was Talbot himself.

Fastolfe, as a result of the Battle of Patray, was degraded by the Duke of Bedford, more as an expression of his rage than as an act of justice.

*   *   *   *

Thus, in a week, the campaign was ended. Joan had taken Jargeau; she had occupied the fortifications on the bridge of Meung; she had taken Beaugency, and she had heavily defeated the enemy in pitched battle at Patray.

The moral effect of these victories on both sides was incalculable.

It began to look as if there was justification for the fears expressed by Fastolfe that all that with so much labour had been won by Henry V would now be lost.

The turning of the tables which had begun at Orléans was almost complete. The awe-inspiring reputation for invincibility, so long borne by the English, was passing to the armies of the Maid. And the moral effect upon the people was no less than that upon the fighting men. All those who had hated the English invaders were no longer restrained by fear from the active expression of their hatred. The English prestige was a bubble pricked. It was no longer safe for Englishmen to venture abroad in small parties. Violences to them, which formerly would never have been dared, were now a common evidence of the change of feeling.

On the morning of Sunday the 19th June, the Maid rode once more into Orléans, returning from the victory of Patray. The Dauphin was to have met her there. But he had come no nearer than Sully-sur-Loire, and thither Joan rode on to join him. The pusillanimous Prince was nervous of the great concourse he would have found in Orléans of men, who, as a result of the enthusiasm Joan had stirred

in them, were ready to bear arms for him, and with whom
he might easily have reconquered the whole of his kingdom. He reduced Joan to tears by his doubts and hesitations when she now renewed her insistence that he should
proceed to Rheims, to be crowned. Although his counsellors were left by Joan's latest achievements without an
argument to oppose to this, it was almost against his will
that she and those few who stoutly supported her prevailed upon him to face the journey.

At last, on the 27th June, he consented to set out, at the
head of an army twelve thousand strong, and accompanied
by all the nobles and captains of his party.

Troyes was the first city in their path that was held by
the invaders; and Troyes was summoned by Joan to surrender to the Dauphin. It was a strong place, garrisoned
by five or six hundred English and Burgundians, who sent
an insulting answer in the course of which they spoke of
Joan as a lunatic possessed of devils.

Here at Troyes there was a well-known Augustinian, a
certain Brother Richard, who had visited the Holy Land,
and then, in Paris, had attracted attention some months
ago by sermons that gave offence to the English. Because
he preached that Antichrist was born and foretold an imminent end to the world, the University of Paris, in its
subservience to the English, elected to perceive in him the
taint of heresy, whereupon Brother Richard, under no
illusions as to what this meant, decamped in haste.

Hearing what was being said of Joan in Troyes, he was
curious to behold her and to judge her for himself, and
he came into the French camp with this object. He approached her nervously, with signs of the cross and sprin-
klings of holy water, first to be reassured by her and then
to be completely won by her obvious purity and piety.

She charged him with fresh letters for the besieged. Not only did he bear them for her, but he seems to have preached to the people of Troyes that Joan possessed the secrets of God with power to make an army enter any city. But when no surrender came in answer to her letters, the pusillanimous Dauphin would have raised the siege had not Joan implored him to stand firm, with the solemn assurance that within five days he should be inside the town. Having persuaded him, she mounted her horse, and standard in hand rode out into the camp to order preparations for the assault.

They were throwing faggots into the ditch next morning when the Bishop of Troyes and the principal burghers came out to capitulate. Possibly Brother Richard's sermon may have had some share in this.

The Dauphin gave the required guarantees, permitting the foreign troops to depart, and on the morrow, which was Sunday, he rode into the city, the Maid beside him with her standard unfurled.

After Troyes came the submission of Châlons, where Charles remained for one night before pushing on to Rheims.

Bedford observed with increasing anxiety a march of events which he was in no case to arrest. He looked about him for reinforcements, to England and to Burgundy. He may have begun to regret his want of tact towards the Duke of Burgundy, and he did what he now could to influence the Duke, reminding him on every occasion of the murder of his father by the Dauphin's friends. In England King Henry's other uncle, the Archbishop of Winchester, had just raised an army for a crusade against the Hussites. Exposing the sorry case in which he found himself as a result of spells cast by an infernal witch, Bedford persuaded the Archbishop to send his army to serve the King in France.

That Joan was a witch it is probably that Bedford by now was genuinely convinced. Glooming in the Castle of Vincennes over the frustration of all his hopes and the demoralization of his defeated armies, he may have found it difficult to believe that this was the natural work of an ignorant peasant girl.

The fall of Troyes and the submission of Châlons were example enough for Rheims. Disregarding Bedford's urgings to hold out until an army could be sent to their relief, the people obeyed their natural inclinations, opening their gates to the Dauphin, and greeting him with cries of "Noël!"

On the 17th of July he came to the Cathedral, supported by the prescribed twelve peers, or their deputies, and accompanied by Joan, there to be crowned King of France, as she had promised.

Regnault de Chartres, the Archbishop of Rheims, anointed him with the sacred oil brought from Saint Rémy, whilst Joan stood beside him, in armour, holding over him the standard which she had borne in the forefront of the battles to which he owed this consecration.

When the crown had been placed upon his brow, she went down on her knees before him. She was in tears.

"Gentle King, now is God's will done that you should come to Rheims and receive your consecration, showing that you are the true King to whom the kingdom belongs."

* * * *

After Rheims, Paris.

That was Joan's view of the proper sequence of events, and it was the view of others.

It was, too, what Bedford, in his Castle of Vincennes expected. "But by God's grace," he wrote on the 16th July (the eve of the coronation), "it will be resisted." And he urges that the young Henry VI be brought at once to France to be crowned, as would have happened before this if his counsel had been heeded, in which case things would be less desperate. He realized how paltry now would be rendered the impression of crowning Henry King of France when another had been so crowned already.

Moreover, in the pass to which things were come, Bedford could no longer feel sure even of Paris. To hold it he needed the Duke of Burgundy, whose influence there was so considerable. He needed also the Cardinal of England (as Winchester was styled) and his anti-Hussites. The Cardinal was on his way. But of Burgundy the Duke of Bedford was doubtful, for there, too, the Maid had been at work to thwart him.

She had written to Philip the Good, to exhort him to remember that in any war between himself and Charles, the blood to be shed on both sides would be French, and she had implored him to make peace. Her letter had been so well received that Philip had sent an embassy to the King, and such fair words were uttered that those about Charles regarded the peace as being as good as signed.

*   *   *   *

After four days in Rheims, King Charles VII moved to Soissons, of which and of Laon the keys were delivered to him. After these cities came the submissions of Château-Thierry, Provins, Coulommiers, Crécy en Brie, Montmirail.

The leisureliness of this victorious progress at a time when speed was all-important was characteristic of the sluggard Charles and exasperating to Joan and to those who perceived the advantages the enemy might derive from it. It actually enabled Bedford to bring the Cardinal's five thousand men into Paris in time. They entered it on the 25th July.

In view of this English reinforcement, and yielding to the representations of his favourites, Charles decided to remain content with what had been accomplished, and turned aside, to return to the lotus-land of the Loire.

But Bedford considered himself now in sufficient strength to dispute the King's passage of the Seine, and in this way he became the ally of Joan, who saw with sorrow the imminent danger of a waste of all that she had done. He sent an insulting letter to Charles, "who called himself Dauphin, and now dares to call himself King," upbraiding him for his wrongful undertakings against King Henry, the natural and lawful King of England and France, and inveighing against the means he employed to delude the simple people by the aid of "a dissolute and infamous woman who wears the garments of a man, and an apostate and seditious mendicant friar" (Brother Richard), "both of them, according to Holy Writ, abominable to God." He invited Charles to appoint time and place for a conference, to which "he may be accompanied by the dissolute woman and the said apostate and any other perjurers or followers he chooses, but on condition that he comes to treat for peace, and not" (he adds for the benefit of the Duke of Burgundy) "a false, simulated, corrupt, perjured peace like that of Montereau when he procured the assassination of Jean Sans Peur."

This letter reached Charles at Crespy-le-Valois on the 11th August, and already Bedford was in the neighbourhood and offering battle, upon ground of his own choice, where he had taken up a strong position. There was some skirmishing. But the French would not press home an attack against positions of such advantage, and in the end Bedford fell back on Paris.

This retreat, following upon the earlier thrasonical defiance, encouraged the French. They followed up, only to meet the same stalemate again at Senlis, where Bedford, strongly entrenched once more, received and repelled the attacks made upon him. The English could not, however, be lured out into the open to a definite engagement, although by exposing herself fearlessly the Maid did all that she could to draw them. She even simulated a retreat so as to encourage pursuit. But the only advantage the English took of this was to resume their retirement upon Paris.

Compiègne and Beauvais surrendered readily to Charles, hailing him as King of France. In Beauvais the *Te Deum* was sung, to the rage of the Bishop-Count Pierre Cauchon, who was completely in the English interest and destined to play so sinister a part in the sequel. He was driven out of his bishopric, compelled to depart like all those who would not submit to Charles.

At Compiègne, where Charles halted, he received the submission of a half-dozen neighbouring towns.

His fortunes appeared now to be prospering, and this almost in spite of himself. But Burgundy was playing a double game. The Duke sent ambassadors to talk vaguely of a general peace, and to propose a truce until Christmas. Yielding to this, the flabby King showed a disposition to return home, and was prevented only by that same energy in Joan which had drawn his reluctant steps to Rheims. Since no truce with Burgundy would include the English, Alençon set out, with Joan once more beside him as a guiding spirit, to march on Paris. They were at Saint Denis on the 26th August. The King followed reluctantly as far as Senlis.

Bedford was on the horns of a dilemma. He was urgently needed in Paris to resist the coming attack, and yet he dared not remain for fear of a general rising in the sorely disaffected north. In the end, he left two thousand English to defend Paris with the Burgundians, and with the remainder of his forces set out for Rouen, so as to keep a firm hand on Normandy.

Alençon, having brought his force to the walls of Paris, could do little more than skirmish there until supported by the main army with which the King was now lagging behind.

At last, on the 7th September, Charles came as far as Saint Denis, and on the next day a really serious assault was delivered by Gilles de Rais, now a Marshal, and Gaucourt. It was aimed at the Gate of Saint Honoré, whilst Alençon with another division watched the Gate of Saint Denis, to intercept any sally.

At the Gate of Saint Honoré the barriers were forced and the bastions carried, and Joan, waving her standard, leapt down into the outer ditch, as elsewhere, to encourage the assailants, without regard to the fire and the hail of stones from the battlements. At the second ditch, however, the attack was checked by the water in it.

Joan was sounding the depth of the water with the staff of her standard, and calling for faggots, when she was struck in the thigh by an arbalest-bolt. In spite of this and of the fact that dusk was falling, she remained at her post, encouraging the men to storm the walls and calling for more faggots, so as to fill up the ditch.

Fear and confusion were loose in Paris, of which the

signs were apparent to the besiegers. The people were already screaming that the city was taken. But darkness was descending, the fight had lasted since noon, and the men were weary. The captains decided to suspend operations until the morrow. Joan protested against this, insisting that only a little perseverance now would place them in possession of the city. History might have been different, indeed, if they had heeded her. As it was, it became necessary for Alençon and Gaucourt to remove her by force. They got to horse, and rode back to La Chappelle, fired upon by the besieged until they were beyond Saint Lazare.

If Joan departed reluctantly and in disappointment, at least she departed in the confidence that the next day would see the end of the Parisian resistance. And so well founded was her conviction that the city could hold out no longer that on the following morning the Baron de Montmorency with some fifty or sixty gentlemen rode out of Paris to join the King.

Operations were resumed. But just as full of ardour the assailants were approaching the walls again, a message came from Charles ordering them all back to Saint Denis. The foolish counsellors of this foolish king had conceived that he would do better to clear the enemy from the south, from those parts of the Loire which he still occupied, arguing that the peace with Burgundy which they regarded as a foregone conclusion would ensure him the ultimate possession of Paris.

In spite of all intercessions, he set out on the 13th September to return to the Loire, abandoning the precious fruit which had been all but shaken from the tree. It is suggested that he was played upon by La Trémouille and others of the same mind, who perceived that if Paris were taken it would have to be held. Nor would that be the end of things. This tireless Maid, who dragged them from enterprise to enterprise, would not rest until she had fulfilled her promise of chasing the last Englishman out of France. This would mean an indefinite prolongation of the war and the establishment of a state of things not only contrary to the wishes of those pusillanimous spirits sighing for the comfortable ease of the south, but one in which the credit of the favourites might have to yield to the credit of the captains.

In the south, meanwhile, some excursions were made against such places as Saint Pierre le Moustier and La Charité. The latter place was besieged in November, but for lack of means the siege was abandoned, and Joan returned to court. She was well received there, notwithstanding a failure the true cause of which was at least recognized.

Not only Joan herself, but her family, too, had by now been ennobled, and her brothers had taken the name of Du Lis, from the blazon they had assumed by royal sanction.

* * * *

The truce with Burgundy, expiring at Christmas, was prolonged to Easter. But the English not being bound by it, hostilities continued in the north. The provinces abandoned by a king whom they had received and acknowledged fell once more a prey to the enemy, and the city of Rheims wrote to Joan that reprisals were feared there for their ready submission to Charles. Joan replied with encouragements to resistance, and from that moment pressed for a resumption of the campaign which had been interrupted in September. The moment was propitious.

The Armagnacs were at Saint Denis, and so difficult were they making things for Paris that, whilst the city was short of food, and prices had reached exorbitant levels, no one dared venture beyond the faubourgs save at the peril of his life.

Bedford and the English were busy in Normandy, and the Duke of Burgundy, pursuing a temporizing policy, could send the Parisians no help.

The King, however, was not to be stirred from his inertia, and at last, in the early days of April, finding all her efforts vain, Joan quitted the court and rode off to more active scenes. She came to Melun, which had just driven out the English, and thence to Lagny on the Marne, the neighbourhood of which was being ravaged by some three or four hundred English under a brigand named Franquet d'Arras. She attacked them with a similar force, completely routed them, and took Franquet a prisoner. He was claimed by the justices of Lagny, and, despite the attempts she made to save his life, he was beheaded.

The news of the Maid's return to action produced such an effect in the north, so encouraging to the French and so intimidating to the English, that we find Bedford in those days publishing a "Proclamation against the captains and soldiers defaulting for fear of the enchantments of La Pucelle."

And now Easter was reached, the truce with Burgundy expired, and it was followed by no treaty of peace such as Charles had too sanguinely expected. Instead, the Duke took the field once more, and Compiègne, being rightly regarded by him as the key to the kingdom, he advanced to take possession of it. There followed some fighting on the Aisne and the Oise at which Joan was present, and in the course of which Choisy fell into the hands of the Duke. Perceiving that the siege of Compiègne was now imminent, Joan hastened thither from Crespy, and arrived at sunrise on the 24th May with some three or four hundred men.

Compiègne was still far from being invested. The river flowed between the city and the enemy, and across the bridge the French had thrown up a strong bastion to defend the approach.

It is now that for the first time in her year of soldiering, we see the Maid actually taking charge of operations and directing strategy, a condition of things due possibly to the fact that whilst there were soldiers of ability present there was none of sufficiently high authority to dispute her own.

The situation was explained to her. The Duke of Burgundy was three miles away, to the north, at Coudon on the Aronde. John of Luxembourg was at Clairoix, at the confluence of the Aronde and the Oise. Montgomery with the English occupied Venette, whilst another Burgundian force was at Margny.

Joan's brave spirit was, as usual, all eagerness to attack, so as to dislodge the besiegers from their positions. Her simple plan was to charge the Burgundians at Margny, drive them beyond Clairoix, and thence fall upon the English at Venette. Nothing could strategically have been worse. If she were successful in dislodging the Burgundians from Margny, by driving them back to Clairoix all that she would accomplish would be to make them retire upon their main body which was stationed there. And in doing so, she would be exposing her rear to an attack from the English, although against this she depended upon the forces left in Compiègne to hold them in check if they should make any such attempt.

On the very evening of the day of her arrival, she rode out at five o'clock with five or six hundred men to execute her aim.

At Margny the surprise attack succeeded, and the Burgundians were thrown back, but only, as should have been foreseen, until they received the support of those at Clairoix. Then a deadlock resulted.

The English did not neglect the opportunity afforded them. They came out of Venette with intent to take her in the rear. Guillaume de Flavy, who commanded in Compiègne, was ready for this. His archers were posted along the bastion of the bridge-head to hold the English in check. But already the rearmost in Joan's troop, fearing to be cut off, were falling back in quest of cover, and in this way actually afforded protection to the English from the Compiègne archers, who could not shoot now without danger of hitting their own men.

Meanwhile, the Burgundians, finding their opponents diminishing, redoubled their efforts. The French began to give way, and Joan was urged to retreat. Refusing, she made a last desperate unavailing effort to rally her men. But the Burgundians were pressing them so hard that in the end she was compelled to fall back with her followers.

A movement with intent to cut off her retreat, made towards the entrance on the right of the bastion guarding the bridge-head, so intimidated Flavy, who feared that thus the enemy might get into Compiègne, that he ordered the drawbridge to be taken up. Thus Joan, with those immediately about her—her brother Pierre, her esquire d'Aulon, and Poton de Xaintrailles—remained outside to be surrounded at the bastion.

Half-a-dozen men-at-arms sprang towards her at once,

and she was dragged from her horse by an archer in the following of one of the knights of John of Luxembourg.

* * * *

She was taken at once to Margny, where the Duke of Burgundy, stirred by a curiosity which appears, however, to have been entirely respectful, came to see her. Thence she was sent by John of Luxembourg, to whom, as a prisoner, she belonged, to his Castle of Beaulieu, in Picardy.

The English, rejoicing in this capture of their arch-enemy, at once demanded her, ready to count out the gold of her ransom.

Luxembourg, however, refused them. It must have been his intention to treat her honourably as an ordinary prisoner of war. But the English and the circumstances between them were to wreck that honourable resolution.

Guillaume de Flavy, the defender of Compiègne, presented so stout a front to his assailants that at the end of six unsuccessful months, Luxembourg was obliged to raise the siege and fall back, leaving his artillery in the hands of the French.

Only then did Luxembourg, whose necessitous circumstances were aggravated by this failure, yield to the demands that were being made. And even then he did not yield to the English, but to the Holy Office, which had been set in motion by English influence with the University of Paris.

It was Pierre Cauchon, that Bishop-Count of Beauvais, who had been driven from his see by Joan, who brought the demand to the Duke of Burgundy and with it the English gold that was to buy the prisoner. It was a prince's ransom, ten thousand livres of six francs, which in purchasing power must have been equal to some ten thousand pounds of our present English money. The extraordinary transaction calls for no comment beyond those which in itself it offers. A person suspected of heresy, and claimed by the Inquisition, is bought by a bishop acting as the agent of the English, who, having bought her, are to hand her over to the Inquisition for trial, so that upon conviction the Inquisition may hand her back to the English for execution. Should the Inquisition fail to find her guilty of heresy, she still remains the property of the English who have purchased her, and they will then be under the necessity of discovering some other ground upon which they can put her to death. That will not be easy without a violation of all the usages of war; therefore, the trial is so to be managed by their agent the Bishop of Beauvais that they will not be further embarrassed. Apart from this there are other expedient reasons why she should be convicted as a heretic and a witch. It is politically necessary to destroy the faith established in her, to soil her, and to destroy her reputation. Without this, her mere death will insufficiently profit her enemies. She had proclaimed that she was sent by God to throw the English out of France. The extent of her successes had appeared to supply the implication that God was against the English. It is necessary to efface this by establishing that the supernatural powers with which it seems idle to deny that she was equipped were derived, not from God, but from the Devil.

And so they bring her from the Castle of Beaurévoir, whither she has been removed subsequent upon an attempt of hers to escape from Beaulieu. At Crotoy, on the 21st November, she is delivered to the English by the officers of the Duke of Burgundy. By the English she is brought to Rouen, where she is awaited by Pierre Cauchon, deputed by the Inquisition to preside at her trial. Here this prisoner of the Holy Office is lodged, not in an ecclesiastical prison, but in the Castle of Rouen, with English men-at-arms for gaolers.

Pierre Cauchon selects his ecclesiastical officers, and prepares his court.

* * * *

In the archives of the nations there is no more repulsive document than the record of this trial. The depths to which human falsity, hypocrisy, guile, and cruelty can descend is nowhere more terribly revealed than in this monument of iniquity.

Nothing could be more misguided or contrary to the fact than to suppose that we have here an ordinary Inquisition trial conducted by men who, however mistaken and deluded by fanaticism, yet act in sincere accordance with their consciences, believing that what they do is right.

For a little while the perusal of the minutes may deceive you, the smooth, patient gentleness of the examiners may lead you into some such assumption. Very soon, however, it becomes apparent that we are in the presence of a gang of hirelings who are prostituting their learning and their casuistical attainments so as to place upon a political assassination a mask of piety and stern ecclesiastical duty. We soon realize that the function of these erudite doctors of civil and canon law is not to investigate whether this poor maid of nineteen years of age may have been guilty of offences against the Faith, but to establish at all costs, and without regard to truth, honour, or humanity, that she has acted as an agent of Satan and that her achievements are due to the support she has received from the powers of darkness. This trial, which superficially appears to be conducted so scrupulously, so justly, and so canonically, is a blasphemy from end to end.

This is not the expression of a lay opinion. The Church herself, after the Rehabilitation Trial of 1455, pronounced upon the matter in terms fully as harsh. After a rigorous investigation and the close examination of a crowd of witnesses, she accuses that tribunal of having proceeded faithlessly, evilly, calumniously, fraudulently, maliciously, iniquitously.

To arrive independently at this opinion, it is not necessary to peruse the records of the Rehabilitation Trial. Craftily though Cauchon conducted the original trial, cunningly though he excluded from it the least hint of the political agencies at work, the political ends to be served, the falsity and fraud of the proceedings will be clear to every intelligent student of the minutes.

⌈ Irregularities of procedure mark the trial from the outset, the most glaring and infamous of which is that this maid of nineteen should have been brought to face that array of doctors without any legal adviser (such as is prescribed for minors by the Holy Office) to support and guide her through the labyrinths of casuistry and theological logic into which she was conducted so that she might lose herself.⌋

Thus, alone, Joan faced for the first time, at eight o'clock on the morning of the 21st February 1431, her formidable judges in the royal chapel of the Castle of Rouen.

Cauchon sat with the officials of his court; Jean d'Estivet, the promoter or prosecutor; Jean de la Fontaine, the examining judge; Boisguillaume and Manchon, apostolic notaries, as recorders; and Jean Massieu, the usher, a young priest who was rural dean of Rouen.

To these Cauchon had added no fewer than twenty-two assessors, and there were present in addition a score of doctors, bachelors and licentiates of canon and civil law. Anatole France describes the assembly as a veritable synod; and this synod sat in judgment upon a matter of the Faith, for which ordinarily two or three canons sufficed.

Joan, in professing her glad willingness to stand her trial, had begged that she might first be allowed to hear Mass. But it was held that, considering the nature of the crimes of which she was accused and the indecent male attire in which she persisted, this could not be permitted.

In this refusal we perceive already an illegality—as distinct from an irregularity. The tribunal had not the right to refuse a prisoner's request to approach the sacraments.

The actual charge upon which she was to be tried is set forth by Cauchon in the announcement of his appointment as deputy on this occasion for the Grand Inquisitor, whose vicar, Lemaitre, was to sit with the Bishop. The terms of it are that: "A woman named Joan, vulgarly known as La Pucelle, having, in absolute oblivion of the decency proper to her sex, broken down the barriers of shame, had in contempt of all feminine pudicity, worn, with an astonishing and monstrous audacity, the indecent garments proper to the male sex. Further her presumption had reached such a point that she had not feared to utter many things contrary to the Catholic Faith and injurious to orthodox belief."

What are these things "contrary to the Faith" which the trial is to establish we find in the instructions to the promoter, which set forth that she is suspected of "various sorceries, incantations, invocations of, and communications with, evil spirits."

* * * *

Brought before her judges on that February morning in the chill gloom of the royal chapel, Joan is "charitably admonished" to speak the truth without recourse to subterfuge, so as to shorten the proceedings. Thereafter she is required to swear that she will speak the truth on all that may be asked.

"I do not know," she says, "upon what you wish to question me. Perhaps you might ask me things which I should not tell you."

The demand is repeated with a slight variation. "Will you swear to speak the truth on what may be asked you concerning matters of the Faith, and upon what you may know?"

After some further argument she kneels, and with her hands upon the Missal compromises by swearing that she will speak the truth upon all things that may be asked her and that she knows concerning matters of the Faith.

The examination on this first day is confined to her name, her birthplace, the names of her father and mother, of her godfathers and godmothers, the place where she was baptized and what priest baptized her, her present age, which she supposes to be nineteen, and the instruction in the Faith which she has received from her mother, who had taught her, she says, the Paternoster, the Ave Maria, and the Credo.

Thereupon, she is requested to recite the Pater Noster. She answers that she will recite it willingly to any of them who will hear her in confession.

Over this they seem to have wrangled with her for some time; they insisting that she should recite it, be it in open court, be it to one or two "notable persons" who shall take her apart for the purpose; she insisting that she will recite it only if she is heard in confession.

At last the matter is allowed to drop, and she is dismissed with a prohibition to leave the prison assigned to her under pain of being convicted of the crime of heresy. This prohibition she refuses spiritedly to recognize, claiming the right of every prisoner to escape if the opportunity should present itself. Upon that she is consigned to the custody of John Grey, John Barow, and William Talbot.

The examination is resumed on the morrow in a chamber adjoining the great hall of the castle.

At the outset we have a repetition of the previous day's argument concerning the form of the oath. Invited to swear, she replies, almost with a touch of scorn it seems, "I swore your oath yesterday; that should suffice. You press me too much."

Finally she swears, again circumscribing her oath to matters relating to the Faith.

Her examination, at the request of Cauchon, is taken up by Jean Beaupère, an eminent elderly theologian, who had been Rector of the University of Paris, a man of authority and subtlety, who brings to his present task the prejudice of a conviction of the malice inherent in feminine nature.

He begins by exhorting her to tell the truth as she has sworn, to which her reply amounts to an assertion that she will answer truthfully where she can answer at all and that otherwise she will not answer. She adds: "If you were well informed about me you would wish me out of your hands. I have done nothing except by revelation."

Asked if in her youth she learnt any trade, she tells him that she learnt to spin and to sew, and adds with a touch of youthful ingenuous jactancy that in these accomplishments she fears comparison with no woman in Rouen.

She goes on to relate how from fear of the Burgundians she had left home to go to Neufchâteau in Lorraine, where for about a fortnight she had remained in the house of a woman named La Rousse.

She answers questions on the extent to which she went to confession, and to the effect that she received communion at Easter. But when asked if she received communion at other times, she tells the examiner to "Pass on!"

To questions concerning her voices she relates how she first heard them when she was thirteen years of age, how at first she was afraid. She tells them that it was summer, at noontide, in her father's garden, and the first voice was accompanied by a bright light. The voices came to her often thereafter, and it seemed to her that they were worthy voices and that they came from God.

Questioned as to what directions she received from these voices for the good of her soul, she answers that they instructed her to govern herself and to frequent the church. The voices told her that she should come to France and that she would deliver Orléans. Also they told her to seek Robert of Baudricourt, and that he would provide men to accompany her. And she related the part played in this by her uncle.

Further questions elicit a simple narrative of her coming into France, seeking the Dauphin at Chinon, and the recognition of her mission.

She is brought back to the voices by her examiner and to the events before Paris, when failure attended her. His presumable aim already is to show the falsity of these voices, her failure before Paris being the proof of this. But she insists that the counsel of her voices was that she should remain at Saint Denis, and that she would so have remained if she had not been constrained to depart.

Asked if it was not on a Sunday that she was battling before Paris, she answers in the affirmative.

"Was that well done?" asks the examiner.

"Pass on!" she answers him.

Again and again we are to hear from her this imperious "Pass on!" (*Transeatis ultra*, in the Latin text, and *Passez outre* in the French.) It comes whenever there is insistence upon some irrelevant or purely impertinent question. Sometimes she varies it by the ironical question, *"Est-ce de votre procés?*—Does it concern your trial?"

Early in the proceedings on the third day, a question, illuminating to us in our reconstruction of the events, is put by Beaupère, who again is the examiner. When, he asks her, did she last eat or drink. It seems a question full of gentle concern. But we are in Lent, and to convict her of disregarding this would, despite her age, be to travel some way in the desired direction; for contempt of the commandments of the Church would be inferred.

"I have neither eaten nor drunk since yesterday at noon," she answers.

Thus we have a glimpse of the physical condition in which this child is subjected to the ordeals of these interrogatories.

* * * *

These public examinations before that imposing court, composing what is described as the Preparatory Trial, are five in number. In the course of these she is questioned and cross-questioned about her voices and her visions. How did she know them to be angelic? How did she know that, as she asserts, these unearthly visitors were Saint Catherine, Saint Margaret, and Saint Michael? It is demanded of her that she describe them. How were they dressed? Did they have hair? Did she touch them ever? If so, was she conscious of any warmth? How did she recognize Saint Michael? Did he carry the scales (by which is meant the scales with which he is represented, the scales in which he weighs souls)?

Their aim is clear, and so far legitimate enough. They are testing her for fraud. From her answers to these, as also to all those other questions concerned with her deeds under arms, we gather her bearing to be marked by that self-possession which in such an ordeal is to be derived only from the tranquil consciousness of virtue. These answers are simple and direct, touched at times by shrewdness and at times by wit. When asked why she should have carried her standard into the Cathedral at the coronation of the Dauphin, she says: "Having been present at the labour it was right that it should be present at the honour." Sometimes she displays an ironic humour. When they ask her whether Saint Michael appeared to her naked, she rejoins: "Do you suppose that God would not have the wherewithal to clothe him?" At moments there is a touch of defiance. When questioned as to what counsel she receives from her voices concerning this trial, she replies, "To answer boldly." And more than once, when pressed unduly, she admonishes Cauchon: "You say that you are my judge. Take care what you do, for in truth I am sent by God, and you place yourself in great danger." More than once she reminds him that matters upon which they press her—her voices, the male garments she wears, which

are to assume more and more importance as the trial proceeds—were settled at Poitiers, where they received canonical approval. This is to ask how can that which the
Church found good at Poitiers be found evil by the Church
at Rouen? How can the authority of the Bishop of Beauvais in these matters be above the authority of the Archbishop of Rheims, his metropolitan?

Sometimes she meets a dangerous question with an answer brilliantly inspired. Once, at the third sitting of the
court, she is asked by Beaupère whether she knows herself
to be in a state of grace. It seems that however she answers a question so wickedly insidious, she must incrim-
inate herself: if in the negative, it is a confession that she
is in a state of sin; if in the affirmative, she convicts herself
of presumptuous pride. And if either answer had been
made, it must have been followed up by questions that
would have driven home the implication.

Piety avails her here, where wit might fail. She answers
completely, and yet avoids the snare spread for her in
either affirmation or denial.

"If I am not in a state of grace, may God bring me into
it; if I am, may God keep me in it." And she sets the seal
upon that sublime answer by adding: "I should be the
most sorrowful person in the world if I knew that I am not
in a state of grace."

At the Rehabilitation Trial it transpired that this question scandalized at least one of the assessors, Jean Lefèvre,
who raised his voice to warn her that she was not compelled to answer. He was angrily told by Cauchon that he
would have done better to have held his tongue.

This is not in the minutes of the trial. There is sup-
pression also of some questions which we must suppose

would have been included only if the answers had been turned to account against her, such as that which asks her whether she is really a virgin.

Another trap is set for her in a question as to whom she believes to be the true Pope.

But she is not so easily to be caught. "Are there, then, two?" she answers.

The more she is pressed to say what was the sign she gave the Dauphin, the more firmly she tells them that they will never draw it from her lips. "Go and ask him," she bids them.

Asked if she knows by revelation that she will escape, she replies: "That does not concern your trial."

Examined as to an attempt she made to escape from Beaurévoir, when she dropped from a height of thirty feet, an expression of hers that she would rather die than fall into the hands of the English is quoted against her to show that she intended suicide.

On the subject of her male attire she is attacked, questioned and cross-questioned from every conceivable angle. In addition to this, the court endeavours indefatigably to persuade her to assume the garments of her sex. When she begs to be allowed to approach the sacraments or to hear Mass, the condition imposed is always that she shall first consent to dress herself as a woman. It is a point upon which she will not yield as long as she is a prisoner. Her reason, which these men refuse to perceive—but which was clear enough to the judges at the Rehabilitation Trial —is that in male attire her modesty and virtue are better safeguarded in a prison in which she is in the custody of rude soldiers. She is ready and willing to dress herself as a woman so as to receive the sacraments, provided that she may change again afterwards. To this, however, these men, who are so anxious for the salvation of her soul, will not consent.

These lengthy interrogatories, coming back always, with a maddening, exasperating persistency, to the same chief points, her voices and her male attire, resemble that form of examination known to us to-day as the third degree.

Since it is not for her judges to deny the possibility of revelation and other supernatural manifestations, the very creed they profess being based on these phenomena, it remains for them to discover either that she is guilty of fraud, or else that the spirits by which she claimed to be visited were evil ones. Preferring the latter alternative as the more definitely damning, they seek with a tireless, relentless zeal to establish it. They address themselves to the discovery of witchcraft in all things concerned with her. Having regard to the part played in her victories by her standard, this becomes a vehicle of enchantments, even to the very inscription graven upon it, as if the names of Jesus and Mary ever had been or ever could be employed in the promotion of unholy traffic. They seem to suggest that the very consecration of the standard was an operation in magic and the uses of holy water a part of that operation. Because people crowded about her wherever she went, there are questions aiming to bring out that she seduced them by necromantic arts. She is examined closely as to a ring which she wore, which they have taken from her, and which it is alleged that people came to touch and kiss, when in fact they came to do no more than kiss her hands.

They delve back into the games which she played as a child under that great beech tree at Domrémy which was known as the Ladies' Tree. They question her about the weaving of flower-chains and garlands which are hung onto the branches of this tree to propitiate the fairies. To such innocent childish acts as these it is sought to attach a dark significance. They plague her with questions about these puerilities, questions which might be sincere only on the lips of foolishly superstitious old women.

The five great public examinations before that regiment of divines are followed by examinations in her prison, conducted by the licentiate in canon law Jean de la Fontaine, the examining judge, and attended by Cauchon, by two doctors of theology, and the other officers of the Bishop's court. There are seven such examinations, between the 7th and the 31st of March. But in these as in the public ones—and the ground covered is always the same—her steadiness and simple candour baffle the tribunal. They have failed utterly, notwithstanding all the guile and craft employed, to draw her into any avowal or declaration which could be pilloried as heretical. The only real matter of incrimination is her male apparel. And there is no heresy in this. As she has said, with simple common-sense, when refused the sacrament in this garb, her clothes do not change her soul, nor do they constitute an offence against the Church. So to construe it, they must invoke an ancient Levitical law, ignore the virtuous purpose for which she prefers the garb, and ignore further the fact that her wearing it was sanctioned by the Archbishop of Rheims.

Things are not easy for these judges until at last, at the examination of the 31st March, the perfidious zeal of Jean de La Fontaine discovers an issue from the difficulty. He invites her to submit herself to the judgment of the Church. Her answer cuts away the ground on which they seek to take their stand. She requests that the answers she has given should be seen and examined by divines, and then that she be told if there is anything in them which is against the Christian faith, adding that, if there is, she would not wish to maintain it, but would regret and reject it.

From this declaration, which must fully have satisfied any honest men, they cannot shake her. It is in vain that they expound to her the distinction between the Church Triumphant and the Church Militant. These are subtleties into which she will not enter.

Perhaps the very insistence which they now employ renders her aware of the snare that is spread for her, brings her to perceive that the Church in their view and for their present purposes is this tribunal of enemies acting in the English interests.

In the last examination of all, that of the 31st March, this question of submission to the Church has become the only question. It has assumed a paramount importance, because the point so lately discovered is the one by which they are to prevail against her.

Here is the text:

Questioned if the Church Militant should tell her that her revelations are illusions, diabolical matters, superstitions or evil things, she will submit to the Church, she replies that she will submit always to Our Lord, Whose commandments she will fulfil.

Questioned if she does not believe that she is subject to the Church which is on earth, namely, our Holy Father the Pope, the cardinals, archbishops, bishops, and other prelates of the Church, she replies: "Yes, Our Lord being served first."

Questioned if she is commanded by her voices not to submit to the Church Militant, which is on earth, or to its judgments, she says that her answers are those commanded by her voices and that they do not command her not to obey the Church, Our Lord being first served.

Beyond this they cannot lead her. They must make the best of it, or the worst. The Preparatory Trial by examination is at an end, and Cauchon, with the assistance of some thirty-nine clerics, passes to the ordinary trial, or trial proper in accordance with the procedure of the Holy Office.

* * * *

An indictment is framed by the prosecutor Jean d'Estivet in seventy articles, and submitted to the Bishop, the assessors, and the rest—in all a body on this occasion of thirty-nine clerics. Joan is brought to the chamber next to the great hall, to hear the reading, which occupies two days, and is invited to reply to, and comment upon, each of the articles.

If it is possible from a perusal of the minutes of the Preliminary or Preparatory Trial to be deceived into supposing that these men may be acting in good faith, no such charitable assumption is possible when we pass from these minutes to a consideration of the articles which claim to summarize them.

A glance at a few of them should suffice to reveal the iniquity at work under the cloak of religion and the impudence of the fraud which they are framed to perpetrate.

The second article asserts

that not only in the present year, but since childhood, she has made and composed many sorceries and superstitions; that she has been deified and has permitted herself to be worshipped and venerated; that she has invoked demons and evil spirits, consulting them frequently and making pacts with them; that she has given advice and assistance to others doing the same things, and has induced them to do the same things, deceiving them into believing that there is no sin in such acts.

To this Joan answers by a denial of all that concerns sorceries, superstitious works, or divinations. As for being worshipped, many have kissed her hands or garments, but if this was worship it was not done by her wish, and she avoided it as far as she was able.

The fourth, fifth, and sixth articles elaborate the charge of sorcery, and enter into particulars.

They assert that in her youth she was not educated or instructed in the principles of the Faith, but was "accustomed and instructed by certain old women to perform sorceries, divinations, and other magic arts." This is an infamous corruption of her admission that as a child she had heard her godmother and others talk of fairies and fairy apparitions. The implication of her godmother leads the prosecutor gratuitously to add that "it is notorious that many inhabitants of these villages have from ancient times resorted to witchcraft."

Proceeding with these absurdities the articles cite a tree, "commonly known as the fairy tree of Bourlemont, near which there is a fountain, about which, it is said, is the dwelling of certain evil spirits known as fairies, in the company of which those who resort to witchcraft are known to dance at night about the tree and the fountain."

When she was questioned about this tree and this fountain, she had said that she knew that sick persons went there to drink or to procure the water with the object of recovering their health, and she had admitted that she herself had drunk of this water, though not for any curative purpose.

Not content with having built to the extent seen upon

this innocent admission, the prosecutor goes shamelessly on to state that she had frequented this tree "particularly at the hours at which divine service was being celebrated in church, so that she might be there alone; dancing about the tree, and suspending from the branches garlands which she had made of several herbs and flowers, uttering and singing certain invocations etc."

She had admitted making these garlands of flowers and sometimes hanging them from the branches, as other children did. But the matter of invocations is an addition invented by Estivet. So as to balance matters, he omits that part of her reply which informed them that more often she had gone there to make garlands of flowers for Our Lady of Domrémy.

During one of her examinations she had been questioned at length about a mandrake alleged to have grown under a tree somewhere at Domrémy, and she was asked if she were acquainted with the uses made of mandrake and what uses she herself had made of it. She had heard, she replied, that mandrakes were kept because they were lucky and made their possessors rich, but she spoke in scorn of such beliefs and denied ever having possessed a mandrake.

That their questions on this matter should have failed completely does not prevent the seventh article from falsely asserting that "the said Joan was sometimes in the habit of carrying a mandrake in her bosom, hoping by this means to have good fortune in riches and temporal things; she affirmed that this mandrake possessed such virtue and effect."

The eighth article contains one of the most infamous and shameless of these distortions. She had related under examination how once from fear of Burgundian raiders she had fled to Neufchâteau, and remained a fortnight in the house of a woman named La Rousse, whom she assisted the while in household matters. In the eighth article the Burgundian reason for her going to Neufchâteau has become an act of filial insubordination. It runs:

> When about fifteen years of age, without permission from her parents, she repaired to the town of Neufchâteau, and there served for a certain time a woman, an inn-keeper, named La Rousse, with whom dwelt continually several immodest young women, and whose lodgers were chiefly men-at-arms.

It does not transpire from the minutes that La Rousse was an inn-keeper, nor is there in them any mention of the immodest young women or the men-at-arms.

Joan referred the court to the actual terms of her answers, and denied the additions.

The ninth article is an unpleasant corollary to the eighth. It scandalously reverses the facts of the attempted betrothal of Joan to a young man of Toul and represents her as the petitioner in the action that was brought, the young man having "refused to marry her because it had come to his knowledge that she had lived with the said dissolute women," at La Rousse's.

Article by article, as we proceed, it is the same. Falsehood, fraud, and distortion of the most shameless. Before quitting the subject it may be well to quote the thirteenth, chiefly for the sake of the terminology employed, in which a reckless fury of accusation seems to betray itself. It deals with the male garments in which she was taken, with her hair cut *en rond,* like a man's.

> And generally, having rejected all feminine modesty, not only in contempt of feminine decency, but also in contempt of that which belongs to men of good morals, she has used

of all garments those which the most dissolute of men are in the habit of wearing, and, further, she has carried arms of offence. To attribute this to a command of Our Lord, to the holy angels and virgin saints, is to blaspheme Our Lord and His Saints, to destroy the divine law, to violate canon law, to scandalize the sex and virtue of womankind, pervert all decency of external wear, and to approve the instances of dissoluteness in humankind.

That, more or less, is the language of all the indictment, and it should suffice to display the ruthlessness of the malice at work.

The articles were, however, of necessity, supplemented by the comments and denials uttered by Joan when they were publicly read to her. But now these learned doctors in Rouen decide to proceed to a further summary, whereby the matter of these seventy articles is confined to twelve. These twelve articles, are not communicated to Joan, so that there are no contradictions or replies from her to add to the texts. They confine themselves to statements of facts, but of facts that have been distorted and adapted to the desired end, and, as if this were not enough, there is a covering letter, indited in the names of sixteen doctors and six bachelors or licentiates who acted as assessors, pronouncing upon these matters which are submitted for judgment to the Venerable Faculty of Theology of the University of Paris.

We say, after diligently considering and weighing the quality of the person, her words and acts, the manner of the apparitions and revelations, the end, the cause, the circumstance, and all that is contained in the above articles and in her trial, that there is reason to think that the said apparitions and revelations which she boasts and affirms to proceed from God, through angels and saints, are rather fictions of human invention or else proceed from the Spirit of Evil.

Thus the application for judgment dictates the form this judgment is to take.

The Venerable Faculty obediently pronounced as was desired, and announced that if upon being "charitably exhorted and admonished" Joan will not willingly rejoin the Catholic Faith, publicly abjure her error, and give suitable satisfaction, she is to be abandoned to the secular arm and receive the penalty due to the importance of her crime.

She was informed in detail of the finding of the University, warned of the penalties she incurred of eternal fire to her soul and temporal fire to her body, and exhorted to save herself from one and the other by submitting to the judgment of the Church Militant.

Her answer was that, although she should see the fire lighted, the faggots burning, and the executioner waiting, she could depart from nothing that she had said at her trial.

This was enough for excommunication and abandonment to the secular arm with its inevitable consequences; but not enough to serve the ends in view. Conviction at the bar of the Church was of little value here unless accompanied by conviction at the bar of public opinion. The impression of her words and deeds had been so profound that their condemnation could not efface it. For this it was necessary that she should condemn herself, denouncing as error and abjuring all that she had said and done. They conducted her to the torture-chamber, and in the presence of its grim furniture, with the tormentors in attendance, they invited her to abjure before being racked. But here again her courage and firmness defeated them. They might break her limbs, but she would not deny her revelations; or, if she did, she would afterwards refuse to ratify and would declare the admissions false and dragged from her by torture. In view of this, their only remaining hope of breaking her heroic spirit lay in putting to the test her assertion that not even the sight of the fire and the faggots would make her false to herself.

* * * *

Two scaffolds were erected in the Cemetery of Saint Ouen, and on Thursday, the 24th May, one of these was occupied by the Bishop of Beauvais, with Henry Beaufort the Cardinal of England, the Bishops of Therouanne, Noyon, and Norwich, and a numerous attendance of ecclesiastics. Joan was placed upon the other scaffold. The multitude surged about them.

A famous doctor of divinity, Guillaume Erard, preached a sermon of the Faith, at the end of which he summoned Joan to submit her acts and words to the judgment of the Church.

"As for submitting to the Church," she said, "I have answered. Let all my acts and words be submitted to our Holy Father the Pope, to whom, under God, I submit myself."

Here was a difficulty. But the preacher overcame it with the rejoinder that Rome was too far away, and again he summoned her to revoke those words and deeds which had been reprobated by the learned doctors.

But she persisted. "I refer myself to God and our Holy Father the Pope."

She was told that this could not suffice; that she must accept upon her words and deeds the findings of those who were learned in these matters. "You will submit, or you will be burnt this very day," the preacher thundered. Thereafter she was three times solemnly admonished.

As she would say nothing further, the Bishop rose, and began to read the sentence, and he had proceeded some way with his reading when she interrupted him, and was heard to be speaking.

Her fortitude had given way at last. Worn down by that long and terrible ordeal culminating in the present threat of imminent death by fire, her spirit broke. She would do as the Church ordered; she would obey in all. Since the churchmen said that her visions and revelations were not to be sustained or believed, she would not sustain them, but in these matters submit herself to her judges and to the Church.

Thus, at long last, the ruthless patience of her enemies was rewarded. Out of her own mouth was she convicted of imposture.

At once the form of abjuration that had been prepared was read to her by Massieu, and aloud she repeated the words after him as required. At the Rehabilitation Trial evidence was given that she spoke dully, mechanically, like a person dazed, and that she even smiled in uttering the words, so that some supposed that she was acting in a spirit of mockery.

At the end of the reading, the document was presented to her for signature, and she traced a cross at the place indicated, where her name was written.

But the Rehabilitation Trial established more than a strong presumption that even here those sanctimonious tricksters defrauded this poor maid, who could not read or write. The abjuration widely published and inserted in the minutes of the trial was couched in the most terrible

terms of self-incrimination, covering virtually all the
twelve articles and confessing guilt of each of the charges
in them. Massieu himself, at the Rehabilitation, swore
that this was not the document which he had read to her
and to which she had set her cross. That was a short
statement of not more than eight lines of thick writing.
And his oath was corroborated by the evidence of others
who had been present.

After the abjuration came the sentence. It delivered her,
in view of her contrition, from excommunication; but, as
a salutary penitence, it condemned her to perpetual imprisonment "on the bread of pain and the water of sorrow."

In view of this "great mercy, which received her into
grace and pardon," she should obediently abandon all her
errors, and, forsaking her male dress, resume that of her
sex. Feminine garments being supplied her, she meekly
assumed them. After this, and so as to efface the round
male cut of her hair, her head was shaved.

This took place in the prison to which she had been
reconducted. Being sentenced by the Church to perpetual
imprisonment, it was to be supposed that she would now,
at last, be conveyed to an ecclesiastical prison. That this
was not done, that she was sent back to the castle and into
the custody of English soldiers, is yet another evidence of
bad faith and of how little it was intended that her imprisonment should be perpetual. It lends full confirmation
to the assumptions by which what follows is to be explained.

*   *   *   *

Her abjuration took place, as we have seen, on the 24th
of May. On the following Monday, the 28th, she was visited

in her prison by Cauchon and a group of her judges, to verify her condition and disposition.

They found that she had resumed male garments.

The Bishop questions her as to when and why she has done this, and, although the answer set down in the minutes is that she had so dressed herself of her own free will and without constraint, because she prefers these garments, it is difficult not to suspect the accuracy of this. The question that instantly suggests itself is, How did she obtain these garments? How did they come into her prison after she had discarded them?

She goes on to say, according to the minutes, that if they will relieve her of her irons, permit her to go to Mass, put her in a proper prison, and let her have a woman, she will be obedient and do as the Church wishes.

This, however, does not answer the Bishop's question as to whether she had not abjured and taken an oath never to wear these garments again. He possesses here the evidence of her relapse, and to test it further he returns to questions concerned with her visions. Have they come to her again? They have, she replies. And does she really believe them to be Saint Catherine and Saint Margaret? She does, and she believes that they come from God. They have told her that she did ill on Thursday to confess that her deeds had not been good.

The Bishop reminds her that on Thursday, in her abjuration, she admitted that she had lyingly boasted when she said that her voices were those of Saint Catherine and Saint Margaret. She answers him that this is more than she had understood, and that for the rest, whatever she revoked, she revoked from fear of the fire. She stigmatizes Erard as a false preacher, who said against her many things which were not true. She adds that she does not know what was in the abjuration, but that if she were to say that she was not sent by God she would damn herself, for in truth she was sent by God.

* * * *

It is the end.

Having, as they suppose, destroyed her repute by her public recantation, it now remains only to let inquisitorial procedure take its course, and completely satisfy the English paymasters by putting her to death.

Two days later, on Wednesday the 30th May, at nine o'clock in the morning, this relapsed offender is brought in a cart to the Old Market-Place, and in the presence of a great concourse of ecclesiastics, and of a great crowd of people, she is conducted by the usher Massieu and a Dominican named Ladvenu to a scaffold. Another scaffold is occupied again by the ecclesiastical concourse. There is a solemn sermon preached by Nicolas Midi, salutarily to admonish her and to edify the people.

This is followed by an exhortation to penitence by the Bishop as a preliminary to passing upon her sentence of excommunication. It is seen from her relapse that she never really turned from her errors and abominable crimes. And so the Church must cast her off, as a rotten member before it shall infect other members. She is delivered in the usual terms to the secular power, and in the usual terms the secular power is exhorted so to moderate its sentence that she may not incur the penalty of death or mutilation of her limbs.

There has been no jactancy this morning in the bearing of this poor maid. She has come weeping from her prison. Weeping and sobbing she sits during the droning of the sentence. At the Rehabilitation it is related that the

French multitude is in tears, but that the English soldiery laugh and jeer at her.

When sentence was pronounced, she went down on her knees.

She begged the people to pray for her, begged the priests present to extend to her the alms of some Masses for her soul. She asked for a cross. An English soldier broke a stick to make one for her. She clutched it against her bosom as two sergeants dragged her to the faggots. Such was the haste of the secular arm to do its work that no sentence was pronounced.

Abjuration now would still have saved her from dying by the flames. She would have been mercifully strangled as the fire was lighted. But not again would she be false to her convictions.

As the flames leapt up about her, she was heard in a loud voice to pronounce the name of Jesus, and a shudder of horror and of fear ran through the multitude at the sound, starting the conviction soon to be voiced that a saint had been burned that day, and so defeating the ends of all this evil, crafty labour.

With that cry, her head sank forward onto her breast.

An English officer ordered the executioner to divide the flames, so that her body might be seen, to establish completely the fact of her death.

* * * *

Bedford might now suppose that his political aims were served. The Holy Office had established the fact that the coronation of Charles VII was a false and unholy act, accomplished by means of witchcraft, and that his consecration was an idle blasphemy. The superstitious fear of Joan which had demoralized Bedford's army, and robbed it of its victorious self-confidence, and the superstitious faith in the holiness of her mission which had so enheartened the failing French, had alike, he supposed, been reduced to ashes at Rouen.

Very soon, however, he was to begin to perceive the flaw in his calculations. The spirit which Joan had aroused was not so easily to be laid. The value of a national hero lies not only in his own heroic achievements, but, and in an infinitely greater degree, in the inspiration of the example he leaves behind.

During one of her examinations, when insisting upon the holiness of her mission, Joan prophesied that the work she had taken in hand, the casting out of the English from the lands of France, would be accomplished before seven years were sped.

Bedford died four years after he had burned the prophetess in the Market-Place at Rouen. But he lived long enough to see the beginnings of the fulfilment of her prophecy; in France the fortunes of his nephew King Henry VI had suffered check after check, and before Bedford expired the Duke of Burgundy had dissolved the alliance which had maintained the English on French soil, and thereby had made their expulsion an easy matter.

It was the mission of Joan the Maid which had prepared the way for this. Had she not come when she came, the Kingdom of France would have sunk completely into the extinction it was fast approaching, and from that extinction it is unlikely that it would ever have been resurrected.

Charles VII, who owed all to the Maid, has been widely vituperated for his ingratitude and passivity when she was a captive in the hands of Burgundy. It is supposed that those minions who had ever reluctantly been dragged from the ease of the Loire were responsible for this inertness. Only thus could they be sure to avoid the toil and hardships of the campaigns to which the Maid might have continued to urge him. Only thus could they be sure that their influence with the King would not be stolen by successful captains.

These are assumptions which may or may not be well founded. It may well be that without breach of his alliance with England it was impossible for the Duke of Burgundy to consider any proposals to ransom her made to him on behalf of France. That steps were taken by Charles there is some evidence. Morosini reports that, as soon as Joan fell into the hands of the Burgundians, Charles sent an embassy to the Duke to warn him that, if he delivered her to the English under any inducement in the world, Charles would take vengeance upon the Burgundians in his hands.

We also know that during the winter of 1430–1431, La Hire, who was master of Louviers, made several excursions in the neighbourhood of Rouen, to the great uneasiness of the English there. And in March of 1431, a frustrated expedition against Rouen led by the Bastard of Orléans was financed by Charles. There was also an attempt upon the Castle of Eu, whilst Joan was a prisoner there.

It is certain, however, that Charles was slow to move in the matter of seeking a canonical removal of infamy from the memory of Joan, and that in the end it was due rather to the efforts of Joan's mother than to those of the King, that the case was reopened by order of Pope Calixtus III at the end of 1455.

By then Cauchon and Estivet were dead. Cauchon had been struck down by apoplexy in 1442; Estivet had been found dead in a drain in 1438, and popular fancy saw in this a punishment of Heaven for the odious part he had played in the trial. Not only had he been one of Joan's harshest persecutors in court, but he had grossly insulted her in prison, calling her strumpet and bawd. Nicolas Midi, too, was dead, and so were many others.

Ladvenu, who had attended her to the stake, Manchon, the recorder, Massieu, the usher Beaupère, and several of the assessors still lived and were brought for examination before the court of inquiry appointed by Calixtus III. Some hundred and forty witnesses were heard. They came from Domrémy, from Orléans, from Paris, and from Rouen. They included the Duke of Alençon, the Bastard of Orléans, now Count of Dunois, Brother Pasquerel who had been Joan's confessor, d'Aulon her esquire, and Contes her page.

The inquiry conducted by a commission composed of the Bishop of Paris, the Bishop of Coutances, the Grand Inquisitor Jean Brehal, and the Archbishop of Rheims, lasted for six months. It established the purity of Joan's life, her profound faith in her divine mission, the animosity of her judges, and the illegality of her trial.

The sentence rehabilitating her memory was in the terms we have already cited, terms that cover with infamy those responsible for her death.

Æneas Sylvius Piccolomini, that eminent theologian, erudite historian, and graceful poet who occupied the throne of Saint Peter as Pius II, closes a study of the Maid in these words:

Thus died Joan, who re-established the Kingdom of France when it was almost destroyed and ruined; who having become a leader of armies, living among men, preserved her purity intact, of whom nothing that was not virtuous was ever reported. Whether this was a case of divine work or human invention I should not know how to decide. What is certain is that under her leadership the siege of Orléans was raised; that by her arms all the country between Bourges and Paris was reconquered; that by her contrivance Rheims was brought into submission and the King crowned; that by her impulse Talbot and his army were put to flight; that by her ability and diligence the fortunes of France were re-established: things worthy to be remembered always, things which posterity will have more difficulty to believe than to admire.

IV
SIR WALTER RALEGH

IV

SIR WALTER RALEGH

FEW men have been the subject of more writing in their own lifetimes than Sir Walter Ralegh, and, for that matter, few men subsequently. The very volume of the available material seems to have served first as a lure and then as a labyrinth to a host of biographers.

Stebbing says of him, and the observation has been widely echoed, that "never was a career beset by more insoluble riddles and unmanageable dilemmas." These riddles and dilemmas, however, are supplied less by Ralegh's actual career than by all the attempts that have been made to render it a subject for subtle analyses, paying heed to all the rubbish, malevolent, scandalous, or speculative written of him by his contemporaries. If we give more attention to his conduct than to the interpretations it received at the hands of demonstrable malevolence, if we examine his actions rather than the demonstrably foolish, ill-informed, or pseudo-subtle inferences from them, it becomes possible to tell a plain tale from which many of these apparently bewildering contradictions vanish.

Because few men were ever so enviable as Ralegh for personal and spiritual grandeur, and, for a season at least, for worldly eminence, few men have ever been more envied. This envy bore its normal fruit of spite, which Ralegh's very personality may have quickened; for whilst of an imperturbable courtesy, his self-command was so complete as to betray its source in the consciousness of superiority with which this intellectual pentathlos was imbued. Then, too, his rise to favour had been too sudden and spectacular to be acceptable either to the Court of which he was the brightest ornament, or to the masses, which shared the Court's resentful mistrust of favourites. Before his exceptional worth was realized, and because his origin was comparatively humble, it was assumed that here was a needy adventurer whose advancement was based solely on the caprice of an elderly lady, over-susceptible to the attractions of a handsome man. For, taking him all in all, there was probably no handsomer figure at Elizabeth's Court than that of this tall, dark Devonian, graceful of shape, proudly graceful of carriage, and splendidly elegant in all his appointments.

Leicester's rise to power had been due to outward lustre: a glittering husk, stuffed with little besides pride and vanity, of a worthlessness which had rendered him deservedly detested. Hence a syllogism hostile at the outset to Ralegh. And when soon the sovereignty of his spirit became manifest, yet the early impressions—after their clinging nature—whilst not to be effaced in distant minds, were to be replaced in near ones by the equally rancorous emotion of fear. By the time he had come to be regarded as Leicester's successor in the royal favour, it was perceived by the self-seekers about Elizabeth's throne that here was one whose rare abilities might well frustrate their own ambitions. Whispers there may have been of fond dalliances between Elizabeth and Ralegh. But to state, as has been stated, that European gossip placed the same construction on her relations with Ralegh as it had placed on her relations with Leicester is not to be aware of what the construction of the latter was. From de Quadra we know that in the courts of Europe the rumour ran, now that

Elizabeth was to marry Leicester, now that she had secretly married him already; and in support de Quadra cites incidents which, if true, would go far to justify the rumour. The gossip that linked the Queen's name with Ralegh never reached, or even approached, such dimensions.

His comparatively sudden rise at Court occurred at the age of twenty-nine or thirty, on his return from Ireland, where his great qualities of military leadership, his masterfulness, resource, and personal courage had been prominently displayed.

His apprenticeship to the trade of arms had been served in France. His going thither was more or less the result of chance.

Whilst his father, Walter Ralegh of Fardell, in Devon, was a landowner of consequence, yet Walter was the fourth of his sons, and therefore under a younger son's necessity to make a career for himself. He possessed the advantage of influential relatives. His mother—the elder Ralegh's third wife—a daughter of Sir Philip Champernoun, was the widow of Otho Gilbert to whom she had borne three sons, one of whom was the famous Sir Humphrey Gilbert.

Walter's kinsmen, the Champernouns, were related to the Huguenot Comte de Montgomerie. One of these cousins was at Oxford with him. Ralegh had gone up to Oriel as a commoner somewhere about 1568, when he would be sixteen years of age. He left abruptly and without taking a degree. This we may trace to the fact that Henry Champernoun had obtained permission to raise a troop of a hundred gentlemen volunteers for service with Montgomerie, and that Ralegh enrolled himself in this troop.

After some six years in France, his military education furthered by a spell of service in the Low Countries under the Prince of Orange, we find him, by 1576, back in England and about the Court, to which he would owe his introduction to his half-brother, Sir Humphrey Gilbert. It was certainly to Sir Humphrey that he owed his first important appointment, a command in the expedition fitting out to search the north-west passage.

It was an expedition that came to nothing. Falling in with a Spanish squadron, the little fleet was so battered that it was constrained to return. All the distinction Ralegh gained from it was that of having held alone to his course until defeated by lack of supplies. This was in 1579.

In the following year, again thanks to Sir Humphrey, who ten years earlier had been President of Munster, he received a captain's commission in the army sent against the Munster insurgents. This proved his real stepping-stone to fortune. In the course of that campaign, by his resource and utter fearlessness, he rendered such valuable service and displayed such competence that a year later, upon the recall of Ormond, we find him, jointly with Sir William Morgan and Captain Piers, appointed to the Lieutenancy of Munster.

Some of the hardest criticisms he has suffered concern the ruthlessness of his conduct in this campaign. Setting aside the fact that this ruthlessness, employed towards rebels abetted by foreign mercenaries, was prescribed by his superior, the Lord Deputy, Lord Grey of Wilton, and approved by the Government, the criticism overlooks that there are varieties in ruthlessness. There is ruthlessness for its own sake, indulged from lust of cruelty; and there is ruthlessness that is salutary and merciful in the sequel, since by speedier pacification it reduces the ultimate number of victims. It would be ludicrous to assume in a man of Ralegh's dispassionate, temperate nature any but the latter motive; and the fruits of his policy were to be seen in a pacification of Munster so speedy that by the end of 1581 it became possible to disband part of the English army.

So far does misunderstanding of Ralegh's conduct go that we find a modern biographer applying the term "perfidious" to the stratagem by which he possessed himself of the castle of the suspected Lord Roche of Bally.

It was a strong place, well-held by devoted retainers, and the road to it from Cork, where Ralegh lay, was known to be guarded by strong bodies of insurgents. Undeterred he set out with a small company on that perilous expedition. Eluding the insurgent forces he reached the castle, and took advantage of a parley to introduce himself with a few followers, on the heels of which he brought in the rest. Thus, in possession of the place, he constrained the bloodless surrender of Lord Roche.

To describe as an act of perfidy this perfectly legitimate *ruse de guerre,* carried out with conspicuous skill and in contempt of overwhelming odds, is merely to corrupt a fact.

* * * *

Sir Robert Naunton, afterwards Secretary of State to James I, writing of Ralegh at this stage, with an admiration oddly at variance with the attitude which self-interest was later to impose upon him, attributes the rise to favour which followed upon Ralegh's return, to his address and force in arguing his side of a difference between himself and Lord Grey. Such a difference would certainly draw attention to him, and once this were achieved his ready wit would do the rest.

His correspondence justifies the belief that he may also have had the favour and support of Leicester.

Be this as it may, he was established now as an authority upon Irish policy, and consulted by Queen and Council upon every measure of importance concerned with it. This brought him close to Elizabeth, and gave her leisure to appreciate not only the grace of his handsome, "well-compacted" person, but also the masterly qualities of his mind. Chosen for admission among her intimates, it was demanded of him, as of others in his case, that in reverencing the Queen he should also do homage to the woman. It was a demand, the fulfilment of which was natural to the innate courtly grace of Ralegh.

When it came to resettling the five hundred thousand acres between Waterford and Limerick, which the war had laid waste and which had suffered forfeiture, Ralegh headed the list, receiving an estate of twelve thousand acres and the patronage of the wardenship of Our Lady's College of Youghal. This, however, was not until 1587, by when the royal favour had already brought him wealth and the opportunity for the display of those gifts which deservedly gave him fame.

Whilst retaining his Irish commission he was authorized, if not, indeed, enjoined, to appoint a deputy to represent him in an office for which the Queen could not spare him from her side. For he was discharging for her by now the duties of private secretary, counsellor, envoy, and the like. To support his position at Court he was given the farm of wines, which he underlet for some seven or eight hundred pounds a year, equivalent in purchasing power to-day to ten times the amount; and he was the holder of a licence for the exportation of broadcloths. Neither of these gifts would tend to make him popular.

In 1584 he received the honour of knighthood, and he was elected to Parliament by his native Devon. In the following year he was appointed Lieutenant of Cornwall, Vice-Admiral of Devon and Cornwall, and Warden of the Stannaries, an important legislative office carrying with it the command of the Cornish militia. By 1586 he is a gentleman of the Privy Chamber, and holds the coveted, intimate position of Captain of the Guard. There is a portrait of him as the holder of this office, a commanding presence in silver armour, his baldrick richly sewn with pearls.

This love of splendour which always marked his dress is of a piece with all his nature. At once an artist and a sybarite, he bent some portion of his many-sided mind to the creation of beautiful settings for himself. When to his Irish lordship came to be added by the Queen's bounty, in 1587, the broad acres forfeited by the conspirator Anthony Babington, his wealth assumed proportions which permitted a full indulgence of his inclinations. If in that sumptuous prodigal age he shared and even exceeded his contemporaries' love of splendour, at least sumptuousness in him was allied with and enhanced by a culture in which he stood alone. If anon, when he went to sea, it was his custom to take with him a retinue of servants, to furnish his cabin with a luxury previously unknown, from the richly upholstered bedstead borne by gilded dolphins to the pictures with which he hung those wooden walls, it was also his custom to carry with him chests of books, so that the studies which filled his every leisure moment should suffer no interruption.

Nor was the indulgence of his sybaritism the only channel into which he poured the wealth that came now so easily to his hands. If he spent profusely upon architecture, upon the creation of gardens, upon books and pictures, jewels, statuary, and furniture, he spent no less profusely both wealth and talents in enterprises making for the maritime aggrandizement of England, arousing and inflaming a national ambition to outrival Spain in the creation of an overseas dominion.

As early as 1583, before he had entered upon his later opulence, he was building the *Ark Ralegh* of two hundred tons, to participate in a fresh expedition of discovery for which Sir Humphrey Gilbert was preparing. In naval architecture, though when and how he learnt it we do not know, Ralegh is reputed to have stood second in his day to none. Possibly this is just another manifestation of his many-sided natural genius.

He did not himself sail in the *Ark Ralegh* when she formed part of Sir Humphrey's expedition, because the Queen refused him leave.

*   *   *   *

In the following year, after the death of the enterprising half-brother to whom Sir Walter was so deeply attached, he obtained a patent to hold by homage any lands not actually possessed by any Christian prince which he might discover within six years; and with the aim of attaching to England an empire in the northern part of America, akin to that established by Spain in the south, he set about the equipment of two ships. Again the Queen refused to allow him to stray from her environment, so that he was forced to content himself with sending deputies.

The expedition sailed on the 27th April 1584. Going by way of the Canaries and the West Indies, his representatives were, in July, on the islands off the coast of North Carolina, of which the largest is Roanoake. They found the soil fruitful, the natives friendly and timid. They traded with them for skins and pearls, and returned to make an enthusiastic report to Ralegh, to whom they brought some pelts, a string of pearls as big as peas, and two Indians, Manteo and Wanchese.

It was Elizabeth herself who bestowed upon this land discovered for a virgin queen the name of Virginia. And of Virginia from that moment Ralegh described himself as Governor.

He set at once about the colonization of the lands that had been discovered upon his initiative and explored for him. He enlisted some support, and in the following April a fleet of seven ships sailed from Plymouth under Ralegh's cousin, Sir Richard Grenville. A deputy went to govern the new colony in the place of the courtier responsible for its foundation, to whom Elizabeth still denied leave of absence.

One hundred and seven colonists, supplied with implements, cattle, and seeds, were left on the newly discovered land. Amongst them was Thomas Hariot, charged by Ralegh to survey and report fully.

This may be said to constitute the first chapter in the history of the North American Colony.

Grenville made the expedition pay for itself, at least in part, by the capture upon the seas of three Spanish vessels, one of which proved rich in booty.

That first and promising attempt at colonization ended in failure, due to strife with the natives; and the colonists returned on the very eve of the arrival of abundant stores.

Hariot acquired from the Indians the use of tobacco, which speedily grew popular in Europe, and to which Ralegh became immediately addicted. His minute report on the New Found Land of Virginia went far to strengthen Ralegh's tenacity of purpose, and a fresh attempt was made under his auspices in 1587. A new expedition was equipped and placed under the command of Captain John White, appointed Governor of the City of Ralegh in Virginia. White took with him a hundred and fifty colonists, many accompanied this time by their wives; and a settlement was made on Roanoake, which he accounted preferable to the site on Chesapeake Bay indicated by Ralegh.

More eagerly than ever had Ralegh desired to accompany these adventurers and survey his governorship in person. But, as before, he was forced to submit to the will of Elizabeth.

Again the colonists encountered difficulties, and again they came into conflict with the natives. Captain White returned home for further equipments, leaving something over a hundred colonists behind him. At the moment, however, Ralegh could not supply their needs. Not only had he already spent the then enormous sum of forty thousand pounds on the plantation, but the menace of the Spanish Armada was overhanging England and claiming all resources.

When this danger was overpast, he was to resume his interest in that overseas dominion, and equip at his own charges expedition after expedition.

If the dream he laboured so tenaciously to realize was not to become a reality until later, it yet remains that it did so become under his inspiration and efforts, and in fulfilment of his conception; and if he had no other claim than this to be honoured by posterity, this alone should abundantly suffice.

* * * *

It is not only in the promotion of colonization and of England's maritime supremacy that we discover Ralegh's lavish munificence. That he was a liberal patron to the art of letters—to which he himself was to become so brilliant and abiding an ornament—we gather from the mass of works dedicated to this insatiable student; whilst the extent to which he employed his favour at Court on behalf of others drew once the question from Elizabeth, "When, Sir Walter, will you cease to be a beggar?" To which he answered, "When your gracious Majesty ceases to be a benefactor."

He is commonly accused of being an intriguer, and this upon no better ground than contemporary common rumour of his being engaged in this or that subterranean endeavour. Frequently a specific charge is ludicrous; often the disproof of it is ready at hand; whilst, to take a general view, the impulse to intrigue is not a normal compound of natures such as his; and those who lightly bring the charge would be taxed to establish a concrete case against him. The intriguer is most frequently detected in operations to advance himself at the expense of others. Of whom can it be said that he suffered this at the hands of Ralegh?

The opportunity was his to have elbowed aside Leicester. But that opportunity we have Elizabeth's word to the Earl that he loyally disregarded.

There is yet another test. Each of us is to himself a standard by which to measure his fellows. To the end of his days, in spite of all betrayals and disloyalties suffered, Ralegh retained in the words of other men a faith which is a reflection of the loyal frankness of his own nature, and this in a man who in nothing else could be called ingenuous. There may have been occasions in adversity when his pride broke, and when for a moment he stooped from the lofty dignity that was to him as the fine raiment that he loved. But such moments were few and fleeting, and in none do we find him stooping quite so far as to the backstair methods of the intriguer. The very pride that made him unpopular, his avowed disdain of the rascal multitude, set him standards of conduct in which intriguing could find no place.

There is here confusion of ideas. The truth is that there was never a man more intrigued against than Ralegh, and such efforts as he did not disdain to make in self-defence have been misconstrued into initiatives.

It was Ralegh himself who sang:

> For whoso reaps renown above the rest
> With heaps of hate shall surely be oppressed.

He sang it to defend another from detraction; but to no case were the lines more applicable than to his own.

At a time when he was bending his talents as soldier, sailor, shipbuilder, and engineer to the matter of the Spanish menace, when he was a member of a Council of War to promote measures of defence, responsible for the fortifications of Portland and Weymouth, and raising troops in his Lieutenancy of Devon and Cornwall, the jealousies he had aroused were spitefully active. His right to eminence by virtue of the masterly intellect of which he supplied such constant and various proofs was not to be denied by those who grudged his favour. Hence a sharper rancour arose at Court against him, and to this rancour Essex largely owed his rise, as well perhaps as to the fact that being so opportune to those who used him, he proved, for once, a royal favourite who did not arouse resentment. Much as the handsome George Villiers was brought in by a Court party under James I to supplant Robert Carr, so was the handsome Essex brought in to supplant Sir Walter Ralegh.

But Ralegh was no such empty husk as James's minion. Established by solid worth in the favour of a woman who, for all her weaknesses, possessed the intelligence to discern it, he stood in no danger of being supplanted. Courtiers might write to one another to assert that this was imminent or already accomplished. The facts show that they merely expressed their jaundiced hopes. The stalwart good looks of Essex may have succeeded in infatuating the elderly Queen; but not on that account was Ralegh thrust aside, nor yet by the efforts which Essex, the tool of the faction that had set him up, exerted to this end. With a presumption upon the royal infatuation which in the end was to cost him his handsome head, the Earl went to incredible lengths of insolence in the expression to Elizabeth of his hostility to Ralegh, a hostility which may well have been sharpened by some sense of his own vast inferiority. She must choose, he told her, between Ralegh and himself. He would not, he had the audacity to tell her (or so he boasts), "give himself over to the service of a mistress who was in awe of such a man."

He does not hesitate to say that he spoke to her as much against Ralegh as he could. "I told her," he adds, "that I was loath to be near about her when I knew my affection so much thrown down, and such a wretch as Ralegh esteemed of her."

Although she resented these impertinences, yet in her infatuation she forgave them, as she was to continue to forgive this handsome coxcomb until in the end he went beyond forgiveness. But that his efforts against Ralegh were ineffective, we see in the continued bounty of the Queen to her Captain of the Guard, and particularly in the bestowal upon him at about this time of these broad acres of the conspirator Anthony Babington.

*   *   *   *

In the matter of the Armada Sir Walter's chief part lay in the dispositions to deal with it. But he was in action, too, with a party of gentlemen volunteers, and it was in the Channel and at Gravelines that he increased his experience as a fighting seaman.

After that, in the following spring, he commanded a ship of his own in the expedition under Drake and Norris which burnt Vigo and destroyed the Spanish supply ships off Lisbon, a profitable matter from which he reaped some four thousand pounds as his share of the prizes.

At last here was something to silence the malicious gibes that Ralegh was a man who sat snugly at home to enjoy the sea-harvests which he sent others forth to garner. Whilst not the obvious, it may have been the immediate, cause of a deepening rancour in Essex, whence sprang the challenge to mortal combat which he sent Sir Walter. The Council intervened to forbid the meeting; and the Queen marked her displeasure impartially to both, as a result of which Ralegh went off to Ireland where the administration of his great estate demanded his presence.

It was here, at this time, that he established bonds of intimacy, based on the homage of one great poet for another, with Edmund Spenser.

Spenser had been secretary to the Lord Deputy Grey, and he had been granted, in the resetttlement of the forfeited lands, an estate of some three thousand acres. There in Ireland Ralegh now read *The Faerie Queen,* and it was his patronage thereafter that raised up its author. Not gratitude alone, however, inspired Spenser's eulogisms. Rather was it his perception of that poetical genius from which has flowed some of the noblest music in the English language. Nowhere else is the richness of Ralegh's mind more brilliantly exhibited than in his exercise of an art in which he treated lightly his own accomplishment. So lightly did he hold this gift, so careless was he of the renown it might have won him, that he never troubled to print his verses; and it has been left for posterity to hunt out and assemble those which have not been irrevocably lost.

"My Lord of Essex hath chased Mr. Ralegh from the Court and hath confined him into Ireland." Thus wrote Anthony Bacon at about this time, expressing the opinion of those who nourished the hope that Ralegh's sojourn in Ireland represented a banishment from royal favour.

They were roundly given the lie by the events on Ralegh's return.

It was Essex, by then, who was in disgrace, as a result of his marriage to Lady Sidney. For Elizabeth, as Ralegh himself was soon to discover, could never bear with equanimity what in a favourite she viewed as a criminal disregard of her own femininity. Meanwhile, Sir Walter came back to receive further proofs of her good will. Chief amongst these was the gift of the noble Dorset estate of Sherborne, with its castle, its park and its manors. Of all his possessions it became the one most dear to him, the one with which his name is mostly closely associated. Like his London residence at Durham House (on the site of the present Adelphi Terrace), it was a property wrested from the Church. It lay under a curse pronounced by Bishop Osmund at the time of its alienation from the See of Salisbury.

Another token of the royal favour was his appointment as Vice-Admiral to an expedition fitting out under the chief command of the Lord High Admiral for a raid upon the Spanish plate fleet. But when the time came to sail, it was his gallant cousin Sir Richard Grenville who took his place.

That English squadron was surprised at the Azores by a powerful Spanish fleet, and it was Grenville who covered the retreat by a fight unequalled in all the glorious maritime history of England. For fifteen hours his ship, *The Revenge,* with not more than a hundred men aboard, engaged no fewer than fifteen great galleons of Spain. Not until he had destroyed four of them, not until his ship was a helpless, mastless, riddled hulk with not a single man left whole aboard and Grenville himself wounded to the death, did he surrender.

The splendid prose of Ralegh's *Report* had its inspiration in that epic of the sea, which served him also for the propaganda he had at heart and upon which he never ceased to labour. He wrote with the aim of inflaming his countrymen into rendering themselves supreme upon the ocean, subduing the predatory tyranny of Spain, "whose weakness," he writes, "we have discovered to the world." And he grows fiercely eloquent on the subject of Spain's cruelty, bigotry, and greed. The *Report* affords also a striking instance of his magnanimity. There had been bad blood at the time between himself and the Admiral, and a challenge was reputed to have passed. Ralegh—this man who has been called an intriguer—not only disdained to make capital, as he might so easily have done, out of the sharp censure current of Howard's conduct in abandoning Grenville to his fate; he actually defended him from his critics, insisting that "it had ill sorted with the discretion of a General to commit himself and his charge to assured destruction."

His propaganda was timely. Spain was fitting out a fleet for reprisals. Ralegh advised a counter-attack on Panama, and under this advice a fleet was assembled to which he contributed the *Roebuck,* and his brother, Carew Ralegh, the *Galleon Ralegh.* To these, ten more ships were added, of which two were supplied by the Queen. Sir Walter was appointed Admiral and enthusiastically pledged his resources to the utmost.

Persistent contrary winds delayed him until it was too late for Panama, but not too late to intercept at the Azores the treasure-fleet which was their objective. In the time of waiting, however, Elizabeth seems, as usual, to have become reluctant to suffer the absence of her Captain of the Guard; and she appears to have extracted a promise from him that if the members of the expedition would accept Frobisher for their leader in his place, he would not go, himself. He went, however, as far as Finisterre, where he handed over to Frobisher not only the command, but the plan of operations to be followed.

This was destined to be the last occasion on which the will of Elizabeth should thwart his ardour. The favour of the Queen, which, whilst enriching and magnifying him in one direction, was cramping and stultifying him in another, was suddenly and violently withdrawn.

* * * *

On his landing (in June 1592) he was arrested, and conveyed straight to the Tower. No charge was preferred, and no reason published. His offence was a treason against Elizabeth the woman, the same in kind as that of Essex, but deeper in degree. He had dared withdraw the glance of devotion from her Majesty, so as to bestow it in more practical form upon Elizabeth Throckmorton, her Majesty's maid of honour. His love was returned, and the exultant view taken by the Essex faction of what followed was that he had seduced the lady.

Robert Cecil in an *ad hoc* access of virtue, describes as "brutish" in Ralegh conduct which in the case of another he treats lightly as a jest. That may be taken to represent the view of malice, hypocritically ready to regard as damnable in the haughty, masterful Sir Walter an act which it could very readily condone in anyone else.

Judgment on such a matter must take into account all the attendant circumstances. That this was no gross act of libertinage we see as much in the character of the parties as in the sequel to the event. In an age of gallantry and licence, Ralegh's conduct had ever been such that there is no suggestion even from his worst detractor that he was in any sense a libertine. The virtue of the lady, like the honesty of the love that linked them, stands as firmly established by the sequel as were her beauty and her wit.

When or where they were married, we do not know. But since the marriage seems to have followed closely upon the scandal, we may assume it to have taken place in the Tower, be it that Mrs. Throckmorton was sent thither with him by an angry Queen, be it that she was left free to visit him in his prison.

The enduring devotion to each other of this husband and wife is reflected in the letters that passed between them down the years, some of which are amongst the most beautiful and tender that ever lovers wrote.

Ralegh's confinement in the Tower was by no means rigorous. He had his own servants to wait upon him, was free to receive the visits of his friends, to conduct through deputies the duties of his various offices, of none of which he was deprived. Naturally he neglected no effort to regain the lost favour, and he sought in the matter what help he could. But it was all in vain. The incensed Elizabeth was not disposed to forgiveness, and his imprisonment might have lasted longer than it did but for supervening events.

The expedition which he had planned was successful. Whilst Frobisher, off the coast of Spain, held the attention of the Spaniards with one squadron, the other, under Sir John Burgh, safely reached the Azores, and on the 3rd August, west of Flores, came up with and captured after a four hours' battle the *Madre de Dios,* a great carack of sixteen hundred tons, laden with a cargo of enormous value, including pearls, precious stones, ebony, silks, amber, musk, and spices. The pepper alone was valued at a hundred thousand pounds.

When this great prize was brought into Dartmouth a month later, there was such plundering, such confusion and wrangling over the division of the spoil that, as Sir John Hawkins wrote to Burleigh, Ralegh was the only man to settle matters. He was, therefore, temporarily released, and sent down to Dartmouth in custody. Cecil, who had gone ahead of him to do what he could, expressed his surprise at the reception given Ralegh by the mariners and at the credit in which it was obvious, from the shouts with which they mobbed him, that he stood with them.

He set to work with the collaboration of Cecil and William Killigrew, and the partitioning was smoothly carried out.

Elizabeth received as her share the enormous sum of

eighty thousand pounds. It was, as Ralegh wrote, "more than ever a man presented her Majesty with as yet. If God have sent it for my ransom, I hope her Majesty of her abundant goodness will accept it. If her Majesty cannot beat me from her affection, I hope her sweet nature will think it no conquest to afflict me."

It was at least four times the sum to which her share entitled her; and if the shares of others underwent some abatement so as to provide it, that of Ralegh suffered complete extinction. He got back barely the amount that he had laid out upon the venture.

But at least he realized the hope he had expressed that the fourscore thousand pounds might ransom him. Such a prize, and the expectation of more to follow by his exertions, might well dispose her to a remunerative mercy towards its purveyor.

His liberty was restored to him in December, but not yet the royal favour.

He seems in the next two years to have spent much time at Sherborne with his "dear Besse" in building and planting, in hawking, of which he was intensely fond, and in other country pursuits. But the duties of his offices, in all of which he continued, and the responsibilities of his possessions took him frequently elsewhere. He held his courts as Warden of the Stannaries, performed the duties of his Lord-Lieutenancy of Devon and Cornwall, gave attention to the development of his Irish lordship and continued to advise upon Irish policy; he sat in Parliament, and was active there; he planned and executed coast defences in his lieutenancy, vigilant the while of Spain, and persevering in his propaganda against her; building ships, and, in short, occupying himself in twenty different directions at once, any one of which would have exhausted the mental energies of an ordinary man. And all the while he was labouring, by the usual courtier devices, for restoration to favour. Perhaps these labours supply one of the causes for dubbing him an intriguer. But in that case, what shall we dub those of the Essex faction, who spared no pains or calumnies to frustrate his efforts?

*   *   *   *

Naunton speaks of the Guiana expedition as a device of Ralegh's; so that by "going aside" he might "teach envy a new way of forgetfulness." This may be the basis upon which that undertaking is described as Ralegh's supreme effort to win back the lost favour. The last expedition of his planning had by its success gained him his ransom; another such should gain him restoration, the plea of gold being one which the avaricious Elizabeth could not resist.

Those who accept this view do him less than justice. They lose sight of the adventurous spirit of the explorer and the planter, which for years had made him strain at the leash in which the Queen restrained him.

The attempt to diminish him by calling him a buccaneer (an anachronism, anyway) is to overlook his patriotic ardour and the hostility to the rapacious Castilians which was its natural offspring. Not for him to recognize the authority of the Pope in bestowing the New World upon Spain to the exclusion of all other Europeans.

It is less likely that in turning now his eyes to Guiana, he was casting about him for new realms to conquer than addressing himself to the execution of a project long considered. For half a century the search of El Dorado had been vainly engaging Spain; and Ralegh, in so far as he was able, had gathered information of that reputedly auriferous but hitherto impenetrable land.

For this perilous adventure he was laying his plans in '94, to the alarm of Lady Ralegh, whose love may have aroused some sense of how ill-fated a land it was to prove to him and to their firstborn, Walter, who saw the light in that same year.

He began by sending out an old follower, Captain Whiddon, to survey the Orinoco. Whiddon was back by the end of the year. Treachery suffered at Trinidad at the hands of the Governor, Don Antonio de Berreo, and the imprisonment of some of Whiddon's men had largely frustrated the captain's exploration. Ralegh immediately set about equipping a second expedition, this time in force, and spared no available funds. The command of one ship he gave to Whiddon, and of another to his faithful and devoted follower Lawrence Keymis. Others came into the venture. The Lord High Admiral lent the *Lion's Whelp* and two other captains brought each a ship to the little fleet. A hundred gentlemen volunteers joined him, among whom was Sir John Gilbert, the son of his adventurous half-brother, Sir Humphrey.

The Royal Commission to Our Servant Sir Walter Ralegh—omitting the usual "trusty and well-beloved"— was to offend and enfeeble the King of Spain and his subjects in his dominions to the uttermost, and to discover and subdue heathen lands not in the possession of any Christian prince nor inhabited by any Christian people.

On this expedition he sailed early in February of 1595, captured a couple of vessels on the way, a Spaniard and a Dutchman, and in six weeks was at Trinidad.

Both because it would be imprudent to leave the treacherous Berreo in his rear, and so as to settle accounts with him for his treatment of Whiddon's men, Sir Walter stormed, captured, and burnt the city of San José, and took Berreo a prisoner.

Leaving the fleet at Trinidad, he embarked with sixty of his gentlemen volunteers in a galley of shallow draught, and accompanied by four other wherries carrying forty more, he crossed the twenty miles of sea to the delta of the Orinoco. Then, piloted through a labyrinth of rivers by a friendly native, they made slow progress through the Caño Mañano, despondency growing amongst them until they emerged from the impenetrable tangle, through which for days they had threaded their dismal way, into an open Eden-like landscape, fertile and lovely, where birds and beasts abounded and where the deer came unafraid to drink at the river they were ascending.

In one of the excursions that they made they discovered an assayer's basket, abandoned by some escaping Spaniards. It contained quicksilver, saltpetre, and a quantity of refined ore. They captured the natives who had accompanied the Spaniards, and in Ralegh's way, which combined policy with humanity, made friends of them.

At Trinidad Ralegh had released five Indian chiefs from the dungeon into which Berreo had flung them to rot in their chains. From these he received accounts of Spanish cruelties which more than justified all that he had written upon the subject. His courteous treatment of them and of other native chiefs won him their greatest trust and affection by very contrast with what their kind had endured from Castilian adventurers. He announced himself to them as sent by his Queen to deliver them from Spanish oppression, and so won their adherence that he was at pains (as he related, no doubt with intent to gratify her Majesty) to prevent them from worshipping as an idol the portrait of Elizabeth which he displayed to them.

The natives now supplied him with a sounder guide than his former one, an Indian named Martino, and, at the end of a fortnight's rowing, the adventurers were conducted by him at last into the main river. As they were the first Englishmen to reach it, Keymis renamed it Raleana.

In the more populous country through which they were now progressing Ralegh maintained his conciliatory policy, sternly repressing in his followers any inclination to plunder or otherwise molest the Indians or their women. He made friends with and enjoyed the hospitality of the Cacique Toparimaca, whose brother became his guide thereafter, and they pushed on in their boats as far as Aromaia, three hundred miles from the sea.

Rumour travelling ahead of them, they were well received here by the centenarian King Topiowari, who was disposed to welcome any enemy of Spain, from the sufferings he had endured at their hands. They had murdered his predecessor, and they had enchained Topiowari himself like a dog, until he had procured for his ransom a hundred plates of gold.

Here Ralegh learnt of the Inca of Manoa, of the El Dorado, where gold was plentiful, of a silver mine at Caroni, and of a tribe of Carolians who would be ready to ally themselves with him from their hostility to both Spaniards and Manoans. He heard also much Indian lore: of the Amazons of Topago and their curious ways; of the Ewaipanomes, whose eyes are in their shoulders, their mouths in their breasts, and the like. He learnt, on the subject of wounds made by poisoned arrows, "the best way of healing, as well as all other poisons." This was information that he would readily absorb; for interest in and a considerable knowledge of medicine were already among his accomplishments.

He was shown specimens of gold wrought by the natives, and he tested for himself the stones abounding on the hills of Aromaia, finding them to be mother-of-gold, *madre del oro,* whose presence was believed to indicate the existence of the precious metal below the surface.

Another cacique offered to lead them to a gold mine on Mount Iconuri. Ralegh sent Keymis to locate and survey the mine. Beyond that nothing could now be done. The rainy season had set in, the rivers were rising, they were without mining tools, and Ralegh had no mind to "dig with his nails."

The same reason prevented him from taking advantage of the offer of Topiowari, old as he was, to lead them to Manoa and its gold if Ralegh would leave fifty Englishmen to defend him afterwards from the vengeance of the Inca and of the Spaniards.

At least, the expedition had been fruitful in the gathering of information and the establishing of friendships. By one and the other they would return next year to profit. In that resolve they took their departure, accompanied by a son of Topiowari, who was christened in England, and named, in honour of Ralegh, Gualtero. In exchange they left behind them an Englishman, Francis Sparrow, to continue the survey, and a boy, Hugh Goodwin, by his own wish, to learn the language.

They set out. They were swept down the swollen, raging river at a rate of a hundred miles a day, and they weathered furious gales in the crossing to Trinidad, where they found the ships safe.

In spite of all hardships suffered and dangers faced, the expedition had lost only one man, and this a negro, who had ventured into a river and had been devoured by a crocodile.

It was in Ralegh's mind, before returning home, to pay
a visit to Virginia, and do what he could there for the
colonists; but the inclemency of the weather was an obstacle to the fulfilment of this design.

* * * *

By August Ralegh was back in England. Since he did
not come laden with plunder there was no excitement.
The mere samples of minerals which he brought aroused
no enthusiasm. Cecil, who had invested in the venture,
probably disgruntled at the lack of return, was little disposed to support Ralegh in promoting the exploitation of
Guiana, whilst the comparative empty-handedness of his
return encouraged calumny. It had been busy with his
name ever since he had sailed. From the cloud of royal displeasure under which he had departed, it had been assumed and asserted that he would never come back, but
would enter the service of the King of Spain. Malice could
have invented nothing more ludicrous. Now that his return gave the lie to this, calumny declared, almost as
ludicrously, that he had made no voyage at all, but had
been in hiding in Cornwall. His samples of gold were first
declared worthless; and when officials of the Royal Mint
pronounced them, on the contrary, extremely rich, the
tale then ran that they had been procured elsewhere than
in Guiana.

To answer these and other falsehoods Ralegh published
his *Discovery of the Large and Beautiful Empire of
Guiana*. The book enjoyed an enormous popularity, deserved by the beauty and liveliness of the writing alone.
It was widely translated, and as a result, if Ralegh was
the object of much detraction, he was also the object of no
little acclamation, both at home and abroad.

Because amongst much that was precious and authentic were to be found the Indians' tales that Ralegh had heard of Amazons and Ewaipanomes, it is ridiculous to assume, as others since Hume have assumed, that the author was abusing credulity and guilty of a deliberate fraud so as to further his project. He had seen enough and could report enough at first hand to justify his faith that Guiana offered an ideal land for colonization. If he was optimistic, if he took much for granted on the score of its mineral riches, this was because his eagerness to found that overseas dominion was the more likely to be gratified where he could hold out a prospect of easily garnered wealth.

Of the affection and nobility of the lady who was the cause of his disgrace we perceive at about this time one of the many eloquent instances she has left. In a letter to Cecil before her husband's return, she wrote, on the subject of a law-suit she was bringing: "I rather choose this time to follow it in Sir Walter's absence, that myself may bear the unkindness, and not he."

Whether he won back to favour or not, and whether or not he could induce the Crown to adopt his plans for Guiana, his public spirit would never suffer him to lose interest in the colonization project; and he decided to pursue it, if need be, at his own charges.

But since at the moment he conceived that more urgent work awaited him at home, he contented himself with sending out Keymis, in January of 1596, with two ships laden with merchandise for trading purposes, so as to maintain with the natives the friendly relations which had been established, and at the same time pursue the explorations.

*   *   *   *

The work awaiting him at home was prompted by the discovery that Spain, in league with Tyrone, was preparing for a raid upon Ireland.

So as to meet and deflect this menace, he pressed upon the Council the view that offence is the best defence, and urged despatch in adopting it.

His advice prevailed. A fleet was equipped of ninety-six sail and fourteen thousand men. The Lord Admiral and the Earl of Essex shared the supreme command, supported by a council of war composed of Lord Thomas Howard and Ralegh for the naval forces, Sir Francis Vere and Sir Comiers Clifford for the land forces, with Ralegh's cousin, Sir George Carew, making a fifth. The fleet was in four squadrons, one of which, comprising twenty-two ships and some three thousand men, was commanded by Sir Walter on the *Warspite*. Allied with the English came a Dutch contingent of twenty-four ships and twenty-six hundred men.

During delays caused by bad weather, the jealousies of the commanders exploded in bickerings. Ralegh, the main object of these, bore himself with that imperturbable self-mastery that was his most irritating characteristic, since it was rooted—or assumed to be rooted—in that disdain which sharpens resentment.

At last, on the 1st June, their destination secret, they sailed; and by the 9th they were off the coast of Spain.

As a result of a council held by the Lord Admiral, Ralegh's squadron was detached to cruise down the coast and intercept any Spanish ships, whilst the main fleet, proceeding ahead, came to anchor off Cadiz. Here the decision was taken to begin operations by storming the town.

They were in the act of attempting to carry out that unsound plan, rendered more difficult by stormy conditions, when Ralegh, his own task accomplished, joined them, and at once assumed that initiative which, maintained in the teeth of jealous rivalries, was to result in victory.

Finding the landing forces being embarked in barges, one of which had already overturned, he repaired at once to the Admiral, succeeded in dissuading him, and drew up an alternative plan of operations. This was that the fleet should enter the harbour, and begin by battering and then boarding from fly-boats the four great galleons moored there—the four Apostles, as Ralegh calls them—the *Saint Philip, Saint Matthew, Saint Andrew,* and *Saint Thomas.* Action by the land forces should wait until the galleons were overcome.

The plan was adopted; but the day being already too far advanced, execution was postponed until the following morning. Ralegh was to lead in the *Warspite,* supported by five other ships. This post of honour, which seems no more than due to the man responsible for the plan of operations, was challenged by Lord Thomas Howard when he heard of it, claiming it as his right by virtue of his rank as Vice-Admiral. Ralegh seems to have settled the matter by the simple device of getting away ahead of everyone else at dawn.

To meet him and to bar his way into the harbour, the four galleons sailed into the straits, and anchored under Fort Puntal, supported by a dozen galleys.

Fort and galleys opened a bombardment on the advancing *Warspite.* But Ralegh, reserving his fire for the galleons, answered each enemy discharge with no more than a flourish of trumpets. Steering for the largest of the galleons, the *Saint Philip* and *Saint Andrew,* he did not open fire until, at last, he had anchored at close quarters. Then commenced a battle that raged for three hours, during which, whilst Ralegh gave his attention to the great ships, those who followed him dealt with the galleys. He maintained the combat until the *Warspite* was nearly shot to pieces. Yet the awaited fly-boats from which to board the galleons did not arrive. Essex meanwhile had come up in his flagship. Getting into a boat, Ralegh went off to him to tell him that in default of fly-boats he intended to board from his own battered vessel. Essex promising to support him, he went back, to find that in his absence the *Warspite* had been headed by the ships of Howard and Vere. Determined, however, to maintain that which he had won at so much cost, he thrust ahead between them, and placed himself athwart the narrow channel, so that none should again pass him. There he abode until the tide turned and the flow of it drifted him up to the Spaniards, and enabled him from his foundering ship to grapple the *Saint Philip*.

His boarding movement put an end to the engagement. The galleons slipped their anchors, and attempted to gain the inner harbour. The commanders of the *Saint Matthew* and *Saint Thomas* avoided capture by blowing up their ships. But the other two vessels, of a thousand tons each, were seized by Ralegh, who had now the support of his companions.

The landing followed, and so demoralized were the Spaniards by the naval defeat that their resistance crumbled. When the midsummer dusk came down upon Cadiz, the English were in possession of the town and the fort. Only the castle still held out, to surrender on the following morning.

Sir Walter, who had been wounded in the leg at the

close of the naval action, and who was in pain, was carried ashore on his men's shoulders.

The booty comprised all the rich merchandise of the town and forty thousand ducats, and had Ralegh's counsel been heeded it would have been enormously increased. Within the Puerto Real lay the Indian fleet, with cargoes worth eight million crowns. But the authority craved by Sir Walter to sail in and take them was denied him by the generals. They were perhaps less culpable in refusing the Spanish offer of two million crowns to ransom the ships. In the end, however, they lost everything; for the Spaniards, acting in a spirit with which the English had not reckoned, fired the lot.

Submitting to necessity, Cadiz agreed to pay a hundred and twenty thousand crowns to ransom the citizens taken prisoners. After this the fortifications were demolished, and most of the city laid in ruins, and at last, on the 5th July, the English departed.

A descent upon Faro, where the splendid library of Bishop Osorius was taken, to form the foundation of the Bodleian, concluded operations, and the fleet sailed for home.

Ralegh, incapacitated by his wound from looking after his interests during the pillage, had been promised his share of the spoil. If he did not come off as badly as he complains—"nought but poverty and pain"—yet the seventeen hundred pounds or so that he received was, by comparison with the appropriations of others, far less than his proper due. He was well rewarded, however, in other ways. He came to London to find himself the acknowledged hero of the Cadiz exploit. For once, in the face of his knightly contribution to the achievement, detraction was silenced. It was admitted that what he had done could not have been bettered, and many who hitherto had been his enemies were converted into admirers.

Sir Anthony Standen, who, as a close follower of Essex, had shared the prejudice common with his kind, now wrote to Ralegh to Burleigh: "I never knew the gentleman until this time, and I am sorry for it, for there are in him excellent things beside his valour; and the observation he hath in this voyage used with my Lord of Essex hath made me love him."

Standen was only one of the many whom the events of Cadiz afforded an opportunity of correcting what they had been taught by the tongue of envious malice.

Of the part played in the enterprise by Essex, Ralegh expressed himself with that generosity which he never denied even to an enemy.

*   *   *   *

Sir Walter Ralegh came back to find Keymis home from Guiana empty-handed. The English activities there had but served to stimulate Spanish interest in the land. A strong force had been sent out for the conquest of Manoa, and when Keymis reached the Orinoco he found his passage barred by a settlement named San Thomé and a fort. So as to reach Manoa, he had been constrained to change his direction. Having done this, he did not persevere, from fear of being cut off. He limited himself to a consolidation of the good relations with the Indians, and to some minor explorations in which he found confirmation of the auriferous character of the country.

Against this fresh disappointment and financial loss, which may have sharpened his grievance at the comparative exiguity of his share of the Cadiz plunder, Ralegh had to set his materially enhanced reputation and the restoration to Elizabeth's favour which now followed. It seems to have been very complete. He resumed in person the office of Captain of the Guard, and came to the Privy Chamber as boldly as of old.

If, as of old, this excited the jealousy of Essex, the Earl subdued the emotion to his interests. Athirst for glory, and no doubt for Spanish plunder, Cadiz had shown him the value of Sir Walter as a collaborator. With Cecil he was straining to obtain the Queen's consent to further expeditions, and Ralegh was brought into an alliance which may well have moved the wonder of the Court.

It bore fruit in the adventure known as the Island Voyage, upon which a fleet of a hundred and twenty ships sailed from Plymouth in August of 1597, with Essex as Admiral, Lord Thomas Howard as Vice-Admiral, Ralegh as Rear-Admiral, and Sir Francis Vere as Marshal of the land forces.

The original intention was to raid Ferrol and capture the Indian treasure-fleet. But delays and storms reduced their aims to the matter of the ultimate decision taken at Flores, which was to lay waste Fayal.

On this errand Essex was the first to sail. But Ralegh was the first to arrive. On his appearance before Fayal, the islanders set about carrying their possessions into the interior whilst the forts subjected Ralgeh's ships to bombardment. Four days he waited, inactive, because, in his own words, "of the desire of some in the company, who would have reserved the title of such an exploit for a greater person." But since continued delay must merely enable the Spaniards to improve their defences, he landed, at last, with two hundred and sixty seamen and volunteers and some pieces of ordnance.

Only his conspicuous gallantry saved that landing from failure. When his followers were hesitating, dismayed by the Spanish fire that welcomed them, he ordered his own boat to be rowed full upon the beach. His example conquered reluctance. The other boats followed. The men waded ashore and gave an account of those who would have hindered them. After that, they made their way up in the wake of Ralegh, who, rendered conspicuous by his white scarf, walked coolly ahead, leading staff in hand, wearing no armour beyond a gorget. Sir Arthur Gorges, who was captain of his flagship, the *Warspite*, joined him in the van, and with a handful of followers set an example of indifference to fire which the main body was again constrained to imitate.

Before the boldness of this advance, the Spaniards fell back, leaving the fort and the town of Horta in English hands.

Essex arrived on the morrow. The disappointment, when he found that the laurels he came seeking had already been garnered, turned readily to resentment in this vain and petulant man. Sycophants were at hand to fan his anger, and when Ralegh came to wait upon his Admiral, it was to find, instead of praise for his action, a charge of breach of discipline, and to learn of orders issued for the arrest of the officers who had taken part with him in the landing. When to his amazement he was reminded that to land troops without the presence and express orders of the commander-in-chief was an offence punishable with death, he reminded Essex in his turn that this was something applicable only to captains, and not to the commander of a squadron, who was in the line of succession to the supreme command. With equal force he protested against the order to arrest his officers. The responsibility for what was done lay upon him alone.

To these arguments there could be no answer. But the hostility was so plain that Ralegh went off to his squadron so as to take measures, at need, to meet force with force. The intervention of Lord Thomas Howard, and—if Monson is to be believed—Essex's fear of the consequences at home averted violence.

Sir Henry Wotton actually perceives nobility in the Earl's answer to the advice of his sycophants to court-martial Ralegh: "I would if he were my friend."

The peace being made, Horta was laid in ashes, and the English sailed forth to intercept a fleet of forty Indiamen, of which Essex had word. But the blundering of the Admiral suffered it to escape into the strong harbour of Terceira. Again at Saint Michael it was the incompetence of Essex—so belauded as an Admiral by contemporaries—which lost him the opportunity of surprising the capital. This whilst Ralegh was seizing a Brazil ship of some value and attempting to salve a rich carack, whose captain, to escape him, had beached and fired her.

* * * *

The deep affection which Elizabeth undoubtedly bore to Essex did not restrain her jeers at the failure he had made of an expedition so liberally undertaken, in which the only, and comparatively trifling, deeds of any consequence had been Ralegh's.

Even without this it is probable that old hostility between the Earl and Sir Walter would have flamed forth, for to a temperament such as that of Essex it was one thing to patronize and use a Ralegh in disfavour, and quite another to tolerate a Ralegh restored to influence at Court, a Ralegh dominant again in affairs of state, advising upon and disposing of the defences of England against Spanish aggression, guiding the Council in the control and government of Ireland, conspicuous in Parliament, a power and a law-maker in the West.

Although still petted and pampered by the Queen, and the object of a curious idolatry from the unreasoning mob, Essex in his vanity felt himself overshadowed by this brilliant, gifted man, who displayed a mastery in all things that he touched. He brooded over his fancied wrongs, and in the valour with which Ralegh had seconded him perceived only the theft of the laurels he had coveted.

It no wise mollified him that Ralegh, imperturbable, disdainful, and unprovocable, should nurse no grievance against him for his minatory conduct at Fayal, or attempt, as an intriguer would have done, to make capital out of Essex's failure at Saint Michael. That with the generosity towards an enemy which Essex had simulated but could not maintain, Ralegh should neglect no opportunity of commending his lordship's valour and ability, must merely have served further to embitter such a nature. His rage was inflamed by the bestowal upon Ralegh, in 1600, of the governorship of Jersey, and it is an easy inference that fear lest Ralegh might be sent—as his authority upon Irish affairs so fully warranted—to Ireland as Lord Deputy should have made Essex jealously snatch at the office for himself.

Thus, so as to thwart Ralegh, he possessed himself of something he did not want, and no sooner was he in possession of it than he was bewailing his fate and inveighing against his banishment. When his measures as Lord Deputy were the subject of criticisms from the Council or of instructions that amended his own dispositions, his imagination perceived here only the thwarting influence of Ralegh.

Hence the jealous frenzy which made him rush upon his doom: his abrupt, unauthorized return; his insult—incredible in any age, but in none more incredible than in this—to the Queen, that her "conditions were as crooked as her carcase," and finally his ludicrous armed rebellion, in which he fatuously and vainly gambled upon his popularity with that "rascal multitude" despised of Ralegh.

By these actions he ruined none but himself. His tirades against Ralegh in letters to Elizabeth were as ineffective as the attempt to murder Sir Walter through the agency of that poor marksman, his lordship's father-in-law, Sir Christopher Blount, who fired four ineffective shots at Ralegh on the river.

It was merely to supply Sir Walter with another occasion for the display of his chivalrous forbearance. When at Blount's execution for his share in the treason of Essex, the sheriff would have stopped him from speaking, Ralegh, who was present as Captain of the Guard, actually interposed in Blount's favour.

Similarly unmoved by the crude taunts of Essex on his trial, Ralegh gave his evidence without heat.

Yet not quite all the intemperate malice of Essex and his friends remained innocuous. Although no action in Ralegh's life could justify the assumption, yet assumed it was by the Essex faction that Ralegh's emotions at the Earl's execution were those which would probably have been his lordship's had the positions been reversed. And on these assumptions calumny took its stand. Because as Captain of the Guard it was his duty to convey to the Lieutenant of the Tower the order for the execution, it was said that he had performed it with eager exultation.

Again as Captain of the Guard it was his duty to attend the execution. From motives of delicacy, he withdrew from the scaffold, and remained a distant, unseen witness. But the story ran that he had lounged in a window, insolently puffing his pipe in cynical satisfaction at the fall of his rival's head.

The circumstances of that report, so alien to the dignity in which Ralegh mantled himself, was not the only harm he suffered by his withdrawal. Essex had asked for him, so that they might be reconciled, which the Earl could have hoped to achieve only by repeating in public the admission already made in private that his reckless charges against Ralegh of treason to the Queen and state were quite unfounded.

A public declaration from the scaffold to that effect might have supplied some antidote to the poison which the letters of Essex had injected into the suspicious, craven mind of the King of Scots. In the course of his wild intriguing against Ralegh, the Earl had scared James Stuart with accounts of a conspiracy to exclude him from the succession. In this conspiracy he had placed Ralegh prominently among others, and more dangerous by virute of his influence in the West and in the Channel Islands.

It would be fantastic to suppose that Sir Walter was dejected for Essex's sake at the fall of an enemy who, almost from his first appearance at Court, and saving for a period when his interests had led him otherwise, had pursued him with a bitter and remorseless malice. But we have Ralegh's word of it, and it does not strain credulity, that he regretted it on his own account. His clear perceptions showed him how the death of Essex, in removing one peril, supplied another from those who hitherto had needed his support against the powerful favourite.

A surviving letter of Ralegh's to Cecil shows clearly that, once Essex had fallen, Ralegh would have kept him down, so that he should have no further opportunity to ply his venom. It by no means shows that Ralegh desired the Earl's death. Apart from this, it is worth quoting for the light it sheds upon the character of Essex:

> I am not wise enough to give you advice; but if you take it for a good counsel to relent towards this tyrant, you will repent it when it shall be too late. His malice is fixed, and will not evaporate by any of your mild courses. For he will ascribe the alteration to her Majesty's pusillanimity, and not to your good nature; knowing that you work but upon her humour, and not out of any love towards him. The less you make him, the less he shall be able to harm you and yours. And if her Majesty's favour fail him, he will again decline to a common person.

It might be an exaggeration to assert that the subsequent and shameful tragedy of this great Englishman was the posthumous work of the false witness borne against him to the King of Scots by Essex, whom James regarded as "his martyr." But it is not fantastic to suppose that the rottenness composing these accusations may well have fertilized the soil on which other intriguers for power, the crafty Cecil and the ineffable Lord Henry Howard, were so diligently to sow.

The execution of Essex took place in February of 1601. The death of Queen Elizabeth, at the age of seventy, occurred in March of 1603.

Never did the credit of Ralegh stand so high as it stood in the time between those two events; never was his life more active or his activity more fruitful in public and in private. He is prominent in foreign affairs, in which his linguistic attainments added force to his other talents. He

is sanely active in Parliament. He is the accepted authority
on armaments. He continues to direct Irish policy, whilst
disposing now of his Irish lordship. He maintains his interest in colonization, continuing to send expeditions to
Virginia, which he is persuaded he shall "yet live to see
an English nation." To his administrative activities in
the West he has added those of his governorshop of Jersey,
reciprocating, by solicitude for the island's affairs, the
joyous welcome his appointment had received there.

Yet, with all these occupations, any one of which would
have filled an ordinary man's mind and time, and in spite
of some trouble with his health, which takes him annually
to Bath, now that he is well advanced in the forties, he
finds leisure for the patronage of letters and the founding
of the association of wits at the Mermaid Tavern, with
which the names of Shakespeare and Ben Jonson are so
intimately associated. Similarly he finds leisure for the development of his estate of Sherborne, so cherished by him
and his "dear Besse," so augmented that by now it em-
braces the Hundred of Yetminster and, besides the manor
of Sherborne itself, five other manors in Dorset and Somerset, with the Castle and Parks of Sherborne and Castleton.

And so, for two years he is vouchsafed, undisputed and
undisturbed, the illustrious eminence to which the un-
rivalled versatility of his gifts, his grace, his wit, his learning, his valour, his elegant munificence, and his public
spirit, entitle him.

But to the ambition and the greed of power of others he
is a menace; and already the rats are industriously bur-
rowing away the foundations of the splendid edifice his
deserts have raised for him.

＊　＊　＊　＊

The future was to show the clarity of Ralegh's judgment when he opined that there would be perils for him not only from those who had been the friends of Essex, and who regarded him as the instrument of the Earl's doom, but also from those who had needed his support in opposition to that powerful favourite.

With Robert Cecil, as with his father, Burleigh, Ralegh's relations had ever been cordial. They had been tightened by alliance in the struggle with Essex; and the King of Scots regarded both Cecil and Ralegh with detestation on that account, whilst nursing against the latter the deeper rancour engendered by those lies of Essex's that Ralegh was hostile to his succession. The falsehood had the more readily gained credence with James since Ralegh, in his fidelity to the Queen he served, followed her own lead in abstaining during her lifetime from any discussion of the succession. He was known even to have gone the length of urging her, in writing, against naming a successor; a matter which it was easy to persuade the timorous, jealous James was to be regarded as antagonistic to himself.

The fear of Essex which had brought Cecil to ally himself with Ralegh was transferred to Ralegh now that Essex was gone. Here Cecil beheld a rival infinitely more formidable, because infinitely more gifted. Between this fear and the fear of that other obstacle to his ambition in the hostility of the King of Scots, who—it was now clear—must succeed the failing Queen, Cecil was drawn into association with that perfidious schemer old Henry Howard, whose credit stood high with James. Howard's letters to the Kings of Scots at this period read like those of a secret agent acting on his behalf. A man who boggled at no falsehood, he persuaded James that Cecil had laboured for the deliverance of Essex. Thus he brought Cecil to share his own credit at the expense of Ralegh, who was the object of continuous, unrestrained invective in the stream of letters Howard sent to Scotland.

When Ralegh was drawn into intimacy with Cecil's brother-in-law, the wealthy, thrasonical Lord Cobham, another who had been in the league against Essex, the denunciations of Howard embraced them both. "You may well believe," he wrote to James, "that hell never did vomit such a couple." And Cecil, at once to ingratiate himself and to increase the discredit of a potential powerful rival, upon finding that Cobham and Ralegh were communicating with the Scottish Court, denounced them to James as hypocrites who hated the King at heart, who were "repugnant to be under his sovereignty," inveighing particularly against Ralegh, "a person whom most religious men do hold anathema." He all but reveals himself for a Judas when he begs James to attach no credit to "their holding themselves out as his friends, or he as theirs." He pretends that if he maintains with Ralegh relations of apparent friendship, it is so that he may restrain him in his "light and sudden humours" against the King, "under pretext of extraordinary care of his well-doing from engaging himself too far."

Whilst actively wielding this double-edged weapon, Cecil outwardly maintained such cordial relations with Ralegh that neither then nor later can Ralegh have had a suspicion of those labours for his ruin.

Cecil's cynical alliance with Henry Howard and his unscrupulous conduct in that alliance would seem to justify Kingsley's denunciation of him as "one of the most accomplished villains in history."

*   *   *   *

The schemes of these intriguers were quick to bear fruit when the Queen died.

Ralegh, one of the signatories of the loyal address of welcome to James, set out at once for the north to meet the King. His reception at Burleigh House, where James had paused in his progress, was not merely cold; it was ominous. The royal boor who conceived himself a wit displayed his malice in a miserable pun when Ralegh was presented and named to him.

"Rawly! Rawly! True enough. For I think of thee very rawly, mon."

As much as other reasons for the King's rancour, there may well have been that clash of personalities which Aubrey's unfinished comment on this meeting seems to imply: "Sir Walter Ralegh had that awfulness and ascendancy in his aspect over other mortals that the K . . ."

To James would be fully known the fame of this man, the distinguished soldier by land and sea, the enterprising explorer and planter, the able statesman, the graceful courtier, the accomplished poet, wit, and philosopher, the mirror of the elegancies.

To know all this by repute was one thing; to behold their personification in this handsome, stately, dominant presence was quite another.

Just as there was never a king more imbued with a sense of the divine right than James, who rated kings as minor gods, so there never was a king more destitute of the attributes of royalty. A mean, treacherous, lying, cowardly knave by nature, grotesquely vain, stuffed with ill-digested learning which made of him a ludicrous pedant, he was vulgar of aspect, filthy of person, and disgusting in his habits.

Whilst he mouthed his poor pun at Ralegh, his mean

soul must secretly have bowed low before the suitor's sovereignty of mind and presence, before that "awfulness" which Aubrey noted. Here was a majesty which James's majesty could neither forgive nor tolerate. It may be that the very parts by which Ralegh counted upon prevailing with Elizabeth's successor, as he had prevailed with Elizabeth, were the very parts that really destroyed him. He did not yet realize, for all his clarity of vision, that the coming of James brought a new spirit into England. The age of Elizabeth had been an age of chivalry. The service of a Queen had evoked a spirit of romance by which men had been fired to the high endeavours that made glorious her reign. Of that, already, merely the afterglow remained, and this was soon to disappear. A sovereign, like a people, has the servants he deserves.

The promise implied in the King's reception of Ralegh was soon fulfilled.

Before reaching London, and so as to court popularity, the monopolies granted by Elizabeth were revoked. Ralegh had long held the profitable office of wine licencer. The question was raised whether this were not a monopoly. Pending decision, his right to levy dues was suspended. That was the first blow, depriving him of a large part of his income. The next, following quickly, was his loss of the office of Captain of the Guard. In his place James appointed a creature of his own, Sir Thomas Erskine, one who had been with him in that dark business at Gowrie House.

Soon after this came an order to Ralegh to quit his London residence at Durham House. It was the episcopal residence of the See of Durham, and James desired to restore it to the Bishop. All that Ralegh begged against this was that he might be allowed to remain until Michael-mas, pleading in favour of it that he had spent two thousand pounds on the building in the twenty years he had occupied it, and that provision ahead was already made there for his great household of forty servants and twenty horses. The plea was rejected.

That Ralegh was, like most truly great men, of an inexhaustible patience, his persistency in colonization alone will serve to show. With this patience he bore now these harsh rebuffs, and continued calmly to frequent the Court. With the same patience he set himself to break down the royal antagonism, and to render royalty aware of his value. The means he took were based upon a misconception. He had not yet gauged the pusillanimity of James. He presumed ardour in a young king and a thirst for glory, for deeds of arms that should make his reign illustrious, and by his *Discourse Touching a War with Spain and the Protecting of the Netherlands* went confidently about the furtherance of his aims for the aggrandizement of England. To accomplish it, he preached against the conclusion of that peace for which Spain, rather battered and weary, was suing, and towards which France had reason to believe—although Ralegh does not appear to have suspected it—that James was more than favourable.

Already before Elizabeth's death this question of a peace with Spain had become a party matter, and among those in favour of it, Lord Cobham had been as conspicuous as Ralegh had been conspicuously against it.

It was a logical sequel that the Count of Aremberg, minister of the joint sovereigns of the Netherlands, the Archduke Albert and the Infanta Isabella, in seeking an English promoter of their desires should have opened relations with Cobham; and there was talk of large sums of money—six hundred thousand crowns, no less—to be supplied by Aremberg in furtherance of the aim.

Unfortunately, there were some others who opened relations of another nature with Cobham at the same time, led to it by the assertions thrown out by this reckless fellow whilst Elizabeth had been still alive, of the rights of Arabella Stuart to the succession.

A group of malcontents, in which were the two priests, William Watson and Francis Clarke, and with them Sir Griffith Markham, Anthony Copley, Lord Grey of Wilton, and Cobham's brother, George Brooke, were hatching a plot—which came to be known as the Bye—to seize the person of James and constrain him to favour Catholicism. Out of this, or in place of it, a further plot—which came to be known as the Main—appears to have been inspired in Brooke by his brother's relations with Aremberg and his brother's old proclaimed leanings toward Arabella Stuart. The Spanish gold, in Brooke's scheme, should be employed to foster a rebellion that would place Arabella on the throne.

That Cobham was seduced by these proposals, he confessed. That Ralegh, the relentless enemy of Spain, could have been drawn into a Spanish plot was not too ludicrous a belief for the malice astir against him.

One July morning, some three months after the accession of James, when Ralegh was among those on the terrace at Windsor, waiting to join the royal hunt, Cecil came to summon him before the Privy Council. From the questions there addressed to him he may have perceived the link connecting him in the minds of his examiners with these two conspiracies.

Of this examination nothing is known directly. But from subsequent allusions the inferences are fairly clear.

Cobham, it would seem, had talked to him of his relations with Aremberg and of the gold that was to come from Spain for the promotion of peace. All that we know of Ralegh's attitude towards Spain renders fully credible his later assertion that, having answered Cobham's vapourings as we should expect, he believed that he had dissuaded him from any such course. Because, anyway, in so far as it was presented to him, no actual treason was perceptible in the matter, it may have made little impression upon him; and on his examination he appears to have denied all knowledge of these practices of Cobham's. In this same conviction later, he may well have assumed that here was a bubble which could be pricked by fuller information, and so he wrote to Cecil disclosing his knowledge that Cobham kept intelligence with Aremberg through the latter's agent, Laurencie. "If Laurencie were taken," he wrote, "the matter would not be discovered. Yet if he were then apprehended, it would give matter for suspicion to the Lord Cobham."

From Cobham, under examination a few days later, their questions drew the admission of his project to distribute Aremberg's gold among English malcontents. It was in the course of this examination that Ralegh's letter to Cecil was laid before him, carefully, so as to supply provocation. It supplied it. With cries of "O traitor! O villain!" the raging Cobham, frenziedly striking at the man he conceived to be his destroyer, declared that he would never have entered into these courses but for Ralegh; that all he had done, he had done at Ralegh's instigation.

Although before he departed from that place, Cobham repented and retracted his reckless retaliation, he had said enough to send Ralegh to the Tower on a charge of high treason.

Sir Walter appears to have seen clearly that his doom was sealed, and in his despair he may have perceived only one way to frustrate some part of the aim of his enemies. By death he would avoid the attainder which would lead to forfeiture of his estates and the consequent impoverishing of his wife and son. And so occurs his lamentable attempt at suicide.

At table with the Lieutenant of the Tower, he plunged a knife into his breast. The blow, however, was deflected by a rib, and before he could repeat it, he was disarmed.

*   *   *   *   *

Arrested in July, his trial followed in November at Winchester, where the King's Bench kept term because the plague was raging at the time in London.

After his momentary surrender to despair, he recovered his courage and his calm, and this, notwithstanding the abundant signs of the remorseless intention to destroy him. That his case was prejudged and his conviction determined, he must have perceived when, "on the ground of his grievous treason against the King" (which as yet was no more than an accusation), he was deprived in August of his governorship of Jersey, of his lieutenancy of Cornwall, and of some lesser offices which he had still retained. Besides this, the Council had decided that the patent of wine licencer did not constitute a monopoly; but on the same still unproven ground of his treason, the King revoked his patent and bestowed it upon Thomas Howard, now Earl of Nottingham.

So as to ensure, or render plausible, that predetermined conviction, his Majesty's jackals laboured to pile up a mass of evidence procured from the actual plotters. But it was evidence so self-contradictory that it went to pieces under examination, until nothing remained as a basis of indictment but the retaliatory outbursts from Cobham. Against this Raleigh believed that he had invincibly armed himself. But he had not armed himself nor could arm himself against the rancour of James, a criminal who did not hesitate at murder.

The people, who had never loved Ralegh, persuaded now of his guilt, made him the object of hostile demonstrations when he passed in his coach to Winchester to take his trial. He bore it with that disdain which was the source of his unpopularity.

On the 17th November of that year 1603, he came to trial before the Lord Chief Justice Popham, with whom sat three other judges and a group of Commissioners of Oyer and Terminer. This included Ralegh's implacable enemy Henry Howard and his false friend Robert Cecil, now Lord Cecil, who admirably maintained an air of regretful friendship whilst steadily assisting to thrust him to his doom.

The trial—by which, on the death-bed admission of Gawdie, one of the judges, English justice was degraded as never before—must be read to be believed.

The prisoner, allowed by law no counsel, stands alone, to receive and deflect as best he can by wit and reason the bombardment of insult and opprobrium that supplies the place of the non-existent evidence.

Never was he invested with a more impressive grandeur than that which is perceived in him by contrast with the court whose business it is to convict him, innocent or guilty.

"We carry a just mind to condemn no man but upon

plain evidence," was the promising opening of the Attorney-General Sir Edward Coke, to which every subsequent word of the trial was to give the lie.

He was explaining at length the treason of the Bye, when Ralegh broke in to remind the jury that he was not charged with part in this.

Coke went on at great length to describe the nature of treasons, and ended upon a singular, and no doubt deliberate, confusion of ideas, so as to anticipate an objection that was foreseen.

"When a man by his accusation of another, shall by the same accusation also condemn himself . . . this is more forcible than many witnesses."

Thus he attempted to multiply into adequacy the utterly inadequate scrap of evidence upon which his case was built.

After this he came to allude to an allegation that between Brooke and Cobham had passed the words: "that there would never be a good world in England till the King and his cubs are taken away." So as to create in the minds of the jury a confusion that the words might be—as was not even alleged—the words of Ralegh, he turned on that to the prisoner.

"To whom," he asked, "did you bear malice? To the royal children?"

"To whom speak you this?" Ralegh demanded. "You tell me news I never heard of."

"Do I? I will prove you the notoriest traitor that ever came to the bar."

"Your words will not condemn me," is Ralegh's contemptuous retort, and he invites the Attorney to prove one of the things with which he is charged.

"Nay, I will prove all," is the Attorney's grandiloquent

promise. But instead of the evidence Ralegh has challenged him to submit, he merely spews forth invective. "Thou art a monster. Thou hast an English face but a Spanish heart." This is followed by a reiteration of the assertion that Ralegh instigated Cobham to raise rebellion, and the assertion is followed by more invective. "You are the absolutest traitor that ever was."

Again Ralegh reminds him: "Your phrases will not prove it, Mr. Attorney. I do not hear yet that you have spoken one word against me. Here is no treason of mine done. If my Lord Cobham be a traitor, what is that to me?"

And now assertion and vituperation are jointly employed. "All that he did was by thy instigation, thou viper. For I *thou* thee, thou traitor."

This use of the second person singular, employable only between intimates or from a man to his servant, is a gratuitous brutality. Yet Ralegh's remonstrance is calm. "It becomes not a man of quality and virtue to call me so. But I take comfort in it, it is all that you can do."

At last Coke produces the evidence that is to justify all his coarse insolence, the unsupported accusation made in anger by Cobham. Building upon it with reckless malice, he goes on to add: "Cobham had told this at least two months before to his brother Brooke: 'You are fools; you are on the Bye. Ralegh and I are on the Main. We mean to take away the King and his cubs.' So mark the manner and the matter. He would not turn the weapon against his own bosom and accuse himself to accuse you."

There Ralegh attempts to pin him. "Hath Cobham confessed that?" he demands.

The Lord Chief Justice explains, lest these convenient mists should be blown away:

"This is spoken by Mr. Attorney to prove that Cobham's speech came not out of passion."

But Ralegh will have daylight on the matter. "Let it be proved that Cobham said so."

Coke cannot do so; he has used words which he cannot substantiate. But he does not say he cannot. He talks as if he could, buttressing his crazy logic with more invective, until Ralegh demands that Cobham, his only accuser, shall be brought face to face with him. Cobham is in Winchester, within the very building in which the court is sitting. Let them produce him.

They urge him reasons why this cannot be. He will have none of them.

"The proof of the common law," he tells them, "is by witness and jury. Let Cobham be here. Let him speak it. Call my accuser before my face, and I have done."

That is merely the beginning of a long wrangle between Ralegh and the court. His arguments were so clear and just and forcible that they could not be ignored. It was necessary to answer them, and the answers merely supply his wit with fresh weapons.

Weakly at last, in pronouncing a definite refusal, the Lord Chief Justice urged as a reason that "the acquitting of his old friend might lead Cobham to speak otherwise than the truth."

That was to open the sluices to a torrent of scornful logic from Ralegh that swept the objection away in ridicule.

"If I had been the infuser of all these treasons unto him! He said I have been the cause of all his miseries, and the destruction of his house, and that all evil hath happened unto him by my wicked counsel. If this be true, whom hath he cause to accuse and to be revenged on but me?"

Coke slammed the door of procedure upon the matter. "He is a party, and may not come. The law is against it."

"It is a toy to tell me of the law," exclaimed Ralegh. "I defy such law. I stand upon the fact."

But all the fact they had upon which to convict him was that accusation—retracted once already—of Cobham's, served up with a sauce of matters taken from the allegations of the other plotters and made to appear as if they concerned the prisoner.

The vague hypotheses upon which Coke demanded his conviction, Ralegh shattered upon the notorious facts of his life. He was a man who had almost ruined himself in actions against Spaniards. To the establishment of the ascendancy of England over Spain he had devoted the best part of his existence. He had always condemned Spanish faction. Quite lately he had written for the King a treatise against Spain. Was there not enough in all this to render ridiculous Cobham's vindictive assertion that he had practised with a Spanish agent? And if more was needed to reveal the absurdity of the charge, was it likely that he would have given heed to wild talk of so vast a sum as six hundred thousand crowns, which Aremberg was to procure from King Philip at a time when King Philip did not know which way to turn for money to pay his troops in Flanders?

But he wasted his breath and his logic on men who had come there to do the will of their knavish master.

Serjeant Philips, following Coke, assured the jury that Ralegh had no answer beyond a bare denial, and he warned them that the bare denial of a defendant must not move a jury.

Ralegh alluded to Cobham's retraction. "If truth be constant and constancy be in truth, why has he forsworn what he hath said? You have not proved any one thing against me by direct proofs, but all by circumstances."

Coke rose again to renew assertion, to protest before God that he had never known a clearer case of treason, and once again to promise Ralegh that he would "lay him on his back for the confidentest traitor that ever came to the bar."

"Thou art," he said, "the most vile and execrable traitor that ever lived."

"You speak indiscreetly, barbarously, and uncivilly," Ralegh rebuked him.

"I want words," foamed Coke, "sufficient to express thy viperous treason."

"I think you want words, indeed, for you have spoken one thing half a dozen times."

"Thou art an odious fellow. Thy name is hateful to all the realm of England for thy pride."

"It will go near to proving a measuring cast between you and me, Mr. Attorney."

"Well, I will now make it appear to the world that there never lived a viler viper upon the face of the earth than thou."

And now, at last, he produces something. Cobham, it will be remembered, had retracted his accusation. But these lords had visited Cobham last night in his prison, with results which Coke was to lay before the jury and which explain the reluctance to produce that witness in court.

Coke drew forth a letter newly obtained from Cobham in which he set forth that at Aremberg's coming Ralegh was to have received a pension of fifteen hundred pounds a year, in return for which he promised that "no action should be undertaken against Spain, the Low Countries

or the Indies but he would give knowledge beforehand.
He hath been," the letter ran on, "the original cause of
my ruin, for I had no dealings with Aremberg but by his
instigation." The letter included a protest that, on his
soul, Cobham wrote "nothing but the truth, before God
and his angels."

Here at least was an alternative to the satisfaction of
Ralegh's demands that his accuser be produced.

"What say you now," Popham asked him, "of the letter
and the pension of fifteen hundred pounds per annum?"

"I say," answered Ralegh, "that Cobham is a base, dis-
honourable, poor soul."

This brought Coke to roar at him: "Is he base? I return
it into thy throat on his behalf. But for thee he had been
a good subject."

But Ralegh had something more than his own assertion
with which to trump that trick.

He had contrived, whilst both he and Cobham were
prisoners in the Tower, to have an apple tossed in at Cobham's window, containing, as he stated, a letter with the
following appeal: "You know that you have undone me.
Now write three lines to justify me." And he produced the
answer he had received, and had kept concealed until
the dramatic moment when he could employ it with the
greatest effect. He desired it to be read by Cecil, who knew
his brother-in-law's hand.

That letter, perforce, was read.

> Seeing myself so near my end, for the discharge of my own
> conscience and freeing myself from your blood, which else
> will cry vengeance against me; I protest upon my salvation
> I never practised with Spain by your procurement; God so
> comfort me in this my affliction as you are a true subject,
> for anything that I know. I will say as Daniel, *Purus sum a*

sanguine hujus. God have mercy on my soul as I know no treason by you.

"Now, I wonder," said Ralegh, "how many souls this man hath. He damns one in this letter, and another in that."

He had flung a bombshell which blew into fragments the only piece of evidence the court could produce against him, and even this was hardly evidence of treason, for the utmost of which Cobham's latest letter accused him was of a willingness to accept fifteen hundred pounds for information that should help the maintenance of peace.

But Coke must do what he unscrupulously could to gather up the shattered pieces of his case, and give them at least the appearance of having been put together again. His assertion now was that the letter to Ralegh had been "politically and cunningly urged from the Lord Cobham," whilst the other was "simply the truth." Lest the jury should find a difficulty in the reasonable and rather obvious conviction that the very opposite was more likely to be the case, the Earl of Devonshire, one of the Lords Commissioners, was invited to assert more than he could possibly know: namely, that Cobham's latest letter "was voluntary, and not extracted upon any hope or promise of pardon."

This concluded the case, and the jury, after an absence of a quarter of an hour, returned a verdict of Guilty.

At great length Popham proceeded to review and re-assert the charges, and probably the only words of pure truth were those he spoke at the end. "I never saw the like trial, and hope I shall never see the like again." Thereafter he passed sentence in all the barbarity of its terms.

Ralegh entreated the intercession of the lords that his death might not be ignominious, and upon that departed under guard, "with admirable erection, yet in such sort as a condemned man should."

* * * *

It seemed that the King and his favourites had prevailed.

But there was in England another bar besides that of the court at Winchester: the bar of Public Opinion, with the entire nation for jury; and the verdict of this jury was not to be mistaken. It would have required a more courageous man than James to have disregarded its finding.

Outraged by the spectacle of that degradation of English Justice, filled with awe and wonder for the nobility, dignity, and dispassionate ability with which the accused had defended himself in that unequal battle, such a revulsion of feeling took place that from being—as Coke had reproached him—one of the best-hated men in England, Ralegh was suddenly become a national hero in English eyes.

This moment came at a season when for the second time despair had taken possession of him, to diminish, as when he had attempted suicide, his heroic stature. It induced him to write a letter pleading for mercy in terms only to be described as abject even when allowance is made for the sycophancy with which seventeenth-century courtesy demanded that a king should be addressed.

Just as it may be presumed that his attempted suicide aimed at preserving his wife and child from the effects of forfeiture, so we have his own word for it now that the thought of those dear ones was responsible for this weakness in a man who certainly never feared to look death squarely in the face.

However that may be, again, as on that former occasion, the weakness was momentary. Believing that he was to die on the 13th December, he wrote on the 9th that beautiful farewell letter to his wife, in the course of which he urges her to "get those letters if it be possible which I wrote to the lords, in which I sued for my life." He wanted no such evidence of his weakness to survive. "God knoweth that it was for you and yours that I desired it; but it is true that I disdain myself for begging it." The remainder of the letter is all tenderness and dignity. "I send you my love that when I am dead you may keep it, not sorrows, dear Bess; let them go to the grave with me and be buried in the dust." He ends with: "God teach me to forgive my persecutors and false accusers. My true wife, farewell. Bless my poor boy; pray for me." And he signs himself: "Yours that was, but now not my own."

It was not his fate, however, yet to die.

James hesitated to sign the warrant. Possibly the reverberations of public opinion helped the poor creature to realize that enough had been accomplished. Ralegh, stripped and ruined, might now be left to rot in the Tower.

But Ralegh was not the man to rot in any surroundings, so long as life remained in him; and now, at the age of fifty-two, rich life still flowed through his veins, and he was, as they have seen at Winchester, in the prime of physical and intellectual vigour.

The nadir of his present misfortunes was not reached until he was plundered of his beloved Sherborne. He had thought to have made this safe when, in 1602, with admirable foresight, he had conveyed it to his son, with a life interest to himself. But now a flaw was discovered in the conveyance, which nullified it. The splendid estate remaining, therefore, in Ralegh's own possession, Ralegh, convicted of treason, must submit to its forfeiture.

It was a cruelty they would not spare him. It was in vain that Lady Ralegh cast herself at the feet of James to implore a waiver of the forfeiture in young Walter's favour. It happened that the worthless minion Robert Carr, to whom James could refuse nothing, was coveting the place for his own. So in answer to the prayers of that distraught lady, his Majesty could merely grunt, "I mun ha' the land. I mun ha' it for Carr."

It went—the mansion he had planned and built, the lovely gardens he had laid out—with all the manors comprising that rich estate on which he had spent so much, and Ralegh was left to depend for his maintenance on little besides his wife's slender private fortune.

If there were petulances, pleadings, and complaints from him, yet in the main his spirit remained serene and his activities undiminished. They were merely constrained to seek new channels, to adapt themselves to the limitations of his present circumstances. And it helped that his confinement was none too rigorous. It was shared by his wife and son, who came to live with him, and by two servants, of all the vast retinue that once had waited on him. Two Indians he had brought from Guiana were, too, of his household there for a time. He could receive the visits of friends, and it was here in the Tower that in 1604 a second son was born to him.

He had the freedom of the garden, and of the terrace; and on the terrace he was frequently to be seen by the people on the wharf below, taking the air, handsome, commanding, and richly dressed as ever.

All his life a student, it was now to study, to reading, and to writing that he gave himself almost entirely. Al-

ways addicted to chemistry and metallurgy, he set up a
laboratory and an assaying furnace, and procuring what
materials he required he proceeded to experiments. These
resulted in at least two discoveries of importance: the cur-
ing of English-grown tobacco, and the condensation of
salt water into fresh. He invented cordials, by one of which
James's Queen believed herself to have been cured of a
dangerous illness.

His interest in Virginia and Guiana continued undiminished. It led him, even now, out of the wreckage of his
fortunes to fit out expeditions that should preserve his
contact with the friendly inhabitants of those lands, against
the day when his dreams of empire-building might yet be
fulfilled. Ores from Guiana came to his assaying furnace
and plants to his laboratory.

For the rest, his writings during those years display a
versatility almost fabulous. They include treatises on government, on the art of war, on shipbuilding, on exploration, on political economy, and on metaphysics, in all of
which is exhibited the stupendous width and depth of his
learning.

It was during these years of captivity that his splendid
intellect found its richest fruition in his *History of the
World*.

The work was projected for Prince Henry, that high-
spirited son of a mean-spirited father, a youth in whom
Ralegh had come to centre all his hopes. The Prince, made
acquainted by his mother with Ralegh, fully shared her
high regard for him. "Who but my father," he is known to
have said, "would keep such a bird in a cage?" Prince
Henry had no illusions on the score of his father, between
whom and himself little love was lost. He sought instruction and guidance at Ralegh's hands, even to the extent

of consulting him on the marriage projected for him by James. His sudden death at the age of eighteen, in 1612, quenched all the high hopes that the prisoner had founded upon this friendship.

When the Prince was *in extremis,* Ralegh sent him, at the Queen's request, a medicine for which he claimed that it would cure any case of fever unless there were poison. It was a claim that may have helped, when the medicine failed, the rumours of foul play that were already current.

The work on *The History of the World,* now well advanced, was continued notwithstanding Prince Henry's death, and was eventually given to the world in 1614, by when Ralegh had been ten years in the Tower. The charm of the narrative manner, the nobility of the prose, the vast intellectual scope of the work captivated all classes then and thereafter. But it did not captivate James. The English Solomon was himself an author, and he did not welcome work with which his own might be compared unfavourably. Moreover, Ralegh presumed to criticize kings as if they were ordinary mortals. In Chamberlain's phrase, James found Ralegh "too saucy in censuring princes."

But the just popularity of a work of such solid worth was not to be stemmed by the displeasure of a royal pedant. It did not, however, promote that liberty for which the prisoner was so ardently longing and petitioning. For another two years, whilst England rang with his fame and did honour in its heart to a greatness that was now recognized, he continued to languish in the Tower.

*   *   *   *

Enlargement came at last. A number of circumstances contributed to it.

Most of those who had sought profit from his eclipse

were, in his own phrase, "already rotten." Cecil was dead.
Henry Howard was dead, and his name covered with infamy. Carr, the petted favourite for whom Ralegh had
been deprived of Sherborne, was in the Tower—not as a
political offender, but as a poisoner. His successor in the
royal smiles, George Villiers, was disposed to be Ralegh's
friend, if only out of his hostility to the Howards who had
been the friends of Carr. There were dark political motives to bring him the suffrages of Sir Ralph Winwood,
the present Secretary of State. Sir Ralph was opposed to
the royal project of a marriage alliance with Spain, and to
let Ralegh loose upon the seas again might be the surest
way of frustrating it. And then there were those—and the
King himself was in this group—who saw a prospect of
riches from Guiana, and from that gold mine which
Keymis had surveyed. An expedition sent out by James
under Captain Harcourt some years before had not only
confirmed Ralegh's assertions of the vast natural wealth of
the country, but had also reported the great repute in
which Ralegh's name was held among the natives. Finally,
bribery is alleged to have played a part in his deliverance.
Edward Villiers, the favourite's half-brother, is said to have
had fifteen hundred pounds for procuring Ralegh's liberty.

Ralegh was free, but he was not pardoned. He might
have had his pardon too, it is said, for another seven hundred pounds. But Bacon, whom he consulted when lib-
erated and commissioned, gave the sound legal opinion
that this royal commission by which he was appointed to
the sole command of the expedition, with powers of life
and death, in itself must imply a pardon.

That opinion will have been the more welcome to

Ralegh, because he needed for the adventure all the money that he could scrape together.

He came forth from the Tower to engage in his preparations in March of 1616. He was now in his sixty-fifth year. His health had suffered in captivity, culminating lately in a slight stroke of apoplexy. His hair that once had been so thick and curling was now thin and almost white. Silvery too was the short spade beard, but the dense eyebrows were still black, the eyes still full of fire, and age had brought an increase of dignity to his fine features. His stature and carriage and the old care for personal adornment made him as striking a figure as ever in any assembly.

Faith in the ability of this, now the last of the great Elizabethans, had increased, rather than diminished. Adventurers flocked to his standard, with heavy contributions towards the expedition, and he received also a statutory bounty towards the building of his ship, the *Destiny* of four hundred and fifty tons.

Gondomar, the ambassador of Spain, of whom James in his eagerness for the Spanish marriage had made a bosom friend, offered Ralegh a safe-conduct to and from the mine, provided that he should go out with only one or two ships. But Ralegh had too much past experience of the faith that was kept by Spain. He must be in sufficient strength to give an account of himself if attacked. And this, James must have admitted, since he authorized the expedition to be made in strength. All that he now required of Ralegh, so as to assure himself that no harm should be done to the lands of the King of Spain, was that he should precisely outline his mining project, and set down on a chart the course he was to follow. These particulars James pledged his royal word that he would keep secret.

* * * *

Ralegh's fleet of seven ships of war and three pinnaces sailed at last in June of 1617. Three further vessels joined at sea. They carried in all a thousand men.

With Ralegh, and in command of his flagship, sailed his son Walter, now in his twenty-third year, said to be a reproduction of his father in body and in mind, but of an impetuosity of disposition absent in Sir Walter.

It was an ill-starred voyage from the outset. Gales drove them for shelter into Cork, where Ralegh was well received, and it was mid-August before the voyage was resumed. At Lancerota, in the Canaries, three of his men, who had landed, were murdered, possibly from a misapprehension of the aims of this English fleet. Ralegh abstained from reprisals. As a result of a difference arising out of this, Bayley, one of his captains, deserted with his ship the *Southampton,* and went home to traduce him. Then sickness attacked them. Forty-two men died of it on board the *Destiny*. Ralegh contracted a fever which laid him low for a month, unable to take solid food, and all but killed him.

By the middle of November, at last, the fleet was off the mouth of the Cayenne, where the Indians showed Ralegh by their welcome—as he wrote to his wife—that his name had lived amongst them. Harry, an Indian chief, one of those who had lived with him for a time in the Tower, sought him, laden with abundance of fresh provisions. They rested there for three weeks to recuperate, and on the 4th December sailed to the Triangle Islands.

Weakened by the fever, Ralegh was in no case to conduct the expedition to the mine. Moreover, it was the general desire of his followers that he should remain with the fleet, so as to secure their line of retreat.

Four hundred men, under their several captains, embarked for the river voyage in the five ships of shallowest draught. Young Walter was given command of the land forces, and Keymis, naturally, was to assume the leadership in the matter of the mine, whilst Sir Walter's nephew, George Ralegh, acted as Lieutenant-General. Ralegh's orders to them were to encamp between the mine and the town of San Thomé, which he supposed to lie beyond it. They were to avoid conflict if possible, but if they were attacked by Spaniards whilst at work on the mine, they were to repel them. He despatched them with the final assurance that on their return they would find him at Gallo Point, dead or alive. "And if you find not my ships there, you shall find their ashes. For I will fire the galleons, if it come to extremity; run will I never."

Their old friend Don Antonio de Berreo had been succeeded in the governorship of Trinidad by Don Diego Palomeque de Acuña, a kinsman of Gondomar's. He had repaired to San Thomé, and was waiting there for the English. This was not the old settlement which both Ralegh and Keymis had located as farther up the river and beyond the point of disembarkation for the mine. It was a new settlement of the same name, lower down.

As the English passed it they were fired upon by the waiting Spaniards. But obeying the instructions to avoid conflict, they disregarded this, and sailed on, to land higher up, on the morrow, which was New Year's Day. Here, however, they were ambuscaded, and attacked. Under the surprise, they fell back at first, then rallied, and drove the Spaniards before them towards the town, where Palomeque waited with the main body of his forces.

Young Walter, impetuously leading the van, was mortally wounded in the advance. As he fell he cried: "Go on! Lord have mercy upon me, and prosper your enterprise."

His death infuriated the English. They stormed on. Don Diego Palomeque fell in the Spanish slaughter, and the town was captured.

The Spaniards who got away were rallied by their alcaldes, and they fortified themselves on the island of La Ceyva.

Walter was buried, and a week later Keymis set out in a couple of launches for the mine, which he estimated to be some eight miles farther up. Near La Ceyva he fell in with the Spaniards who had repaired thither, and, having suffered a loss of nine men killed, he retreated with the intention of returning in greater strength.

But all things considered, the responsibility was becoming too much for Keymis, and he decided to abandon the expedition. George Ralegh's opposition to this postponed departure for a month, during which the English sustained several attacks from the Spaniards, and lost some prisoners to them who, it was said, were barbarously slaughtered. They yielded then to the representations of Keymis, and departed, having first fired the town, and carrying off a large quantity of tobacco and some other spoil.

* * * *

At Gallo Point, where he waited, Ralegh had received in a letter from Keymis the terrible news of his loss. It reached him on the 14th February, and on that day the journal of the voyage, which he had kept so faithfully, was abruptly broken off. With his son's death, "all respect of this world hath taken end in me."

In addition to his letter Keymis sent a parcel of papers taken in San Thomé. Amongst them Ralegh found a copy, according to some, the original, according to others, of his own letter to King James, in which he had set forth the details of the project and the route he was to follow. It was covered by a letter of warning from King Philip to Don Diego Palomeque. This explained how Don Diego came to be posted at San Thomé to receive the expedition.

To curry Spanish favour King James had treacherously foredoomed Ralegh's enterprise to failure. Of anyone but King James it would be quite incredible.

Little wonder that when Keymis reached Gallo Point with the followers, of whom he had lost two hundred, he found there a distracted man, who had shed his normal lofty urbanity and who received him with fierce reproaches. Keymis was told that he should have persisted in reaching the mine, so that, by proof of its existence and wealth, he might silence the slanderers who alleged that no mine existed. Thus, whilst Ralegh had lost his son, at least his honour would have been safe.

Keymis took so deeply to heart the reproaches of the adored leader whose fortunes he had so long followed that he committed suicide immediately upon leaving his presence.

* * * *

With tenacity of purpose, for his honour's sake, and in spite of the tragedies that already burdened the adventure, Ralegh planned now to go to Virginia, to re-equip, and thence make another attempt to reach the mine in the spring. But the enthusiasm of his followers was dead; and, at last, the desertion of two of his captains, Whitney and Wollaston, decided the sequel. Those two went off in quest of Spanish plate ships; but they could not persuade Ralegh to go with them even when they represented to him that he was a lost man if he returned to England.

Other things apart, Ralegh's faith was pledged to return.

The broken-hearted man wrote to his wife:

> God knows I never knew what sorrow meant till now. Comfort your heart, dearest Bess, I shall sorrow for us both. I shall sorrow the less because I have not long to sorrow, because not long to live.

She hastened to Plymouth to meet him on his landing there in June, after that year of absence. Her tenderness for him brought her down from London at a time when the only comfort for both lay in this reunion.

A royal proclamation had already doomed him, a week before his landing.

A month ago the news of the burning of San Thomé had reached London from Madrid, and Gondomar had broken into the King's presence, shattering etiquette and bawling: "Piratas! Piratas! Piratas!"

James had pacified him and his master with the promise of Sir Walter Ralegh's head.

Hence that proclamation, denouncing "the scandalous and enormous outrages and the malicious breaking of the peace which hath been so happily established and so long inviolately continued."

The treachery of Ralegh's kinsman Stukeley (afterwards known for it as Sir Judas), the simulated sickness and madness by which Ralegh prolonged his stay at Salisbury in the hope of an audience with the King, who was then expected there, the frustration of his eleventh-hour attempted flight to France, each a story in itself, are trifles of little moment in the major, dreadful story of Ralegh's end.

On the 10th August he was back in the Tower, in resumption, be it understood, of an imprisonment that had merely been suspended for the purposes of his voyage.

His head was promised to Spain, which hated and feared him as it had hated and feared Drake whose successor it beheld in him; that noble English head was to be a peace-offering that should leave the way clear for the marriage of Prince Charles and the Infanta on which James had set his heart. The barbarity of taking off this head under the Winchester conviction of fifteen years, and more, ago, did not daunt King James. What daunted him was the inevitable public condemnation that must attend such a course. Therefore, he commanded the lawyers to find a case against Sir Walter.

Bacon, Coke, and the rest went zealously about the task, only to end by despairing of formulating any charge on which they would dare to bring the victim to trial. They remembered Winchester, and the effect which his masterly defence had produced upon the nation. Yet the accusation against him then placed no such weapons in his hands as would be placed by the only conceivable present accusation.

He had written to Winwood (not knowing that Sir Ralph was already dead at the time)

It pleased his Majesty to value us at so little as to command me upon my allegiance to set down under my hand the country, and the very river by which I was to enter it; to set down the number of men and burden of my ships;

with what ordnance every ship carried; which was made known by him to the Spanish ambassador, and by him in post sent to the King of Spain.

That charge of treachery against the King would be the backbone now of Ralegh's defence, and how would the King look if it were uttered? No denial would crush it, because it would be followed by expositions whose truth must be self-evident. If Ralegh was guilty of provoking war by violation of Spanish territory, James, who had seen the charts, to which Ralegh had kept, and who must have approved them, since he had sanctioned the expedition, knew that violation there would be. Moreover, his Majesty had himself been guilty of the same when he sent Harcourt on an exploration.

If the English had no right to enter Guiana, the responsibility lay with the King who had commissioned Ralegh to enter it.

Equally futile and dangerous would it be to rest an indictment upon the vague allegations that Ralegh's El Dorado was a fraudulent invention of his own for the purpose of getting out of the Tower and sailing on a pirate raid. Ralegh's conduct upon the seas supported no such accusation, and it was worse than idle to urge an intention which no act of his confirmed, although opportunity had not been lacking.

Not daring, then, to bring him to public trial, they hit amongst them, and with the collaboration of James himself, upon the expedient of bringing him for examination before the Council, which could be done in private, behind closed doors, and of which they could afterwards publish what they chose.

Following upon that examination, which took place on

the 22nd October, and of which no records exist, he was informed—and the public was informed with him—that the King in his mercy had spared his execution of the sentence passed upon him in 1603, but that "new offences had stirred up his Majesty's justice to revive what the law had formerly cast upon him."

In those vague words, at Westminster, on the 28th October, the Lord Chief Justice Montagu granted execution of the old sentence.

Ralegh had protested with Bacon's argument that the King's commission for the late voyage implied a pardon from the old conviction. He was answered that treason was never pardoned by implication.

Not knowing that the warrant for his execution was already drawn and signed, Ralegh begged with dignity for a little time in which to set his affairs in order.

It was in vain that the Queen, from her death-bed, had pleaded for his life. In vain had other appeals been addressed to James. He had promised Ralegh's head to the King of Spain. All that he had required was a plausible pretext, and this he believed that he now held.

* * * *

With a firm step and a cheerful countenance, Sir Walter walked across to the Gate House, where he was to prepare to die for being the enemy of Spain, under a sentence originally passed upon him for being Spain's friend.

In Palace Yard he met Sir Hugh Beeston, and invited him to the execution.

"I do not know what you may do for a place," he said. "For my part, I am sure of one."

Similar was his bearing with those who came to the Gate

House to take leave of him. "The world itself," he said to one, "is but a larger prison, out of which some are daily selected for execution."

Dr. Tounson, Dean of Westminster, was sent to comfort him, and wondered uneasily at his fearless cheerfulness in the face of death.

Late in the day came Lady Ralegh, having exhausted vain prayers with the Council to mediate for Sir Walter's life with the King. All the grace she received was authority to dispose of the corpse.

He instructed her now, this brave, able, reliable wife, how to vindicate his fame if on the morrow he were refused speech on the scaffold.

At midnight she rose to go, so that he might rest, and in the anguish of their last parting told him of the Council's grace.

He smiled. "It is well, dear Bess, that thou mayst dispose of that dead which thou hadst not always the disposing of when alive." And so they parted.

Tounson, coming early in the morning to administer the sacrament, found Sir Walter's cheerfulness so unclouded that at first he regarded it almost with disapproval. In the Dean's view, cheerfulness was no proper frame of mind in which a man should go to meet his Maker. But Ralegh reassured him.

He ate his breakfast heartily, smoked a pipe of tobacco, and "made no more of his death than if he had been to take a journey."

With rare and fleeting exceptions, Ralegh throughout his life had been a heroic, arresting figure against whatever background he had been set, but never so heroic, arresting, and gallant as now, against the background of death.

When the sheriffs came to lead him forth, a cup of sack was offered him, and when he had drunk it, they asked him how he liked it.

"I will answer you," he jested, "as did the fellow who drank Saint Giles's bowl as he went to Tyburn. It is good drink if a man might tarry by it."

The scaffold had been erected in Old Palace Yard, before the Parliament House. Barriers had been raised, to restrict the available space. It was also hoped that because it was Lord Mayor's Day, the show in the City would prove a counter-attraction for the people. Nevertheless, when Ralegh came forth on that raw October morning (the 29th) he found an enormous multitude assembled.

He had dressed himself for the scaffold with that elegance and richness which all his days he had observed. He wore a ruff band, and a black velvet, wrought gown over a doublet of hair-coloured satin, a black, wrought waistcoat, black, cut taffeta breeches, and ash-coloured silk stockings. He had neglected, however, that morning the curling of his hair, and when this had troubled his barber, he had said of his own head, "Let them comb it that shall have it." It was perhaps on this account that he covered his head with a lace night-cap under his hat. It was to supply him with the theme for yet a jest.

In the crowd he beheld a very bald old man, and paused to ask him what had brought him forth on such a morning.

"To see you and pray God for you," was the answer.

Having thanked him, Ralegh plucked the lace cap from his head. "I grieve that I have no better return than this to make for your goodwill." And he tossed the cap to him. "You need it, my friend, more now than I."

With that pleasantry he moved on through the press of

people which rendered slow and difficult his passage, cheerfully greeting those of his acquaintance.

A fire had been lighted for the sheriffs beside the scaffold. They invited him to stay and warm himself. But he refused, on the ground that his ague would soon be upon him, and so he should prefer to get on before it happened, lest any might suppose that he quaked from fear.

He began his address to the multitude by thanking God for sending him there to die in the light, and not in darkness; before such an assembly of honourable witnesses, and not obscurely in the Tower. Then he passed on to speak in his own vindication. His speech was at once shrewd, skilful, and dignified. It included no attacks, voiced no grievance. It did not even allude to the King's betrayal to Spain of the details of his Guiana project. It may well be that in this he was restrained by the thought of those he left behind him, upon whom James might visit his resentment of that disclosure. Firmly, quietly, and eloquently he denied all treason of word or deed, and he laid bare the falsity of any charge of trickery in the matter of Guiana. He was vehement only in rebutting the ancient slander that he had rejoiced in the death of Essex, and that in derision of him he had stood puffing tobacco in a window whilst watching the execution.

He closed with a request for their prayers "to that great God of Heaven whom I have grievously offended, being a man full of all vanity, who has lived a sinful life in callings that have been most inciting to it; for I have been a soldier, a sailor, and a courtier, which are courses of wickedness and vice. So, I take my leave of you all, making my peace with God. I have a long journey to take, and must bid the company farewell."

He gave his hat and money to some attendants, and

then proceeded to remove his gown and doublet in preparation for the block, "as free from all manner of apprehension," says an eye-witness, "as if he had been come thither rather to be a spectator than a sufferer; nay, the beholders seemed much more sensible than he."

When he stood forth in shirt and breeches, he called for the axe. As he fingered the edge of it, he smiled, remarking to the sheriffs, "This is a sharp medicine; but it is a cure for all diseases."

Going then to each side of the scaffold in turn, he begged the spectators to sustain his strength with their prayers. He begged Lord Arundel, who was present, to desire the King that no scandalous writings to defame him might be published after his death. A slander which had pursued him all his life, attracted by his intellect, was that he was an atheist. He now declared to Dean Tounson that he died in the faith professed by the Church of England, and hoped to have his sins washed away by the precious blood of our Saviour.

The executioner, having spread a cloak on the ground for him, knelt to beg his forgiveness, and Ralegh placed his hand on the man's shoulder as he granted it.

Asked whether he would not lay himself eastwards on the block, he answered: "So the heart be right, it is no matter which way the head lies." Eastwards, nevertheless, he placed it as his friends wished.

He refused to be blindfolded. "Think you I fear the shadow of the axe, when I fear not itself?"

He told the executioner to strike when he should hold forth his hands. But when he did so, the man hesitated.

"What dost thou fear?" cried Ralegh. "Strike, man! Strike!"

* * * *

As the axe fell, a shudder ran through the crowd.

It did not cease in Palace Yard. Like a ripple over water it ran, spreading, through London, and thence through England. Unlike a ripple, it gathered volume and impulse as it went, until it was swollen into a tidal wave of horror and execration of those who had encompassed that great man's death.

Never had the heroism of Ralegh been so startlingly apparent as he had rendered it by the manner of his end. Never had the greatness of his soul been more fully revealed than in the hour of its departure. The utterance of a reckless fellow in Palace Yard, that "England had not such another head to cut off," was presently the utterance of the nation.

King James—that foolish Solomon—was surprised and startled by the storm.

A *Declaration* was published, a nauseous document, that began: "Although Kings be not bound to give account of their actions to any but God alone, yet such are his Majesty's proceedings that he has always been willing to bring them before sun and moon." It went on, thence, to make out a case against Ralegh that, having been condemned of high treason and spared for fourteen years by royal clemency, he had won out upon an imposture merely to aggravate the offence by his demeanour and carriage as well in his voyage as in and since his return.

The attempt to destroy the lustre and dignity of the victim was received with scorn by an indignant, sorrowing nation. The lingering awe of royalty may have circumscribed the expression of it at the time, but the martyrdom of Ralegh went to swell the growing constitutional party; it helped to reveal the necessity of rendering kings answerable other than to God for their actions; it helped to weaken the foundations of the throne and to prepare it for its overthrow in the succeeding reign.

* * * *

On the night before he died, Sir Walter Ralegh, the poet, wrote his swan song in the Bible which he gave to Dean Tounson:

> Even such is time, that takes in trust
> Our youth, our joys, our all we have,
> And pays us but with earth and dust;
> Who, in the dark and silent grave,
> When we have wandered all our ways,
> Shuts up the story of our days.
> But from this earth, this grave, this dust,
> My God shall raise me up, I trust.

V

VICE-ADMIRAL LORD NELSON

V

VICE-ADMIRAL LORD NELSON

No MAN that ever lived is more deserving than Horatio
Nelson of the title of Hero. His glory does not rest solely
upon his genius, his sagacity and his courage, his quickness
to perceive opportunity and his audacity in seizing it, his
careful preliminary planning that left nothing to chance.
It rests much more solidly upon his greatness of soul: the
selfless nobility which impelled him always to prefer his
country's advantage to his own, to place duty far above interest. In the performance of his duty and to the profit of
his country, he never hesitated to face any hazard or to
oppose himself to forces by which he might be destroyed.
Not for him the merely spectacular triumph that crowns
the victor's brow with laurel but is more or less barren
of results to the cause he serves. To this he would have
preferred defeat, if in suffering it he could so dispose that
his conqueror should cease to be a menace. Going into
action in that lofty, selfless spirit, undismayed by odds, he
knew none of the hesitations that beset a man concerned
for his own safety and his own glory. From this firmness of
purpose, this unfaltering, heroic readiness to sacrifice himself and his fleet to his country's advantage, he derived that
quality of invincibility, that force that made him probably
the greatest fighting seaman that ever paced a quarter-
deck.

You may perceive early indications of this spirit in such
events as his audacious refusal, when a young captain of

twenty-seven, to obey an admiral who ordered him not to enforce the Navigation Act. Although he realized that he might be broken for his disobedience, he boldly took the risk because he conceived this to be his duty. You may perceive the same again in his refusal to recognize the broad pennant of a captain not in commission. Much more marked does it become during those four strenuous years of detached service in the Mediterranean, when he flew his commodore's pennant from the masthead of the *Agamemnon*. If at that time his name was still unknown in England, he was rendering it famous along the Italian seaboard by his conduct at Calvi, at Bastia, and at the blockade of Genoa when he so ably supported the Austrian operations on land against Bonaparte, who was then initiating his first Italian campaign. If the government at home had been languid in its appreciation of the great and difficult services he had rendered there, at least that stern and stately veteran of the sea, Sir John Jervis, had very fully valued the zeal, the indomitable energy, judgment, resource, and audacity which Nelson had displayed.

Sir John Jervis, as Nelson's commander-in-chief, had studied his performances at close quarters, and had given him that esteem which Nelson seldom failed to win from those with whom he was brought into immediate contact. As early as 1783, when he was barely twenty-five years of age, and in command of the *Albemarle* of twenty-eight guns, that great admiral Lord Hood, in presenting him to Prince William Henry (afterwards King William IV), at the time a midshipman on Hood's flagship, informed His Royal Highness that here was one who could give him as much information on naval tactics as any officer in the fleet.

The Prince has left us the following vivid portrait of Nelson as he saw him on that first occasion:

> . . . I had the watch on deck when Captain Nelson, of the *Albemarle,* came in his barge alongside, who appeared to be the merest boy of a captain I ever beheld; and his dress was worthy of attention. He had on a full-laced uniform; his lank, unpowdered hair was tied in a stiff Hessian tail of an extraordinary length; the old-fashioned flaps of his waistcoat added to the general quaintness of his figure, and produced an appearance which particularly attracted my notice. . . . There was something irresistibly pleasing in his address and conversation; and an enthusiasm when speaking on professional subjects that showed he was no common being.

It was an opinion from which his Royal Highness never had occasion to depart in the course of the long intimacy that followed between himself and Nelson. And it was an opinion held in common with most men of discernment who had Nelson's acquaintance. For if on the one hand he was of a self-confidence which he never hesitated to assert, on the other he was of a winning courtesy and an evenness of temper which few could resist.

If no man held Nelson in higher esteem than did Sir John Jervis, no man had better cause to do so, for it was Nelson's genius as a fighting seaman combined with his selfless heroism that placed upon the brow of Jervis the laurels of the victory of Cape Saint Vincent.

*   *   *   *

When at the end of 1796, England determined upon the withdrawal from the Mediterranean of the fleet which Sir John Jervis had commanded for two years, abandoning her recently acquired sovereignty of Corsica, Nelson, who

by that time had quitted the battle-scarred *Agamemnon,*
was despatched, with two frigates, to superintend the
evacuation, and to bring away the British Viceroy, Sir
Gilbert Elliot (afterwards Lord Minto), between whom
and himself a friendship had been formed that was to last
as long as life endured.

On his way back, he learnt, at Gibraltar, that the fleet
of Spain, now in alliance with France, had passed the
Rock, going westward, four days earlier. He crowded sail
so as to reach the British fleet in time for the battle he
foresaw, and by noon on the 13th February he was on
board Sir John's flagship, the *Victory.* Having made his
report, he went to take over the command of his own ship,
the *Captain.*

At daybreak next morning—Saint Valentine's Day 1797
—when they were twenty-five miles to the south-west of
Cape Saint Vincent, the enemy was in sight.

*   *   *   *

The Spanish fleet comprised twenty-seven ships of the
line: the *Santisima Trinidad,* the flagship of Don José de
Cordoba, an enormous four-decker of one hundred and
thirty-six guns, the largest vessel afloat; six three-deckers
of one hundred and twelve guns; two eighty-fours and
eighteen seventy-fours, with ten frigates and a brig.

Sir John opposed to this formidable array fifteen ships
of the line: two of one hundred guns; two of ninety-eight;
two of ninety; eight seventy-fours and one sixty-four; with
four brigs, a sloop, and a cutter. Even so it was a greater
force than Don José de Cordoba had expected to meet,
having come out to destroy a fleet, as he supposed, of only
nine ships. But when he beheld the extent to which he
had been misinformed, his own preponderance was still

such as to leave him without uneasiness. He took precipitate steps to form a carelessly scattered fleet into regular order of battle. Sir John, however, denied him leisure. Cleared for action and in close order, as the British had kept during the night, they now crowded sail, swept through a wide gap in the enemy line, and tacking thereafter, cut off nine of the Spaniards from the main body. To rejoin it, these nine attempted to form on the larboard tack, only to be met by so hot a fire that they went about and stood off to await a better opportunity.

This left Sir John free to turn his full attention to the depleted but still vastly superior main body of the Spaniards to windward.

In this situation the Spanish fleet headed northward, sailing parallel with the British, but steering in the opposite direction, and exchanging cannonades as they went.

With intent to take them in the rear, Sir John gave the signal to tack in line ahead. Troubridge on the leading ship, the *Culloden,* instantly obeyed, and the remainder of the line followed, to tack at the same point.

As the manœuvre was proceeding, Nelson, whose ship was the third from the end of the line, observed that the leading Spaniards were veering eastward, with the aim of passing behind the British rear. If he succeeded in this manœuvre, as he must unless immediately prevented, Don José de Cordoba would rejoin his nine ships cut off to leeward, and then either accept battle in full restored preponderance or run before the wind for Cadiz in his faster vessels. Instantly perceiving this, Nelson as instantly took a resolve that dazzlingly displays his genius and his audacity.

*　*　*　*

It is said that there were three precepts which he impressed upon his midshipmen: always implicitly to obey orders, without attempting to form opinions respecting their propriety; to consider every man their enemy who spoke ill of the King; and to hate a Frenchman as they would hate the devil.

Himself, no doubt, he rigorously observed the second and third of these precepts. As for the first, he had been known, as we have seen, to depart from it before now; but never so flagrantly or, as the sequel shows, more gloriously.

*　　*　　*　　*

He ordered his ship to be wore out of the line, and, going about, passed between the two vessels that had been following him, and went to put himself across the bows of the leading Spanish ships, a thwarting obstacle in their course.

Instantly he was heavily engaged with the mighty *Santisima Trinidad* and two other first-raters, by the *San Nicolao* of eighty guns and by two seventy-fours.

Troubridge in the *Culloden,* which, as the leader of the British van, was now the nearest of the approaching ships, immediately steered to join him. Soon the *Blenheim* followed, and then Sir John signalled to Collingwood, in the *Excellent,* which being the last in the line was now the nearest to the point of action, to lend his support as well.

Thus, by Nelson's initiative, by his lightning perception of opportunity, by a decision as swift and a gallantry that took no account of his own probable destruction, were the Spaniards checked and brought to grips.

In these grips, borne for a moment alone, the *Captain*

was sorely mauled. By the time the *Excellent* came to relieve her, she was so maimed as to be useless either in the
line or in the chase.

Her foretopmast was gone; not a sail, shroud, or rope
was left, and her wheel had been shot away. She had
fetched up alongside of the *San Nicolao,* her spritsail en-
tangled in the Spaniard's mizzen shrouds, and Nelson ordered his captain—Captain Miller—to put the helm hard
a-starboard. Then he called for boarders, and whilst the
Spanish gunners below were still firing upon the British,
Nelson and his followers were engaged in a running fight
above. Beginning in the quarter gallery, by a window of
which the boarders had broken into the ship, the battle
swept up to the poop and thence went forward until the
last of the surviving Spanish officers surrendered.

But this was not yet the end of the epic that began
when the *Captain* wore out of the line.

The British in the waist of the captured *San Nicolao*
found themselves being fired upon from the stern galleries
of the *San José,* which lay board and board with her.
Whilst they returned the fire, Nelson called for reinforcements from the *Captain,* and with these set about boarding a second Spanish ship from the one already boarded.
"Nelson's Bridge" the feat was afterwards to be called.

With the cry of "Westminster Abbey or Victory," the
slight, boyish figure led the boarding-party, helped into
the mizzen chains of the great three-decker by Edward
Berry, a young commander who had been Nelson's first
lieutenant on the *Agamemnon.* The Captain of the *San
José,* demoralized perhaps by the fact that Rear-Admiral
Winthuysen was dying of his wounds below, yielded to
Nelson on the quarter-deck, and summoned his officers to

surrender with him. An old *Agamemnon* bargeman, to whom Nelson delivered their swords, unceremoniously tucked them under his arm.

Thus he crowned the exploit begun when he wore out of the line on his own responsibility; for it is by no means impossible that, but for his intrepidity in seizing these two ships, they might have forged into their own fleet, as did others that were as battered, and so have got away.

The afternoon was well advanced by then, and the nine ships that had been cut off at the beginning of the engagement were at last enabled to rejoin the main Spanish body. Both sides had received a deal of punishment in that very unequal contest. Whilst the Spaniards, being by far the heavier sufferers, and having lost four ships by capture, were intent on flight, Sir John, considering the damaged state of some of his vessels, was content to form on the starboard tack, so as to cover the prizes and the crippled *Captain,* and so discontinue the action.

Of the four captured ships Nelson had taken two. Of the casualties suffered by the British—very slight in their total—more than one fourth was sustained by the *Captain*.

When Nelson, after the battle, went on board the flagship, Jervis, who held that the test of a man's courage is responsibility, came out to meet him on the quarter-deck, and there embraced him, confessing himself without words in which adequately to thank him for a bold, shrewd action at the critical moment which had decided the fortunes of the day.

* * * *

It is related that, in conversation with the Admiral that evening, Robert Calder, the Captain of the Fleet, de-

scribed Nelson's wearing out of the line as an unauthorized departure from the Admiral's orders.

"It certainly was so," Jervis dryly agreed. "And if ever
you commit such a breach of your orders, I will forgive you
also."

*   *   *   *

Sir Gilbert Elliot, who had watched the battle from the
deck of the frigate in which Nelson had brought him from
Corsica, wrote to him on the morrow:

> To have had any share in yesterday's glory is honour
> enough for one man's life; but to be foremost on such a day
> could fall to your share alone.

Sir Gilbert had witnessed no more than he knew himself entitled to expect from the gifts of leadership and the
capacity for responsibility which Nelson had displayed
under his eyes in the course of his Mediterranean operations.

Starting for home a few days later, and arriving at a
time when the country was uplifted by the news of the
victory, Elliot told England what he had seen. The re-
sounding fame it suddenly brought Horatio Nelson, whose
name was as yet unknown beyond official circles, is best
perceived in the letter from his old father, the Rector of
Burnham Thorpe in Norfolk:

> I thank my God with all the power of a grateful soul for
> the mercies He has most graciously bestowed on me in
> preserving you. Not only my few acquaintances here, but
> the people in general, met me at every corner with such
> handsome words that I was obliged to retire from the public
> eye. The height of glory to which your professional judg-
> ment, united with a proper degree of bravery, guarded by

Providence, has raised you, few sons, my dear child, attain
to, and fewer fathers live to see. Tears of joy have involun-
tarily trickled down my furrowed cheeks: who could stand
the force of such general congratulation? The name and
services of Nelson have sounded through this city of Bath
—from the common ballad-singer to the public theatre.

Sir John Jervis might be created Earl Saint Vincent and
granted a pension of three thousand pounds a year for
life, but it was Nelson whose glorious part in that victory
had justly conquered the popular imagination.

It was, indeed, a far cry from that cold spring day, when
the little boy of twelve had alighted at Chatham from the
London coach on which his father had placed him, and
had wandered off, chilled and bewildered, to find the ship
of his uncle, Maurice Suckling, the *Raisonnable*, on which,
as a midshipman, he was to learn the trade of the sea.

The coveted Order of the Bath was bestowed upon him,

to mark the Royal approbation of your successful and gallant exertions on several occasions during the course of the
present war in the Mediterranean, and more particularly
of your very distinguished conduct in the glorious and brilliant victory obtained over the fleet of Spain by His Majesty's
fleet on the 14th February last.

*   *   *   *

To his wife he wrote after the knighthood had been conferred:

Though we can afford no more than a cottage, yet with a
contented mind, my chains, medals and ribbons are all
sufficient.

There was no affectation here. Acquisitiveness of
worldly possessions had never had place in his lofty soul.
The only greed he knew was the greed of honour. Of this

his career supplies constant evidence, from the moment in 1782, when as that very boyish young captain of twenty-four, on the *Albemarle,* he convoyed a fleet of transports to New York. By Admiral Digby, the Commander-in-Chief, he was informed on arrival at Sandy Hook that he was come to a fine station for making prize-money.

Although quite poor, he was not tempted. "Yes, sir," he answered. "But the West Indies is the station for honour." And he begged Admiral Lord Hood, who was then at Sandy Hook with a detachment of Rodney's fleet, to ask for the *Albemarle,* so that he might go to a station where honour was most likely to be obtained.

* * * *

After his glorious share in the victory of Cape Saint Vincent, came his failure at Teneriffe, five months later. Whilst it momentarily broke him physically and spiritually, it could not tarnish his reputation. The tremendous odds he was called upon to encounter there, and in encountering which he was ill-served by fortune, were not overlooked.

It was from the outset a desperate enterprise.

Lord Saint Vincent, his fleet increased to twenty-one ships of the line, was blockading Cadiz, and Nelson was now flying the pennant of a rear-admiral from the *Theseus,* which he had chosen for his flagship. News of his promotion had reached him on the 1st April.

The *Theseus* had been among the reinforcements received from England. She had taken part in the recent mutiny of the Nore, which had distressed and alarmed the country, and trouble was still feared from the temper of the men. Nelson's heroic reputation, natural kindli-

ness, and irresistibly attractive manner, made an end of
that menace. His flag had not been hoisted a month on
the *Theseus* when a paper, signed "The Ship's Company,"
was picked up on the quarter-deck invoking blessings upon
Admiral Nelson and asserting that the men would shed
the last drop of their blood to make that ship as renowned
as the *Captain*.

The idea of a raid on the Canary Islands had been Nelson's almost from the commencement of the blockade of
Cadiz. When in July intelligence was received of a treasure-
ship from Manila having put into Teneriffe, he received
orders to occupy Santa Cruz and hold the island to ransom
unless all public treasures were surrendered to him. They
were estimated to amount to six or seven million sterling,
which was as much as England was spending yearly on the
war.

Unable to obtain troops, which had been an essential
factor in his original plan, Nelson was yet sanguine of
being able to contrive without them.

He sailed on the 15th July with a squadron of four ships
of the line, three frigates, and a cutter. His intention was
to effect a surprise landing by night, and the force detached
for the purpose was sent forward in the three frigates. They
were thwarted by a gale of wind in the offing and a strong
opposing current. The vessels were still a mile from the
landing-place by daybreak, when they were discovered by
the Spaniards, and the element of surprise was lost.

A second attempt on the morrow, when Nelson stood in
with his ships of the line, so as to bombard the fort and
cover a landing, was again frustrated, this time by lack
of wind and by contrary currents, making it impossible to
get nearer than three miles from the shore.

On the 24th he tried again, and this time he determined to lead the landing-party in person.

Coming to anchor some two miles north of the town, he made every show of disposing to attack the heights. At eleven o'clock that night the boats of the squadron set out accompanied by the cutter and bearing in all close upon a thousand men.

Aware that he went on a forlorn hope, which he conceived honour to demand of him, he had, before setting out, written the last letter that was ever to come from his right hand. It was to Lord Saint Vincent, announcing the circumstances in which he was about to lead the landing-party. Then he had sent for his stepson, Lieutenant Josiah Nisbet, who had the watch on deck, to come and receive his last instructions.

* * * *

Ten years ago, in 1787, at the age of twenty-nine, whilst serving in the West Indies, Nelson had married Frances Woolward, a niece of John Richardson Herbert, the wealthy West Indian planter who was President of the Island of Nevis. A wife at eighteen, she had become a widow before she was twenty and had so remained for nine years when Nelson met her, wooed and married her, a quiet, gentle-mannered woman, reserved to the point of primness, if her letters are an index to her mind.

Her child by Dr. Nisbet, her first husband, found a friend and father in Nelson. In 1793, when Nelson was appointed to the *Agamemnon,* he took the lad, then aged thirteen, as a midshipman, so that, like his stepfather, he, too, might receive a cockpit education. Under Nelson's care and tutelage, Josiah's promotion had been rapid, and Josiah repaid him with an affection of which he now gave proof.

The boy came armed into his stepfather's presence. Guessing the reason, Nelson informed him that he was to remain on board. Not only did his duty lie there, but his mother must not be exposed to the danger of losing both son and husband at the same time.

Josiah, however, was insistent in his wish to accompany Nelson, and in the end prevailed.

The sequel shows that had he not done so, Nelson might never have returned alive.

* * * *

The night was exceedingly dark, and under cover of this darkness the boats got within a half-gunshot of the town before the sharp lookout of the Spaniards discovered them. Then the blackness of the night was streaked with fire. A cannonade of thirty or forty pieces thundered a welcome; volleys of musketry rattled from one end of the town to the other.

It did not, however, suffice to check them. Their real misfortune came from missing the mole in the dark, so that most of the boats went ashore in a raging surf that stove them in.

The men scrambled out, and some three or four hundred of them, led by Troubridge, made their way to the square, and held it, awaiting the Admiral.

But the Admiral did not come.

His boat was one of a half-dozen that had successfully gained the mole. But a gallant attempt to storm it had been beaten back with heavy casualties by the withering fire of the citadel. Grapeshot shattered Nelson's right elbow as he was in the act of landing.

In his left hand he caught the drawn sword, which had belonged to his uncle, Maurice Suckling, and fell back into the arms of Josiah Nisbet. The boy lowered him, faint and bleeding terribly, to the bottom of the boat. Then, with great presence of mind, and employing a kerchief stripped from his neck, Josiah tightly bound up the arm above the wound. Thus he saved his stepfather from bleeding to death, for the brachial artery had been severed. A bargeman tore his shirt to shreds to make a sling.

Next, getting a few men together, and himself taking one of the oars, Josiah set out to convey Nelson back to the ship.

As they were standing off, a shot took the cutter *Fox* below the water-line, and she went down with her commander and ninety-seven men. Nelson, rousing himself, ordered the boat to stand by, and, subduing pain and faintness, exerted himself to give directions by which eighty-three men were saved.

It was two o'clock in the morning when, at last, Josiah brought the boat alongside the *Theseus*.

With an energy that amazed the witnesses, Nelson peremptorily refused to be helped on board.

"Let me alone! I have still my legs left and an arm."

It was the impatient cry of a proud spirit, resentfully determined not to yield to the hampering infirmities of the flesh.

He caught the rope in his left hand, and steadying himself upon it went up the ship's side.

"Tell the surgeon to make haste and get his instruments. I know I must lose my right arm; so the sooner it is off, the better."

* * * *

His indomitable capacity for physical suffering had been seen before. It had been signally displayed in Corsica at the siege of Calvi, three years earlier, when a cannon-ball, which narrowly missed him, hurled sand and stone into his face, so violently that as a consequence—and although leaving no blemish that could be perceived—the sight of his right eye was eventually destroyed. Yet that same evening he was writing lightly about his injury to Lord Hood, who was then his Commander-in-Chief, and on the morrow he had resumed his duties. He did not, however, write lightly now to Lord Saint Vincent, although it may have been the bitter consciousness of failure, added to his physical pain and crippled condition, that dictated the letter he scrawled three days later with his left hand and sent on by a frigate despatched ahead of the squadron:

> I am become a burthen to my friends and useless to my country. When I leave your command, I become dead to the world; I go hence and am no more seen.

But it must have softened his anguish, when three weeks later he rejoined the fleet before Cadiz, to be generously greeted by Saint Vincent in an adaptation of a line of Addison's:

> Mortals cannot command success. You and your companions have certainly deserved it by the greatest degree of heroism and perseverance that was ever exhibited.

Invalided home, he joined his wife and his father at Bath. Months followed of pain so acute that he could hardly sleep without the use of opiates. But, by Christmas of that year 1797 he had so far conquered the notion of his utility being ended, that he was chafing to go to sea again.

At the end of the following March, his wound now fully healed and no longer a source of pain, he hoisted his rear-admiral's flag on the *Vanguard* of seventy-guns, and sailed once more for the Bay of Cadiz, where Saint Vincent was still stationed.

* * * *

In the early part of that year '98 the British Government had received intelligence from Italy of the preparation of vast French armaments. The secret of their destination and purpose was well kept by Bonaparte. But, whatever these might be, their frustration was a paramount necessity if Europe was to be saved from the menace of Revolutionary France.

In the secret instructions to Saint Vincent, Earl Spencer, the First Lord of the Admiralty, wrote:

> If you determine to send a detachment into the Mediterranean, I think it almost unnecessary to suggest the propriety of placing it under the command of Sir Horatio Nelson, whose acquaintance with that part of the world as well as his activity and disposition seem to qualify him in a peculiar manner for that service.

The record of Sir Horatio's "activity and disposition" was summarized in the memorial he had been called upon to prepare a year earlier, on the occasion of his formal investiture with the Order of the Bath. It set forth that he had been in four actions with the fleets of the enemy, and in three actions with boats employed in cutting out of harbour, in destroying vessels and in taking three towns; that he had served on shore with the army for four months and commanded the batteries at the sieges of Bastia and Calvi; that he had assisted at the capture of seven sail of the line, six frigates, four corvettes, and eleven privateers; that he had taken and destroyed nearly fifty sail of merchant vessels, and had actually been engaged against the enemy upwards of a hundred and twenty times; in which service he had lost his right eye and right arm and had been severely wounded and bruised in his body.

* * * *

Because of this "activity and disposition," and because of the exceptional experience of Mediterranean conditions which he had acquired, he was so obviously the man to command the squadron which the situation as obviously suggested should be sent to watch Toulon, that the Admiralty orders when received had already been anticipated.

Upon Nelson's return to the fleet, the Commander-in-Chief, as his letter to Earl Spencer tells us, had at once conceived the idea of so employing him.

On this reconnoitring expedition Nelson sailed, with two other seventy-fours, the *Orion,* commanded by that fine sailor, Sir James Saumarez, and the *Alexander,* commanded by Alexander Ball, an old Mediterranean associate of Nelson's, between whom and himself a close friendship was to be established.

Edward Berry, who at Saint Vincent had helped Nelson into the mizzen chains of the *San José,* was now his captain.

In addition to these ships of the line the little squadron included four frigates and a sloop.

A gale that caught them in the Gulf of Lyons carried away the *Vanguard's* foremast and her main and mizzen topmast. But her distress on the following morning—such that, as Nelson wrote to his wife, the meanest frigate out of France would have been an unwelcome guest—was the least of the misadventure, as the future was to show. The frigates had parted company in the night with the ships of the line. Later, he learnt that they had made for

Gibraltar, on the assumption that the *Vanguard,* in view
of her damage, must do the same.

"I thought Hope would have known me better," was his
comment.

The helpless *Vanguard* was taken in tow by the *Alexander,* which steered a course for Sardinia and the harbour
of San Pietro. There, in four days, equipped with jury
masts, she was fit to take the sea again.

*   *   *   *

Whilst this was happening, the great armament Nelson
had been sent to observe had quitted Toulon. On the day
after the storm, Bonaparte's three hundred transports,
carrying thirty-eight thousand men, were convoyed by
thirteen line-of-battle ships, six frigates, a corvette, and
forty-five smaller vessels.

In ignorance of this, Nelson returned to his station in
the Gulf of Lyons, and there was sought by Lieutenant
James Masterman Hardy on the *Mutine*—a French brig
which Hardy himself had cut out from the harbour of
Santa Cruz.

Hardy brought orders from the Commander-in-Chief
and word of reinforcements on the way from Cadiz.
These reinforcements under Captain Troubridge followed
two days later: ten ships of the line of seventy-four guns
and one of fifty.

Nelson's orders were now to seek out the enemy's fleet
and destroy it wherever found, and to provision his ships
by force if necessary in the seaports which he entered.
Saint Vincent mentioned Naples and Sicily, or Gibraltar,
Portugal, Ireland, or even the Morea and Asia Minor, as
possible French objectives.

Nelson knew by now that Bonaparte had sailed, and if

he had not already followed, so as to ascertain his destination, it was because he awaited the return of his frigates, which were practically indispensable for this. It was from Hardy, who had spoken them in passing, that he received only now the vexatious news that they had gone to Gibraltar.

Not daring to delay further, in view of the start which the French had obtained, the *Mutine* must supply, however inadequately, this lack of frigates. And so, his hunt for the French began.

* * * *

News that he picked up at Naples made him set sail for Malta. But off Syracuse, he learnt from a Genoese brig that the French had departed from Malta a week before, steering, it was believed, for Sicily. This confirmed his own deductions that Egypt would be the French destination. He crowded sail for Alexandria, to find when he arrived there neither the enemy armament nor any news of it.

It did not occur to him that he had outstripped the French. It could not occur to him, because the Genoese report had been wrong by a matter of three days in the time of Bonaparte's leaving Malta.

His impatience beginning to turn to anxiety, and exasperated by the lack of frigates to scout for him, so that he must grope about the seas, half-sightless, when time was of such value, he resumed the hunt.

Carrying press of sail night and day against contrary winds, he steered northward along the coast of Caramania, then westward again along the southern coast of Crete, and so back to Syracuse, in mental anguish by now to find himself so baffled.

Later he spoke of that return to Syracuse as having broken his heart.

Letters awaiting him in Sicily afforded him a glimpse of the weapon which the fruitlessness of his stern and unsparing endeavours was placing in the hands of envy and malice. The sneers at his failure to find the enemy and the open censure of those who had given so young a flag-officer so momentous a charge were apparently justified. It was being asked what he was about, that the French fleet should have passed under his nose.

Saint Vincent wrote to him:

> Sir William Parker and Sir John Orde have written strong remonstrances against your commanding the detached squadron instead of them. I did all I could to prevent it, consistently with my situation, but there is a faction fraught with all manner of ill-will to you, that, unfortunately for the two Baronets, domined over any argument or influence I could use.

With his duty clearly and compellingly before his eyes, and with confidence in his own ability to perform it once he found the elusive enemy, Nelson may not at this stage have been perturbed by hostile criticism. But the sense of his responsibility to Saint Vincent and Earl Spencer was an addition to the burden that he carried and to the anxieties in which he lay.

* * * *

Having taken in supplies at Syracuse, the chase was resumed, in the direction of the Morea. Three days later, on the 25th July, in the Gulf of Coron, he heard at last that the French fleet had been seen four weeks ago steering south-east of Crete. Persuaded by this of what had happened, and that Egypt, after all, as he had believed throughout, was Bonaparte's destination, he bore up under full sail once more for Alexandria. And on the 1st of August his long suspense was at last ended by the discovery of the French fleet at anchor in Aboukir Bay.

It was a quarter to three in the afternoon when the French were first sighted from the lookout of the *Zealous;* and soon after this, although there was little likelihood of reaching them before sunset, Nelson signalled his fleet to clear for action. There would barely have been time, and, anyway, there was not the need to call a council of his captains. During the weeks of that baffling chase it had been the Admiral's habit to assemble them aboard the *Vanguard,* there to concert what should be their action in every probable set of circumstances. Nothing had been omitted. New signals even had been added to the code.

As the disposition of the French became increasingly apparent, Nelson perceived at once their strength and their weakness. Their strength did not daunt him, but their weakness they might repair if time were allowed them. Therefore, there could be no postponement of action because of the approach of night.

He made the signal to form line of battle.

* * * *

The French Admiral, François Paul Brueys d'Aigailliers, a sailor of valour and experience, had anchored his ships in line at a distance of about one hundred and sixty yards from each other, and some three miles from the westward shore. The head of the line might be said to rest upon the edge of the shoal to the south of the island at the entrance of the bay. This position, pronounced by the Commissary of the Fleet as one in which they might defy a force more than double their own, secured their larboard flank.

The force now bearing down upon them, whilst superior in number by one ship of the line, was actually and considerably inferior in weight of metal; for whilst Nelson's ships were all seventy-fours with the exception of the *Leander,* which was of only fifty guns, Brueys' thirteen ships included the *Orient* of one hundred and twenty, three of eighty, and the remainder of seventy-four guns. In addition, he possessed three frigates of forty and one of thirty-six guns.

Further, however, Nelson came into action with only ten ships of his squadron.

The *Swiftsure* and the *Alexander* had been scouting when the French were sighted, and were now some miles to windward. The *Culloden* had fallen astern with a small French prize in tow, and in her haste to rejoin the line now that battle was imminent, went aground on the dangerous shoal at the entrance of the bay. The *Leander* stood by to attempt to refloat her.

Nelson's plan of attack possesses something of that quality of obviousness to be discovered in most great inventions once their secret is disclosed. It is the same obviousness that is discernible, after the event, in Bonaparte's irresistible tactics; but an obviousness which his opponents never learnt to practise.

If Nelson perceived the French Commissary's boasted strength of Brueys' position (and there is a clear, recognized advantage with ships fighting at anchor as Brueys meant to fight), he perceived also how to deal with it, and signalled his prompt decision to his fleet. One advantage he possessed in that the wind was blowing along the French line. Profiting by this, he could throw what force he pleased on the enemy's van and centre, and, by doubling on them, destroy them ship by ship.

As the British approached, groping their way in with the lead, Nelson took a closer survey, and found that the French might not be as inaccessible to larboard as they seemed persuaded, from the fact that they had cleared for action on the starboard side only. Between their van-ship and the shoal ahead of it there must be room for that ship to swing at anchor. Where there was room for this, there must be room for another ship to pass.

Hailing Captain Hood of the *Zealous,* Nelson inquired if they were far enough eastward to clear the shoal, of which they were then abreast. So as to ascertain, Captain Hood, then in eleven fathoms, went ahead, sounding his way. He was outstripped, however, by Captain Foley in the faster sailing *Goliath,* who proceeding with the same caution over this unknown ground, aimed at placing himself inside the French line.

As they bore down upon the enemy van, the *Vanguard* dropped to sixth, whence Nelson could observe and thereafter act upon the initial operations by those ahead of him.

To Brueys, seeing ship after ship steering in the wake of the *Goliath* to seek a passage across the bows of his van-ship, the *Guerrier,* it seemed that the English were delivering themselves into his hands and that they must stick fast on the shoal at any moment.

At six-thirty, as the sun was setting, the two leading French seventy-fours opened fire on the *Goliath.* Holding his fire until he was across the bows of the *Guerrier,* Foley then raked her with a broadside as he sailed on with intent to anchor on her inner bow. But because his anchor hung, he drifted, to anchor instead on the inner quarter of the second ship, the *Conquérant,* and in ten minutes he had shot away her masts.

The *Zealous,* following, took up the station which the *Goliath* had missed and in as many minutes had totally disabled the *Guerrier,* whilst the *Audacious,* coming round third, completed the destruction of the *Conquérant.*

The swift crushing of these two leaders must be assigned to the fact that, deluded by their conviction of inaccessibility on the inner side, they had not been prepared to serve their larboard guns.

Whilst two more of the British ships, the *Orion* and the *Theseus,* were moving to stations inside the enemy line, Nelson proceeded to deal with the outside. The first and second ships being already sufficiently engaged, he brought the *Vanguard* to anchor within pistol-shot of the third, the *Spartiate,* whose larboard was already receiving the fire of the *Theseus* at longer range.

The seventh and eighth British ships, passing him, engaged the fourth and fifth of the French, which were also already receiving fire on their inner flanks.

Thus, within a half-hour of the first shot, beset by eight British ships, the French van of five ships, two of which were already out of action, was well on the way to destruction.

The first and most critical stage of the battle may be said to end there. The advantage wrested by the British gave them such a preponderance that the end might almost be considered assured.

The ninth and tenth (and for the moment the last) of Nelson's ships now came into action. But owing to the deepening dusk and the clouds of smoke in which they moved, the *Bellerophon* missed the sixth French vessel, and anchored opposite to Brueys' hundred-and-twenty-gun flagship, whilst the *Majestic*, going still farther, engaged the ninth enemy.

It was whilst the battle was raging thus that Nelson was struck down on the quarter-deck by a piece of langridge. Captain Berry caught him as he fell, and must have shared his belief that his hurt was mortal from the horrible aspect of the wound, which covered the Admiral's face with blood. A rectangular flap of skin, detached from the forehead, fell across his sound eye, so that he was completely blinded.

In that blindness, in sharpest pain, suffering, there can be no doubt, from concussion, he lay in the sweltering shambles of the lantern-lit cockpit, awaiting examination at the hands of Jefferson, the surgeon, who was at last to assure him that there was no fracture of the skull or danger to life.

The wound dressed, he was carried to a storeroom on the orlop deck, and recommended to lie down and keep quiet. But still fearing, from the intense pain in his head, and notwithstanding Jefferson's assurances, that his end must be approaching, Nelson sent for his secretary, and began to dictate a despatch to the Admiralty. The secretary, however, proved unable to write, unnerved by the sight of his Admiral, as he supposed *in extremis,* by the roar and rattle of guns and the cries and ravings of the wounded in the cockpit. Thereupon Nelson seized the pen, and set about scrawling the letter himself.

He was still at this when, at a little after nine o'clock, Captain Berry brought him word that the French flagship was in flames.

* * * *

The *Bellerophon*, which had first engaged the *Orient*, dismasted and battered into helplessness by her powerful adversary, had cut her cable and worn out of the action, to be presently replaced in the line by the *Swiftsure*, which, with the *Alexander*, had at last come up. They brought into action with them the *Leander*, which until then had been making futile endeavours to refloat the *Culloden*.

The three vessels, arriving fresh at this stage, came to play the part of a reserve. Whilst the *Swiftsure* anchored abreast of the space between the *Orient* and the *Franklin*, and divided her fire between the two, the *Alexander* passed through the line under the stern of the French flagship, to station herself close on her quarter, whence she swept her decks with musketry.

Brueys, already twice wounded, still gallantly fought his ship until a cannon-ball tore away his left hip. Even then he would not leave the quarter-deck, but begged to be left to die there.

* * * *

Berry's report that the *Orient* was on fire made Nelson insist upon going on deck. There he found the grim scene luridly lighted by the great blazing torch which the battle-ship had become.

Only one of the *Vanguard's* boats remained in a condition to be launched, and in this he ordered his first lieutenant to rescue whom he could of the unfortunate crew of the burning vessel. About seventy were so rescued.

The *Orient's* was the burning deck on which the boy Casabianca stood. He perished there with his father who was the commodore.

Shortly before ten o'clock the flagship blew up. As if that terrific explosion had overpowered the senses, it was succeeded by an awe-stricken pause. The guns abruptly ceased. The scene, visible until then, was suddenly blacked out, and the ensuing silence was maintained until broken by the crash and hiss of timbers falling into the sea from the prodigious height to which they had been flung. Then the guns resumed, and hell was loose once more in Aboukir Bay.

Nelson was prevailed upon to seek his bed. But notwithstanding his condition, he directed thence, by messages, events which were already working to their inevitable end. For already the battle had entered upon its closing stage.

When the Egyptian day broke, only the three rearmost ships of the French line still flew their colours. They cut their cables, and with the two surviving frigates, the *Guillaume Tell* and the *Genereux*, stood out to sea unpursued by their exhausted opponents. The third ship, the *Timoléon*, ran aground, and was burnt by her crew, lest she should add another to the prizes captured by the enemy.

Of the thirteen French ships of the line so confidently riding at anchor on the previous evening to receive the British onfall, nine were captured and two had been destroyed by fire.

* * * *

Thus ended the Battle of the Nile, as it came to be called, incomparably the greatest engagement ever fought until that day upon the seas, and the most complete and crushing victory in naval annals.

Its importance and its far-reaching consequences were not to be overestimated. The immediate result was to cut off the French army in Egypt under Bonaparte, and to lift from Europe the menace of Revolutionary France.

When the news of it reached England, it produced there a delirium of joy and thankfulness.

What it did not produce, to the everlasting shame of the Government of that day, was a reward commensurate with either the magnitude of the achievement or the national gratitude. It is almost to be suspected that the envy and malice which had so loudly censured Nelson's appointment to that command, if perforce now silenced, had not become inactive.

For the comparatively poor achievement of the Battle of Cape Saint Vincent, practically sterile, and, such as it was, due mainly to the valour and ability of Nelson, Sir John Jervis was made an earl, with a pension of three thousand pounds a year for life. For the greatest and most fateful naval victory that had distinguished British arms since the defeat of the Spanish Armada, Nelson was given a barony and a pension of two thousand pounds.

The First Lord, in writing to congratulate him upon what he termed "this high distinction," went on to add that it was the highest honour that had ever been conferred upon an officer of Nelson's rank—that is to say, who was not a commander-in-chief. It does not seem to have occurred to him that no officer of Nelson's rank, or of any other rank, had ever achieved a victory of this magnitude. But it occurred to others, and even more deplorable was Pitt's reply in the House of Commons to General Walpole's protest against the meagreness of the reward:

> Admiral Nelson's name will be co-equal with the British name, and it will be remembered that he obtained the greatest naval victory on record: when no man would think of asking whether he had been created a baron, a viscount, or an earl.

It is a typical example of the glib, resonant insincerity

of the politician. When its vapid rhetoric is analyzed, the ludicrous meaning emerges that, whilst lesser services may be richly rewarded, in the case of a service so inestimable, virtue must be its own reward.

Nelson had not been human had he not resented the meanness of which he was the victim, and he might well have concluded that he served an ungrateful country but for the popular idolatry into which he knew that he was come.

And as if to stress the illiberal treatment he received from the British Government, rich tributes reached him from other sources. The East India Company acknowledged the security his victory ensured them by a gift of ten thousand pounds. From the City of London he received a sword ornamented with diamonds. The Sultan of Turkey sent him a pelisse of sables valued at one thousand pounds and a diamond aigrette taken from one of the royal turbans, worth four thousand pounds. From the Sultan's mother he received a box set with diamonds worth one thousand pounds, and from the Czar of Russia another such box worth twenty-five hundred pounds. The King of Naples sent him a sword richly set with diamonds and a sum of five thousand pounds, whilst lesser gifts and letters of praise and congratulations showered upon him from other exalted quarters.

The most singular present he received—probably the most singular ever made—came from Captain Hallowell of the *Swiftsure*. It was a coffin fashioned out of timber from the mainmast of the *Orient*, sent him so that when he came to depart this life he might be buried in one of his own trophies.

* * * *

In accordance with the orders from Lord Saint Vincent, Nelson left Captain Hood, with three ships of the line and three recently arrived frigates, to blockade Alexandria, and himself, with the *Vanguard, Culloden,* and *Alexander,* sailed for Naples, where work awaited him.

The remainder of the fleet, seven ships of the line, with six of the captured French ships (the remainder having been burnt beyond repair), proceeded to Gibraltar under the command of Sir James Saumarez.

The Kingdom of Naples—more officially styled of the Two Sicilies—by the exertions of its Austrian Queen, Maria Carolina, a sister of Marie-Antoinette, and by her influence over her weak, ignorant, pusillanimous Bourbon husband, King Ferdinand IV, had joined in 1793 the coalition against France. Intimidated, however, by Bonaparte's sweeping victories in the first campaign of Italy, Naples had subsequently become a party to the peace of Campo Formio.

Bonaparte's Egyptian expedition having depleted the French army of occupation in northern Italy, Austria was collecting her vast resources for a renewal of the war in the spring of '99. Among the alliances she was establishing, Naples, ruled by an Austrian Queen, was to be included; and Field Marshal Baron von Mack was sent to organize the Neapolitan army.

Hitherto the presence of the French troops in the bordering Papal States, and a powerful French fleet free to range the seas along the Neapolitan coast, had been strong arguments against any departure by Naples from her treaty of peace with France. Nelson had been made to feel this when during his recent pursuit of the French he was denied in Neapolitan seaports the support essential to him. But now that French arms had been dealt so demoralizing a blow and the French fleet from Toulon had been practically annihilated, Neapolitan apprehensions were at an end. Naples enthusiastically declared for the allies and prepared a great reception for the victor of the Nile.

That victor, worn and ill, afflicted by sickness and almost constant headaches—the indications of the concussion suffered—wrote to Lord Saint Vincent: "I detest this voyage to Naples; nothing but absolute necessity could force me to the measure." And he alludes to a fever, "which has very near done my business; for eighteen hours my life was thought to be past hope."

In Naples, however, the seductions awaited him of a nursing that was to be fateful.

Sir William Hamilton, the British Ambassador there, had written: "A pleasant apartment is ready for you in my house, and Emma is looking out for the softest pillows to repose the few wearied limbs you have left."

* * * *

Nelson's acquaintance with Sir William and Lady Hamilton was slight as yet. It had been made five years earlier, when as Captain of the *Agamemnon* he had paid Naples his first visit. We know that Sir William was impressed—as were most persons he met—by Nelson's personality, at once vigorous and winning; for he is reported to have told his wife that he was about to present a little man to her who could not boast of being very handsome, but who would, he believed, one day astonish the world. The captain had been a guest at the embassy, and both he and Josiah Nisbet, who was with him, had received every kindness at the hands of their hosts.

Towards Lady Hamilton he had occasion also for official gratitude, more recently incurred. When during his pursuit of the French, his ships were being refused the vitally necessary supplies at Syracuse, secret orders had reached the Governor, which relieved him of the obligation to observe a strict neutrality. This Nelson owed to Lady Hamilton's influence with the Queen and to the efforts which she exerted.

Those concerned to diminish a woman whose association with him certainly diminished Nelson have been at pains to establish that she rendered neither this nor other services claimed for her. They base the assertion upon the fact that no trace of any such intervention can be found in the official records. But evidence of an intervention which was secret and unofficial is not to be sought in official documents. Evidence enough should be discovered in the categorical statement in the codicil of Nelson's will; and this is corroborated by Nelson's letters from Syracuse to Sir William Hamilton, first in resentment of difficulties which he had expected a "private order" would have removed, and then in grateful acknowledgment that all his wants had been supplied. "Thanks to your exertions," he writes to Sir William and Lady Hamilton jointly, "we have victualled and watered."

The only possible refutation of such evidence would be that it is forged; and this refutation has duly been put forward. But just as the codicil is confirmed by the letter, so is the letter confirmed by the codicil. And, besides, there is enough in the remarkable career of Lady Hamilton to colour the opinion that, to some degree at least, she acted in Naples as a British agent.

Southey, in his *Life of Nelson*, written, be it remembered, in Emma Hamilton's lifetime, describes her as "a woman whose personal accomplishments have seldom been equalled, and whose powers of mind were not less fascinating than her person."

You will look in vain for confirmation of this staggering claim in the facts of her ladyship's career or in the testimony of her more responsible contemporaries.

Of the accomplishments "which have seldom been equalled," all that can be discovered is a third-rate histrionic ability; and those who, like Sir Gilbert Elliot, Mrs. Saint George, and others, found it difficult to reconcile the loud and vulgar deportment of the woman with the grace and appeal of the "attitudes" with which she delighted audiences, were evidently too slightly acquainted with histrionic art to know that this is a comparative commonplace of the theatre.

Originally a Cheshire servant-girl, her endowments were great personal beauty, vanity, impudence, sensuality, and a large measure of that quality known as sex-appeal.

At the early age of eighteen she gave birth to her first child, whilst living under the protection of a naval officer named Paine. From him she passed into an association with a quack named Graham, who exhibited her—more or less draped—as a representation of Hygeia, an experience which may have sown in her mind the seed of her subsequent "attitudes." Next she became the mistress of a Sussex gentleman, Sir Harry Fetherstonehaugh, who eventually sent her packing. After this there are no records until we find her, in 1781, at the age of twenty or twenty-one, installed as the mistress of Charles Greville, with whom she remained for four or five years.

Greville was moved to add grace of mind to such exceptional grace of body, and with this laudable aim procured her a measure of education. It was in these years that

Romney, who was Greville's friend, discovered in her a heaven-sent model, and frequently painted her. Then Greville's uncle, Sir William Hamilton, on a visit to England, first beheld her. He was a widower in the middle fifties, handsome in a delicate way, a dilettante, a collector of antiquities, and something of a musician. Since 1764 he had been British Ambassador at the Court of Naples, and in that appointment so admirably suited to the pursuit of his hobbies he was to remain until 1800.

His æsthetic perceptions discovered in the warm, palpitating loveliness of Emma a counter-attraction to the cold beauty of his antiques. It also happened that his nephew was contemplating marriage and desired Emma to be taken off his hands. A bargain was struck. Sir William paid his nephew's debts, and Romney's model was packed off to Italy on a pretext of studying music, together with her mother, who now called herself Mrs. Cadogan. The pretext was necessary, because Emma had become really attached to Greville and might have given trouble had she understood that the separation was to be final.

Her marriage with Sir William did not follow until 1791, in the course of a visit to England. Since the infatuated elderly gentleman could not bring himself to determine the association, it became necessary to make an honest woman of her, because not even the lax society of the Neapolitan Court would accept her in the false position in which she stood. Once, however, she had become Lady Hamilton, the Queen of Naples was not only willing to receive her, but glad for political reasons to make a friend of her. Her Majesty's hopes of deliverance being set on England, this friendship with the British Ambassador's wife would provide a cloak and supply a channel for the close association with the British Ambassador

from which she had been hitherto restrained by the dread
of French vigilance.

Thus the relations of these two women, one from the
summit, the other from the very base of the social ladder,
became close and intimate, such a situation being rendered
possible by the fact that when Emma spoke Italian her
native vulgarity was superficially veiled.

*   *   *   *

The great victory of the Nile, in removing the dread
of France, produced the frenzy of joy in which Naples
gave the victor a reception such as was probably never accorded a conqueror outside of his own country. From the
outset Lady Hamilton was the most conspicuous figure
in this reception. Already before Nelson's arrival her un-
solicited touch was cheapening him. When Captain Capel
of the frigate that carried the despatches was leaving the
palace with another officer, she made them get into her
carriage, and drove about the streets of Naples with them,
wearing on her hat a bandeau with the legend, NELSON
AND VICTORY. When, on the 22nd September, the battered *Vanguard* sailed into the bay, to the roaring of guns
and the pealing of bells, her ladyship was the first to go
up the side from the foremost of the flotilla of barges that
crowded to meet the flagship.

On deck, face to face with the Admiral, who advances
with his short, quick step, she at once finds occasion for
one of her "attitudes."

She had last seen him five years ago, when he was a
very brisk and youthful-looking captain of thirty-five. Now
his appearance is of an age beyond his forty years. His hair
is grey and a piece hangs across his brow to hide the ugly

scar of his latest wound. He is prematurely aged by ill-health and fevers, and worn by recent physical sufferings from which he is not yet emancipated. His melancholy countenance, with its mouth sensitive as a woman's, yet in the forward thrust of the nether lip expressing the strength of his nature, is gaunt and pallid. His gold-laced right sleeve is pinned, empty, across his breast. His aspect, and the change which five short years have wrought in it supply the cue for her.

"O God!" she cries. "Is it possible?" And she swoons against him, so that he must catch her in his single arm, no light matter to so frail a man; for she was no longer of the sylph proportions Romney had painted. Approaching forty, her big-boned frame was growing buxom. It remained, however, still of a good shape and the loveliness of her face was unimpaired. If her complexion was coarse, this was redeemed by the fineness of her features and the vivacity of her blue eyes, in one of which there was a speck of brown, a blemish that merely heightened the attractiveness. Her eyebrows were black, like her hair, which she wore short, and which (according to Mrs. Saint George) was never clean.

* * * *

After the Hamiltons came the portly King Ferdinand, effusively to take Nelson by the hand and hail him as his deliverer and preserver.

In the same terms—*"Viva il nostro liberatore!"*—was he hailed by the Neapolitan crowds as he drove through the streets to the British Embassy, where he was to be lodged in the Hamiltons' care.

Days of festivity followed, very wearing to the ailing

man, who meanwhile was intermittently being nursed by her ladyship, as Sir William had promised.

Her egregious vanity, emotionalism, and love of self-display urged her to thrust herself close within the effulgence of the hero. From that moment of her swooning upon him she seems to have marked him for her own, and upon the conquest of the conqueror she concentrated all her forces.

A man of the world might have been repelled by the obviousness of the onset. But Nelson was not a man of the world. His life had been spent at sea; his profession had engrossed him. She came to him at a time when physical suffering renders a man dependable on and susceptible to the tenderness of a woman. And Nelson, even in full health and strength, had given signs of an inherent susceptibility. It was an inalienable part of the romanticism of his nature which had made him the hero that he was.

At Quebec, in '82, when as a young man of twenty-four he had commanded the *Albemarle,* it had required all the masterful determination of his lifelong friend Alexander Davison to prevent him from contracting an undesirable marriage.

By nature essentially chivalrous, it would seem to follow that where a woman was concerned he was slow to assumptions that would have warned him to resist beginnings. By the time the situation had developed beyond misunderstanding, withdrawal was impossible without inflicting pain, a course to which chivalry again made him always reluctant. He was probably of those who believe that where love is offered a debt is contracted.

If this is accepted, it becomes easy to understand how

a bold, forward, assuming woman, such as Lady Hamilton, could in the particular circumstances of their early association have bound him fast almost before he was aware of it.

It is possible that his wife did not supply the strong sheet-anchor which might have saved him now from being swept away; although it is certainly true that his letters to her, up to this time, abound in expressions of tenderness.

From the siege of Calvi, a few days before the sight of his right eye was destroyed, he wrote to her: "Except with you I would not be anywhere but where I am for the world." After the Battle of Cape Saint Vincent he assured her that "the imperious call of honour to serve my country is the only thing that keeps me a moment from you." After the loss of his arm at Teneriffe, when he contemplated having to leave the service, he says: "I shall feel rich if I continue to enjoy your affection." Of the aigrette presented to him by the Sultan, he tells Lady Nelson: "If it were worth a million my pleasure would be to see it in your possession." And as lately as on the occasion of his arrival in Naples, when a lady asked him if the day of Aboukir was not the happiest of his life, he was heard to answer: "No, madam. The happiest was the day on which I married Lady Nelson."

Those expressions of a lover so frequent in his letters to his wife are matched by no expressions in her letters to him. These are primly restrained; her expressions of affection are the conventional expressions of a dutiful wife. On the other hand, there is certainly no evidence that she was the termagant represented by one biographer or that "her exacting temper and selfishness had proved insufferable" to him. His own assertion later, when he had drifted far, that he believes "she has a most unfeeling heart," is hardly confirmed by her later attitude.

*   *   *   *

However regarded, the twenty months that Nelson now spent in Naples cannot be considered happy. In indifferent health, overburdened with work—responsible for the security of the Neapolitan coast-line, the siege of Malta, and the blockade of Alexandria—and sorely tried in many ways, he had lost his earlier vivacity.

He was a different man, indeed, from the buoyant young captain of the *Albemarle,* who, when anchored off Elsinore, had said to a Danish officer who came to ascertain his strength: "The *Albemarle* is one of His Britannic Majesty's ships. You are at liberty, sir, to count the guns as you go down the side; and you may assure the Danish Admiral that if necessary they shall be well served."

We discover in him now little of that spirit of light-hearted gallantry.

Instead we find him in prey to petulances and irritability, for which, however, there was certainly no lack of reason, apart from his physical condition. We find him at cross-purposes with Vice-Admiral Lord Keith, who had been given the chief command in the Mediterranean, a position to which Nelson may not unreasonably have felt that he had the better claim. We find him flagrantly disobeying Keith, and being as flagrantly disobeyed himself, by the presumptuous Sir Sidney Smith. It resulted from the latter's conduct of affairs, to the exasperation of Nelson, that the French army which he had cut off in Egypt, there to wear itself away in fruitless operations against the Mamelukes, was permitted to return to France.

Not only was he crushed under a burden of work and

anxiety, but the victim of criticisms which, when closely examined, lead one to suspect that the "faction fraught with all manner of ill-will" towards him, of which he had earlier been warned by Lord Saint Vincent, was more alive than ever now that by his triumph he was established in the eyes, not merely of England, but of the world, as the greatest seaman and most glorious hero of his time.

* * * *

The three gravest charges contemporary censure brought quite recklessly against him are still being repeated by writers who are content to take opinion ready-made from their predecessors. They are worth considering.

Upon the defeat of the Neapolitan army under Baron von Mack, which marched, at first victoriously, against the French in the Papal States, Nelson was pronounced rash and hasty for having urged the King of Naples to declare war. He was blamed for the disaster, as if he should have foreseen that a well-equipped force of forty thousand men, led by an Austrian soldier of high repute, should be beaten by half that number of Frenchmen. Neither could he have foreseen that Baron von Mack should have learnt so little from the defeats suffered by other Austrian generals in the first campaign of Italy as still to pursue those tactics of divided forces which had made victory easy for Bonaparte.

The consequences were a French invasion of Naples, the overthrow of the monarchy, and the establishment of a republic styled the Parthenopean, in accordance with Jacobin predilection for classical nomenclature.

Nelson carried away to Palermo the escaping King and Queen, the royal treasure and the Hamiltons.

He was to return later as King Ferdinand's plenipotentiary, when the need of reinforcements in northern Italy, where the war was going against the French, had compelled them to evacuate Naples. They left only a garrison to hold the Castle of Saint Elmo, and placed the Neapolitan Jacobins under the necessity of shifting for themselves.

Besieged in the Castles of Uovo and Nuovo by the Royalists under Fabrizio Ruffo—a lay Cardinal—the Republicans had asked for an armistice which had been granted. When Nelson sailed into the bay in the *Foudroyant,* a treaty of capitulation had been drawn up, and was already signed by Ruffo and his associates, amongst whom was included Captain Foote of the frigate *Seahorse.* But we know that until a treaty is ratified by the competent authorities, the signatures of the negotiators, however important they may be, have little value.

The charge against Nelson in this connection is summarily given by Southey who has supplied the text for others:

> His directions were to co-operate to the utmost of his powers with the Royalists, at whose head Ruffo had been placed, and he had no other instructions whatever. . . . Nelson annulled the treaty, declaring that he would grant rebels no other terms than those of unconditional surrender. The Cardinal objected to this. . . . He retired at last silenced by Nelson's authority. Captain Foote was sent out of the bay; and the garrisons, taken out of the castles under pretence of carrying the treaty into effect, were delivered over as rebels to the vengeance of the Sicilian Court. A deplorable transaction! A stain upon the memory of Nelson and the honour of England . . . there is no alternative for one who will not make himself a participator in guilt, but to record the disgraceful story with sorrow and with shame.

Southey is mistaken. There is an alternative, and this

is to investigate the facts before perpetrating that turgid piece of rhetoric against a man whose honour was without stain.

The assertion that Nelson's directions were merely to co-operate with Ruffo, who was the supreme commander, is easily disproved. That Nelson's commission from King Ferdinand was that of a plenipotentiary is clear by His Majesty's Instructions, published by Mahan. Article 4 of these runs:

> All the military and political operations shall be agreed by the Prince Royal and Admiral Nelson. The opinion of this latter always to have a preponderance on account of the respect due to his experience, as well as to the forces under his command, which will determine the operations.

As for the graver calumny, the imputation to Nelson of a disgraceful act of treachery, there can be little doubt that its source was political. It may be traced to a speech by Fox in the House of Commons and to the cynical readiness of a politician to make capital for himself and his party, however dishonestly and whatever the havoc:

> Naples, for instance, has been what is called "delivered"; and yet, if I am rightly informed, it has been stained and polluted by murders so ferocious and by cruelties of every kind, so abhorrent that the heart shudders at the recital. . . . Nay, England is not totally exempt from reproach, if the rumours that are circulated are true. . . . It is said that a party of the Republican inhabitants at Naples took shelter in the fortress of Castel del Uovo. They capitulated to a British officer. They made terms with him under the sanction of the British name. It was agreed that their persons and property should be safe. . . . But before they sailed, their property was confiscated, numbers of them taken out and thrown into dungeons, and some of them, I understand, notwithstanding the British guarantee, absolutely executed.

The charge is infamously false, as three letters from the relevant correspondence published by Mahan will suffice to show.

Nelson on the *Foudroyant* handed the following note to Cardinal Ruffo:

> Rear-Admiral Lord Nelson arrived with the British fleet the 24th June in the Bay of Naples, and found a treaty entered into with the Rebels, which, in his opinion, cannot be carried into execution, without the approbation of his Sicillian Majesty.

Cardinal Ruffo, who, as one of the authors of the treaty, violently disagreed with him, communicated his decision in the following terms to Massa, the commandant of Castel Nuovo:

> Although Cardinal Ruffo himself and the representative of the allies hold as sacred and inviolable the treaty of capitulation of the castles, nevertheless the rear-admiral of the English squadron is not willing to recognize it, and therefore the garrisons are at liberty to avail themselves of the 5th article of the capitulation, as the patriots of Saint Martin's Hill have done, who have all departed by land.

That the rebels when they came out of the castles did so in this knowledge and under no delusion by a "pretence to carry the treaty into effect" is further seen from Massa's reply:

> We have given to your letter the interpretation which it deserved. Firm, however, in our duties, we shall religiously observe the articles of the treaty. . . . For the rest we cannot be either surprised or intimidated, and we shall resume a hostile attitude whenever it may happen that you constrain us thereto.

And he requested an escort for a messenger to bear the information to the rebels in the other castle.

The third of the major charges brought against Nelson is even more unfounded.

Prince Caracciolo, Admiral of the Royal Neapolitan Navy, who had accompanied King Ferdinand in his flight to Palermo, afterwards obtained leave to return to Naples. Fearing, it is said, confiscation of his estates by the Republicans, he went over to them and assumed command of the insurgent navy, and in that capacity was actually in action against the British and Neapolitan flags. When the Parthenopean Republic fell, he attempted flight, but was captured.

The charge correctly formulated against him read:

> Francesco Caracciolo, a Commodore in the service of his Sicilian Majesty, stands accused of rebellion against his lawful sovereign and for firing at his colours hoisted on board his frigate *Minerva*.

For this offence Nelson, acting upon his commission as the representative of the King of Naples, ordered Caracciolo to be tried by a court-martial of Neapolitan officers under the presidency of Count Thurn. By this court Caracciolo was sentenced to death, and he was hanged.

There hardly seems room for comment. Caracciolo's guilt was never in question. It was too flagrant and notorious. Similarly, it is impossible to denounce the sentence and execution, since these are the normal consequences of conviction of that offence. But so that Nelson's fair name might be damaged, irregularities were discovered in the proceedings. Caracciolo is represented as a victim. So far has this gone that the worst that a recent biographer can find to say of the man's treachery is that "it cannot be maintained that his action was without reproach."

Southey, making himself in this, as egregiously as in the matter of the capitulation, the mouthpiece of Nelson's calumniators, puts the charges brought against him in the form of six rhetorical questions.

It is easy to answer them in such a manner as to destroy their implications.

The first three are: Had Nelson the authority of His Sicilian Majesty for proceeding as he did? If so, why was not that authority produced? If not, why were the proceedings hurried on without it?

These questions are answered by Article 4 of the Instructions, already cited, which fully establishes Nelson's authority. That the authority was not produced and that the proceedings were hurried on without it, are merely the corollary assumptions of those who hoped that it did not exist.

The fourth and fifth questions are: "Why was the trial precipitated so that it was impossible for the prisoner, had he been innocent, to provide witnesses who might have have proved him so?" and, "Why was a second trial refused when the known animosity of the president of the court against the prisoner was considered?"

The assertion of "known animosity of the president of the Court" is an unwarranted acceptance of the allegation used by Caracciolo himself on which to base a plea for a new trial. Count Thurn, as the senior officer in Naples, was by every precedent the inevitable president of the court. No evidence is advanced of his animosity, unless the fact that Thurn was in command of the *Minerva* when Caracciolo turned the insurgent guns upon her is to be received as evidence.

Last comes the question: "Why was the execution hastened so as to preclude any appeal for mercy, and render the prerogative of mercy useless?"

This question is raised simply for the purpose of colouring the recklessly malicious suggestion, which immediately follows it, that, in acting as he did, Nelson was rendering himself the tool of Neapolitan vindictiveness and of the Queen's spite, of which Lady Hamilton made herself the advocate.

That there is not a shred of evidence to support the calumny has not troubled those who have disseminated it, so that unless we read them critically we are in danger of the preposterous persuasion that the traitor Caracciolo was a poor martyr inhumanly sacrificed by Nelson to Neapolitan malice upon the altar of his infatuation for Lady Hamilton.

*　*　*　*

Worn out in health and spirits, his Mediterranean task accomplished, and rewarded by King Ferdinand for the great services to Naples with the title of Duke of Bronte and lands having an annual yield of three thousand pounds, Nelson obtained leave to go home.

Sir William Hamilton asked for leave at the same time, and this was granted him the more readily because the Government had already taken the decision to replace him in the embassy at Naples.

Nelson applied to Keith for permission to carry his friends to England on the *Foudroyant,* but was refused. Thereupon he struck his flag, and the party, which included Mrs. Cadogan, set out overland, accompanied by the Queen of Naples as far as Vienna. They crossed from Ancona to Trieste on a Russian frigate.

At Trieste, the acclamations that greeted the great sailor, the illuminations and fireworks in his honour, were the first indications of the triumphal progress across Europe into which the journey was to resolve itself.

He was cheered by crowds whenever he showed himself, and in Vienna his appearance at the theatre was greeted by an ovation.

There at the British Embassy he met again his old friends the Elliots, now Lord and Lady Minto. So much stress has been laid by some upon Nelson's vanity that Lady Minto's reference to him at this time is worth considering. "He has the same shock head and the same honest, simple manners." She speaks of his devotion to Lady Hamilton, "who must sit by him at dinner to cut his meat."

Lady Minto's nephew, Lord Fitzharis, an attaché at the embassy, affords the same testimony: "Open and honest, not the least vanity about him." But on the subject of Lady Hamilton, he is in agreement with the general, well-bred opinion: "She is without exception the most coarse, ill-mannered, disagreeable woman I ever met."

They lingered in Vienna for a month, and then by way of Prague and Dresden they reached Hamburg, whence they sailed for England.

At Prague, the young Archduke Charles, already acknowledged the greatest soldier Austria possessed, gave a royal celebration to Nelson's birthday on the 29th September. At Dresden there was a repetition of the scenes of enthusiasm which had greeted him elsewhere and also of the hostile criticisms of his closest companion. The expressions of Mrs. Saint George and of Hugh Elliot (Lord Minto's brother, who was British Minister in Dresden), whilst barbed with a sharper malice, are not essentially different from others. Mr. Elliot thought that in England Emma would "captivate the Prince of Wales, whose mind is as vulgar as her own." Nelson, however, fast-bound in the proprietary attentions to which he had by now completely surrendered, saw none of this.

The Electress, refusing to receive Lady Hamilton, and yet not wishing to put a slight upon Lord Nelson, contrived that there should be no Court whilst the travellers were in Dresden.

* * * *

Embarking at last on the 6th November 1800 on the mail-packet at Hamburg, the party landed at Yarmouth, and Nelson's triumphal progress was resumed on his native soil. It is to be doubted if any homing conqueror was ever more deliriously greeted by a grateful people. Every ship in the harbour flew her colours; the freedom of the town was bestowed upon him; a guard of honour was appointed to him; and bonfires at night celebrated his landing.

Within a mile of Ipswich crowds flocked to meet him, took the horses from his carriage, and drew it through the town. The same was to happen again in London, on the occasion of his being feasted by the City, when the people drew his carriage from Ludgate Hill to the Guildhall; and there was a scene in a theatre similar to that in Vienna, when upon his entrance the audience rose to applaud him, and when Lady Hamilton, thrusting herself forward as usual to share his glory, stood beside him to acknowledge the plaudits. It is said that, behind them, Lady Nelson fainted in the box.

His wife and father, who were devoted to each other, had waited in London for his arrival, and there, after a separation of two and a half years, they had met at Nerot's Hotel on the 8th November. Lady Nelson must have been informed of an infatuation which Lady Hamilton, glorying in it, had been at pains to render notorious. But it would appear that her attitude was one of quiet, dignified forbearance. She received the Hamiltons, entertained them and was entertained by them. The inevitable conclusion, however, must have been accelerated by such events as that scene in the theatre, and the fact that Nelson left her to spend Christmas at Fonthill, where William Beckford gave a party in which the Hamiltons were included.

The crisis followed a week or two later. One morning, when Nelson's solicitor Haslewood was having breakfast with them, Nelson was alluding warmly and volubly to "dear Lady Hamilton," when Lady Nelson rose to make her protest.

"I am sick of hearing of dear Lady Hamilton, and I am resolved that you shall give up either her or me."

Nelson, restrained perhaps by the presence of a third person, kept his calm. "Take care, Frances, what you say. I love you sincerely; but I cannot forget my obligations to Lady Hamilton, or speak of her otherwise than with affection and admiration."

They were the last words he ever spoke to her. With a half-audible murmur that her mind was made up, she walked out of the room and out of his house.

The dignity of her attitude to the end of her life, in 1831, commands respect. We know of three letters to him: one to thank him for the "generosity and tenderness" shown in the allowance he made her (it was eighteen hundred pounds a year), another to express her happiness and thankfulness that his life had been spared at Copenhagen, and a third which was a dignified appeal for a reconciliation. This, however, was no longer possible, or even desirable, since it could not have made for the happiness of either. "She was always warm and enthusiastic in her praise of his public achievements, and bowed down with submission to the errors of his public life." Thus Hotham.

If the relations of man and wife are matters of the heart and mind, so intimate and subtle as often to elude the full perception of the parties themselves, it is an intolerable presumption for another to attempt judgment or to do more than record their outward manifestations, in so far as these affect an individual's public life.

That at this stage Nelson's entanglement adversely affected him socially must be admitted as freely as it must be deplored. His very chivalry made it impossible for him to shield himself; since it was not in his nature to slight a woman who by him, or through him, was now compromised, and a woman, moreover, of whose worth he was firmly persuaded. Where a man of coarse fibre, loose morals, or cynical promiscuity would have passed unscathed and held the respect of his class, Nelson succumbed to his very asceticism in sex matters, and was placed by his idealist's susceptibility in the pillory of scandal. He had surrendered to his infatuation, as such natures will, until it had become an overmastering passion; and he would abide by the consequences like one who never shirked responsibility. If it entailed a sacrifice of society's respect and of the advantages that accompany it, he would make the sacrifice without hesitation.

Sir William's apparent complaisance has been attributed to his being now in his dotage; and, indeed, it seems impossible to explain in any other way a simple-mindedness that could accept—as we must suppose that he did accept —the deception practised upon him and upon the world in the matter of the child Horatia, of which Emma was delivered at the end of January of 1801. Her ladyship disappeared for a little while on the pretext of being confined by a chill, and the child, within a week or two of its birth, was taken away and placed with a woman engaged to nurse it. Three years later, the little Horatia was to be sent back by Nelson to Lady Hamilton, as a child adopted by him in Italy whom he now entrusted to his dear friend's care.

*   *   *   *

Before the birth of Horatia, Nelson was already at sea again.

Whatever his infatuation may have done for him, it did not dim the splendour of his patriotism or diminish his heroic ardour. On the contrary, his conduct supports his protests that his devotion to Emma was a stimulus to deeds that should make her thrill with pride at the mention of his name.

Scarcely had he landed in England than he was reporting his health restored, and applying for an appointment. And England's need of him was urgent. War-clouds were gathering in the north, so black and menacing that never was England's safety in greater jeopardy.

Throughout the troubles agitating Europe, Denmark and Sweden had stood neutral, and so had profited substantially by a large carrying trade.

This, however, was restricted, under international law, by the rights of belligerents to search all ships for contraband of war, with the inevitable disputes as to what constituted contraband. The pretensions of Denmark and Sweden were suddenly stiffened by the support of Russia. The mad Czar, Paul I, was incensed by England's retention of Malta, which he coveted, so that he might revive there the order of which he was grand master. Bonaparte, now First Consul and virtual ruler of France, playing skilfully upon his indignation and offering him Malta as a bait, had lured him from the anti-French alliance.

With Russia's support Denmark and Sweden adopted armed neutrality, whereunder their merchant ships would be convoyed, and the right to search resisted.

Such was the beginning of a northern coalition, which England must take steps to crush before it could be consolidated. A fleet was despatched under Admiral Sir Hyde Parker; and Nelson, as second-in-command, hoisted his flag of Vice-Admiral of the Blue—to which he had just been promoted—on the *Saint George*. His captain was that Thomas Masterman Hardy, who had been with him at Teneriffe, and who at the Nile had commanded the brig *Mutine*.

The fleet sailed from Yarmouth on the 12th March: fifteen ships of the line, two of fifty guns, and an array of frigates, sloops of war, fire-ships, and bomb vessels.

As yet there had been no declaration of war, wherefore a Mr. Vansittart went with them, charged to negotiate and to allow the Danes forty-eight hours in which to accept the British demands and withdraw from the coalition.

On the 19th March the fleet was off the Skaw. Thence it proceeded down the Kattegat with a leisureliness that kindled the impatience of Nelson, who realized the paramount importance of striking quickly.

Mr. Vansittart was despatched ahead in a frigate. He returned on the 23rd to the fleet, which then was riding at anchor some eighteen miles north of Kronenburg.

The negotiator came wrapped in gloom. Not only did the Danes reject the British demands, but they were so armed for defence that, in Mr. Vansittart's view, disaster must attend any attempt against them.

The council held on Sir Hyde's flagship, the *London*, was plunged into dejection, and already there was talk of retreating, when Nelson interposed.

Hitherto Sir Hyde had studiously kept his second-in-command at a distance, a slight which, whilst resented, had been borne with the patience founded upon conviction that his hour would come.

The strategic conception now strongly urged by Nelson, and distinguished by that combination of shrewdness and audacity which places him where he stands among great sea-fighters, was that they should sail boldly up the Baltic, and deal first with Russia. The moment was opportune. The Russian fleet was divided between Revel and Cronstadt. Since no concentration would be possible until the ice broke up, the Revel division lay at their mercy, and Nelson was prepared to undertake its destruction within two hours of entering the harbour. Thus, in breaking Russia, they broke the backbone of the coalition, and they might count with assurance upon a consequent paralysis of its limbs.

It was too bold a conception for so timid and incompetent a commander as Parker. All that he could perceive was that it would leave an armed Denmark in his rear. And whilst Nelson could, and did, discount the admitted disadvantages of this, he could not discount them sufficiently for the hesitations of his Commander-in-Chief. Indeed, it was only with the utmost difficulty and insistence that he could bring him to consider the alternative attack on Denmark.

Pertinently and searchingly questioning Mr. Vansittart and those who had been with him to Copenhagen, Nelson ascertained not only the precise extent of the force which had so intimidated them, but also exactly how it was disposed. Having elicited that the greatest strength of the Danes was at the head of their line, drawn up before Copenhagen, he vigorously urged that they be attacked from the other end.

* * * *

Copenhagen stands on the east side of the island of Zealand, at the entrance of the Baltic. It is approached from the Kattegat either by a narrow eastern passage between Denmark and Sweden, known as the Sound, or by the wider western passage known as the Great Belt.

The Sound being defended by the formidable fortress of Kronenburg, it was opined that, if the attempt was to be made at all, it must be made by way of the Great Belt.

"Go by the Belt or the Sound, or anyhow, only lose not an hour," said Nelson, who realized how delays must increase the enemy advantages which delays had created.

The difficulty, however, was to induce Sir Hyde to take either route; and only Nelson's insistence, backed by a definite and detailed plan of operations, brought the Commander-in-Chief to listen to Nelson's passionate assertion that never did England depend so much upon the success of any fleet as upon this.

Being persuaded at last, and upon a decision that the batteries of Kronenburg, however formidable, would offer less danger than the shoals of the Great Belt, it was by way of the Sound that the approach was determined.

For best part of a week they were baffled by contrary winds. On the 30th March, at last, a north-westerly breeze bore them into the Sound. Nelson had meanwhile transferred his flag to the lighter *Elephant,* commanded by that Captain Foley who, at the Nile, had led the way inside the French line.

They had expected to run the gauntlet not only of the
guns of Kronenburg, but also of those of the Swedish batteries. The Swedes, however, were still indisposed to commit themselves to hostilities, and their guns remained
silent, in view of which the British fleet, keeping close to
the Swedish shore, passed Kronenburg out of range of all
the shot it wasted on them.

They dropped anchor at a distance of five miles from
Copenhagen, and Parker and Nelson went forward in a
schooner to reconnoitre. They found the defences to con-
sist of a line of battleships, most of which had been dismasted, supported at the northern end by the Trekroner
battery. This, substantially agreeing with Mr. Vansittart's
report, and the fact that the Danes had removed all the
buoys from the two difficult channels about the shoal
known as the Middle Ground, seems to have reawakened
Parker's apprehensions. Nelson, however, unshaken in his
confidence, announced that with ten ships of the line he
would account for the enemy. With these he would pass
through the northern channel to the main attack against
the southern flank, whilst the remainder of the fleet supported him by an attack upon the northern end.

Parker, pronouncing the enterprise a piece of Quixot-
ism, was nevertheless overborne by his masterful second-
in-command, and gave him twelve ships for the enterprise.
It was fortunate that he thus increased the number Nelson
had requested, for in the advance, which was made on the
2nd April, one of the ships was entirely out of the action
and two others partially so as a result of going aground.

When the moment came to go forward and execute the
plan which Nelson had worked out in such detail that the
station of each ship was predetermined, he was held up by
the indecision of the pilots.

"I experienced in the Sound," he wrote, "the misery of having the honour of our country entrusted to pilots who had no other thought than to keep the ship clear of danger and their own silly heads clear of shot."

When eventually one of the masters of the fleet offered to lead the line, the grounding of those three ships, one of which was the *Agamemnon,* entailed an instant change of the plan so meticulously prepared. It was a moment of overwhelming anxiety for the daring commander who had undertaken this responsibility in the face of all opposition. His fresh dispositions made, there was end of manœuvring. It became, in Nelson's own words, a matter of downright fighting.

Parker, some four miles off, watching with anxiety an engagement to which he had been overpersuaded, fancied his misgivings justified when he perceived the Danish resistance to be fiercer than had been represented to him as likely. He made the signal to break off the action.

Nelson was pacing the deck of the *Elephant,* then hotly engaged with the Danish flagship, the *Danneborg,* when the signal lieutenant reported to him that signal 39 was made, asking whether he should repeat it, which meant passing on the order to the fleet.

"No," said Nelson shortly. "Acknowledge it."

Resuming his walk he shook his fin, as was said of him when he moved the stump of his amputated arm, always a sign of agitation. He grumbled whilst doing so: "Leave off action! Now damn me if I do!" Then he paused and put the telescope to his blind eye. "I really do not see the signal." He tucked the telescope under his arm again. "Damn the signal! Keep mine for 'closer battle' flying. Nail mine to the mast!"

And so the line remained unbroken at a time when

withdrawal would have lost everything, when tenacity alone might bring, and, indeed, already promised, victory.

An hour later the Danish fire began to slacken. The Danish flagship was in flames, and several others, shattered and helpless, had struck their colours. But the British, too, were feeling the strain by now and beginning to stagger under it, when Nelson perceived a condition of things that afforded him the opportunity of bringing the action to a close. The ships that had struck were his lawful prizes of war. But attempts to take possession of them were frustrated by the shore batteries, which fired across them, and whose fire could be returned only in the same way. So that the vessels which had surrendered were in the terrible position of being under a cross-fire.

Nelson sent a flag of truce ashore with a message for the Crown Prince to the effect that, if the firing from the batteries was continued, he would have no recourse but to set fire to the surrendered prizes without power of saving their survivors. This, from humanity, he hoped that the Danes would not constrain him to do.

It had the desired effect. The Crown Prince, acknowledging that declaration of checkmate, sent orders to the batteries to cease firing, and despatched his aide-de-camp to the *London*.

Nelson at once set about withdrawing his ships, which had suffered so severely that but for his address in handling the situation he might have been unable to grasp the victory which he had won.

The truce was extended from day to day until the 9th April, both sides meanwhile preparing to resume hostilities in the event of a breakdown of negotiations. These in the main were being conducted ashore by Nelson himself with the Crown Prince. The extraordinarily advantageous terms which he obtained revealed him to be as skilful in diplomacy as he was formidable at sea.

"Your lordship's whole conduct, from your first appointment to this hour," wrote Lord Saint Vincent, "is the subject of our constant admiration. It does not become me to make comparisons: all agree there is but one Nelson."

* * * *

Whilst less spectacular in itself than the Battle of the Nile, the victory of Copenhagen was probably greater in itself, and as great in its consequences to the security of Britain. It was fought against heavier odds and under circumstances of greater difficulty, increased for Nelson by the manner in which he was trammelled and opposed by an incompetent superior.

Sir Hyde Parker's conduct had not escaped notice at home. Other matters apart, there were against him two grave grounds of censure: the fact that he had not himself led the attacking squadron, and the signal of recall.

In a letter to Lady Hamilton, Nelson had written:

> How they will manage about Sir Hyde I cannot guess . . . they may make him Lord Copenhagen if they please, it will not offend me.

On the 5th May came orders relieving Parker of his command and entrusting it to Nelson.

That his old friend Troubridge, now a lord of the Admiralty, should write to congratulate him on his promotion, led to the outburst: "Does he take me for a greater fool than I am?"

A man of his proven calibre had been sent out upon a great and difficult enterprise as second-in-command to an incompetent; and now, when all was done, and done by him almost in despite of that superior, he was given a task for which any officer was competent. He could not refuse it; but he could and did request to be relieved.

That relief came a month later, after Nelson, by an admirable combination of firmness and tact, had scored yet another victory in the valuable, friendly concessions he obtained for England from the Emperor Alexander, who by now had succeeded his murdered father—the mad Paul—on the throne of Russia.

From Colonel William Stewart, who sailed with Nelson on the Baltic expedition, and who has left us a very clear account of it, we have the following vivid picture of Nelson's daily life in Russian waters:

> His hour of rising was four or five o'clock, and of going to rest about ten; breakfast was never later than six, and generally nearer to five o'clock. A midshipman or two were always of the party; and I have known him send during the middle watch to invite the little fellows to breakfast with him when relieved. At table with them he would enter into their boyish jokes, and be the most youthful of the party. At dinner he invariably had every officer of the ship in their turn, and was both a polite and hospitable host. The whole ordinary business of the fleet was invariably despatched, as it had been by Earl Saint Vincent, before eight o'clock. The great command of time which Lord Nelson thus gave himself, and the alertness which this example imparted throughout the fleet, can only be understood by those who witnessed it or those who know the value of early hours. . . .

*   *   *   *

With dreams of retirement and rest, Nelson came home to a country thrilled with gratitude and admiration for his valour and his genius, to find that the need for his services was still urgent.

Across the Channel Bonaparte was preparing for the invasion of England, and a disquieted nation could be pacified only by the knowledge that Nelson had command of the coast defences, just as Bonaparte might be given pause only by the same knowledge. Such by now was the magic of his name and of his renown for invincibility.

And whilst so invoking his ægis on the one hand, on the other, for the great services by which England had so enormously profited and by which it had been so gloriously magnified in the eyes of Europe, the administrators of a grateful country could do no more than raise him to the rank of a Viscount. The wonder is that so as to drive the irony well home they did not point out to him again that this was a greater honour than had ever been conferred upon a second-in-command. No pecuniary reward was voted to him; so that Nelson, by no means a wealthy man, was actually out of pocket on the Baltic campaign. No medals were issued for Copenhagen. The feelings of the incompetent Parker had to be spared. And the City of London, usually so punctilious in these matters, forgot to thank Nelson, a matter for which he took an opportunity later, for the sake of those who had fought beside him, to rebuke the Lord Mayor.

* * * *

Two raids he directed upon Boulogne during that time when he was in charge of the coast defences. The first was in the nature of a reconnaissance, conducted in person. In the course of it he did some small material damage and considerable moral damage, by demonstrating to the French that their flotilla could not come out of port without grave risk. The second raid, on a more ambitious scale, in which Nelson did not personally take part, was repulsed.

After this the Peace of Amiens, the preliminaries of which were settled in October 1801, put an end to hostilities, and Nelson was able at last to seek a spell of peace in the place at Merton, which Lady Hamilton, commissioned to act for him, had lately acquired on his behalf. There Sir William and his lady were installed, and upon the owner's insistence her ladyship managed the affairs of the household for him. There, with them, he certainly seems to have spent some months of peace and quiet such as his chequered, active life had scarcely known before. There he received the welcomed visits of such friends as the gallant Lieutenant Layman, who had lately been in the Baltic with him, of Alexander Ball and Samuel Hood, both of whom had been with him at the Nile, of Lord Minto and of others.

There is a letter from Lord Minto which gives clearly the melancholy impressions which that household must have made upon any true friend of Nelson's. The place was stamped with the vulgar vainglory of the woman who presided over it, so much of which may be responsible for contemporary imputations of a rather childish vanity to Nelson. An expression of his to Lady Hamilton that is freely quoted—"Brave Emma! Good Emma! If there were more Emmas there would be more Nelsons"—is the ejaculation of a coxcomb. It has no better authority than Lady Hamilton's word after his death, and may confidently be pronounced as false as we know to be false the scene in which she places it: a scene in which she assigns herself the heroic part of supplying to this man, whose soul was a flame of self-denying zeal and duty, the necessary stimulus to take up arms for his country in the hour of need. Of this the evidence that flatly contradicts her is overwhelming.

Notwithstanding all this, the indignation and regrets of Lord Minto and of others who truly loved Nelson were wasted. Nelson had draped this lay-figure in the brilliant fabrics of his own ideals, until he could perceive none of its fundamental tawdriness; and in his worship of her he found a happiness and an inspiration which only such an emotion can bring a man. The evidence is clear and abundant. Only because her vulgarity diminished a man of his rare greatness need we deplore that the mantle of idealism in which he clothed her should not have fallen upon shoulders that could have worn it with a dignity, grace, and reticence worthy of its weaver. Thus he must have escaped the detractions of those who are connoisseurs only of mean things. The nature of no man of any consequence is simple. And the greater the man, the greater the complexities and contrasts which his nature offers. There is probably no better guide to Nelson's nature than Layman's assertions that he was little in little things, but by far the greatest man in great things that ever Layman had seen; and Layman had seen him petulant in trifles, and magnificently collected amid dangers that would have prostrated a common mind.

Faults in her ladyship to which the fond eyes of Nelson were blind became only too apparent to Sir William. The peace which he desired in his old age and the liberty quietly to amuse himself in his own fashion were denied him by her boisterousness. His protests led to acrimonious discussions which embittered him, so that in a long letter that he wrote to her occur the words: "If really one cannot live comfortably together, a wise and well-concerted separation is preferable." He was reluctant, however, to take this step, since, as he said, not having much longer to live, it was hardly worth while to make a change, and also because any such change would be distressing to their best friend, Lord Nelson. He begs her, therefore, for God's sake, that they may bear and forbear. In the same letter he qualifies a complaint of all her attention being given to Lord Nelson with the assertion: "I well know the purity of Lord Nelson's friendship for Emma and me."

Sir William, however, was approaching the end of all vexations. He died very peacefully, in April of 1803, in the arms of Emma and Lord Nelson.

His death left Lady Hamilton with a life-rent of eight hundred pounds a year. His pension of twelve hundred pounds a year died with him. But for this she was compensated by Nelson, who settled a like sum upon her for life.

*   *   *   *

Within a month of Sir William's death, war flamed forth again, and Nelson was appointed to command the Mediterranean Fleet. He hoisted his flag on the *Victory*, a three-decker of one hundred guns, and sailed to his station before Toulon, as in 1798. Now, as then, the situation was much the same. It was not known against what point the French fleet would be launched when it came forth.

Actually, the aim was, more strongly than ever before, the invasion of England. To render it possible, Bonaparte perceived that he must hold the seas, and for this the concentration of all the naval strength of France would be required. To realize it, his fleets were to sail from their various harbours and assemble in the West Indies, whence in their overwhelming total they should return to Europe and dominate the Channel.

In their ignorance of this, the British could but stand

on guard before Brest, Toulon, Rochefort, and Ferrol, and wait for the French fleets to come forth.

For Nelson were to be repeated all the anxieties of the hunt of 1798, save that now he was to pursue the enemy all the way to the West Indies and back without, this time, bringing him to battle.

Before that long chase, however, he was to know the only fear that seems ever to have touched him: the fear that his quarry had eluded him. Word was brought him by his frigates that the Toulon fleet under La Touche Tréville had come out. The frigates had lost track of it in the night. But at least they could report the direction in which the French were sailing when last seen. As a result Nelson was scouring the seas for ten days about the coast of Sicily, then across to Egypt, and thence to Malta, where at last, to his relief, he learnt that severely buffeted by a gale Tréville had put back into Toulon.

"These gentlemen," said he, "are not accustomed to a Gulf of Lyons gale, which we have buffeted for twenty-one months, and not carried away a spar."

The watch was resumed, and all through the remainder of that year 1803 maintained with muscles taut for the spring. But Tréville could be neither coaxed nor annoyed into coming forth.

In the spring of 1804 the French Admiral began to venture out of the harbour's mouth, so as to exercise small divisions of his fleet. Nelson commented: "My friend Monsieur La Touche sometimes plays bo-peep in and out of Toulon, like a mouse at the edge of her hole." And again: "Yesterday a rear-admiral and seven sail including frigates put their nose outside the harbour. If they go on playing this game, some day we shall lay salt upon their tails, and so end the campaign."

In June, Nelson mentioned in a letter that "Monsieur La Touche came out with eight sail of the line and six frigates, cut a caper off Sepet, and went in again. I brought-to for his attack, although I did not believe that anything was meant serious, but merely a gasconade."

A little later he read in a copy of the *Moniteur*, Tréville's version of the affair, in which the French Admiral boasted that the British fleet had fled before him. To this Nelson wrote: "If my character is not established by this time for not being apt to run away, it is not worth my time to attempt to put the world right." And further: "You will have seen Monsieur La Touche's letter of how he chased me and how I ran. I keep it; and, by God, if I take him, he shall eat it."

Tréville, however, died before that dish could be set before him, and was succeeded by Pierre Silvestre Villeneuve, who at the Nile had commanded the *Guillaume Tell*, one of the three ships of Brueys' fleet that escaped capture.

* * * *

By the time Villeneuve was in command, Spain had been dragged into the war at the heels of France. This brought a prospect of the capture of rich galleons that should compensate the officers of the Mediterranean Fleet for the long, arduous, and trying vigil which they had so faithfully kept now for fifteen months.

Whilst the threat of war was still unfulfilled, Nelson had written: "I hope war with Spain may be avoided. I want not riches at such a dreadful price."

Now, however, that war was declared, the Government elected to send out a small squadron of five ships to blockade Cadiz, and the command of this was given to that

Sir John Orde who after Saint Vincent had so bitterly expressed his resentment that his junior, Nelson, should have been preferred to himself to command the squadron which ultimately fought the Battle of the Nile. The appointment of this senior officer meant reducing Nelson's station, which until then had extended to Finisterre, and depriving him of that fruitful source of prizes.

He was justifiably indignant. "I have learnt," he writes, "not to be surprised at anything; but the sending of an officer to such a point, to take, if it is a Spanish war, the whole harvest, after all my trials (God knows unprofitable enough, for I am a much poorer man than when we started), seems a little hard." And again: "He is sent off Cadiz to reap the golden harvest. I fancied—but, nay, it must have been a dream, an idle dream—yet, I confess it, I did fancy that I had done my country service; and thus they use me! And under what circumstances, and with what pointed aggravation!" Considering what his record had been, there was scarcely the need for him to go on to protest, as he does, that his indignation was for the "brave band of brothers" with him rather than for himself.

Apart from this, Sir John Orde, abusing his seniority, troubled and hampered Nelson by seizing some of the frigates he sent out of the Straits, and despatching them upon errands other than those with which they were charged. So serious did this become that to get despatches home, Nelson was constrained to instruct the commander of a frigate to go wide of Orde's squadron and by night, so as to get past him without interference.

Circumstances, however, were to avenge him for these vexations.

On the 4th April Nelson received definite news that

Villeneuve had put to sea with eleven ships of the line, seven frigates, and two brigs, steering for the coast of Africa. Whilst he was still making sure that the French had not gone down the Mediterranean, word came that they had been sighted off Gibraltar. Beating up against westerly winds, and these so foul that he could not pass the Straits until the 5th May, Nelson confidently looked for news there from Sir John Orde of the direction the enemy had taken. But Sir John Orde, that man of pretensions, had retired upon Brest before the approach of Villeneuve, and this without taking the elementary measure of detaching frigates to observe the French course. For this culpable omission, of such a stupidity that it is difficult to suppose it free from malice, Sir John Orde fully deserved the censure under which he fell, even if he did not deserve the outcry against him in England for having avoided battle. He applied to be relieved from duty, urging a number of grievances, and his application was immediately granted.

Sir John had missed the chance of exhibiting the worth of that seniority which he so jealously asserted against Nelson. Whilst it cannot be denied that prudence justified his withdrawal of his six ships before Villeneuve's eleven, it was not the sort of prudence that would have restrained Nelson. This we realize when we see Nelson presently, with eleven ships of the line, eagerly in pursuit of Villeneuve's force when it had been increased to twenty ships and was believed by the pursuer to have been increased to twenty-two. These were longer odds than those which Sir John had declined. But Nelson, without counting odds, was straining every nerve to overtake the Frenchman, vowing that if they met "we won't part without a battle."

We touch here upon that main factor of Nelson's success to which allusion has been made. When we hear him declaring, as he repeatedly declared at about this period, that "by the time the enemy has beaten our fleet soundly, they will do no harm this year," we understand the heroic devotion which rendered him so formidable.

* * * *

On fairly definite information that Villeneuve, joined by the Spanish Admiral Gravina with six ships of the line from Cadiz, had sailed for the West Indies, Nelson set out to follow.

At Barbados, on the 4th June, General Brereton, commanding the troops at Santa Lucia, sent him word that the allied fleet had passed there on the 29th May, steering south. Information so precise overbore his own sound assumption that Martinique would be the enemy rallying-point. He pushed on for Trinidad, to find that nothing had been seen of his quarry. On the 9th June came positive information that eighteen ships of the line had passed Dominica on the 6th, and he enraged to think that but for the inaccurate information by which he had been misled, he must have overtaken them and brought them to battle.

He need not, however, have taken the matter so deeply to heart, for his very presence had done all that was immediately necessary. The magic of his name had sufficed to protect the British West Indian possessions and to disorganize the plans of Bonaparte. For despite his superior numbers, again increased by a further two ships which had joined him in these waters, and without awaiting the expiry of the term he was instructed to remain there,

Villeneuve at once set sail for Europe. Informed of this, Nelson went raging after him.

By the 18th July the British were once more off Cape Spartel without having sighted the quarry. Here Nelson found his old friend Collingwood with six ships, replacing Orde in the blockade of Cadiz.

"Oh, General Brereton! General Brereton! Damn General Brereton!" is the outcry in Nelson's letters.

Yet he had almost outsailed Villeneuve. But going south of the Azores, so as most speedily to reach the Mediterranean, he had missed the French who had gone north and were heading for Ferrol. There on the 22nd Villeneuve came up with a British fleet of fifteen ships under Sir Robert Calder. There was an inconclusive action in which Sir Robert contented himself with the capture of two Spanish vessels, but made no attempt to follow the French, who safely reached the port of Vigo.

In England, where the fears of invasion and concern for the safety of British merchant shipping had now become acute, the outcry against Calder was so loud and vehement that he was presently constrained, for his honour's sake, to ask for an inquiry.

Meanwhile, however, Nelson had dropped anchor at Gibraltar, to revictual and re-equip, and there he went ashore for the first time in thirteen months.

This marks the close of an achievement admirably summed up by Hugh Elliott, now British Ambassador at Naples:

> After an unremitting cruise of two long years in the stormy Gulf of Lyons, to have proceeded, without going into port, to Alexandria, from Alexandria to the West Indies, from the West Indies back again to Gibraltar; to have kept your ships afloat, your rigging standing, and your crews in

health and spirits—is an effort such as was never realized in former times, nor, I doubt, will ever again be repeated by any other admiral. You have protected us for two long years, and you have saved the West Indies by only a few days.

* * * *

Sailing north, Nelson reached on the 1st August the Channel Fleet off Ushant, under the command of Cornwallis, by whom he was authorized to proceed to England, so that he might enjoy at last a leave which had been accorded to him before the pursuit of Villeneuve began.

On the 16th August the *Victory* dropped anchor at Portsmouth, and at once the Admiral had the first of the affecting and almost overpowering evidences of the place he had won in England's heart. As soon as it was known who came, the people of Portsmouth flocked in crowds to welcome him, and it was to the roar of their cheering that he was pulled ashore in his barge.

As at Portsmouth, so elsewhere. In London he could not show himself without being mobbed by adoring crowds. The wonder, admiration, love, and respect which his life deserved were expressed on every opportunity by every class of the population.

Three weeks at Merton with Emma and the child Horatia, and the company of some old friends and members of his family, was all that his country could spare him to himself. And not even all of this; for consultations at the Admiralty with Lord Barham, now the First Lord, were frequent. The State lay at last, like the people, under a full appreciation of his immeasurable worth, and at the Admiralty in those days he went rather to instruct than to receive instructions. Organization was left to him; he was even invited to choose the officers he would have to serve under him, to which, with characteristic generosity, he made answer that where excellence was so uniform there could be no choosing. Let the First Lord make the appointments.

He had expected to remain at Merton until October. But the needs of his country became too pressing to permit it.

Prompt to the call of duty, he went forth again on Friday the 13th September of that year 1805. A premonition that this parting was to be final seems to have brought a note of anguish into it. Lady Hamilton—from the picture Lord Minto gives us—was prostrated with grief. For two days she had wept and been near to swooning. Of Nelson's feelings on his departure from a place so dear to him, which he was never to see again, let the words from his diary speak

> At half-past ten drove from dear dear Merton, where I left all which I hold dear in this world, to go to serve my King and Country. May the great God whom I adore enable me to fulfil the expectations of my Country; and if it is His good pleasure that I should return, my thanks will never cease being offered up to the Throne of His Mercy. If it is His good Providence to cut short my days upon earth, I bow with the greatest submission, relying that he will protect those so dear to me, that I may leave behind. His will be done. Amen, Amen, Amen.

Next morning he was at Portsmouth, surrounded again by crowds, less boisterous, but no less fervent, than those which had welcomed him a few weeks ago. A little subdued now by anxiety natural to the love he had inspired, they pressed upon him to behold that frail man's resolute, melancholy face. Some wept, we are told, and others knelt as he passed, to call down blessings upon his head.

He took his seat in the barge with Captain Hardy, and was pulled away to his ship.

* * * *

On the 28th September, the eve of his forty-seventh birthday, the *Victory* reached the fleet of twenty-nine ships of the line under Collingwood, before Cadiz. Nelson had ordered beforehand that there should be no salutes. Fully conscious by now of the effect of his name, he was anxious above all that Villeneuve should be supplied with no deterrent to his coming forth.

But whilst no guns might be fired, a welcome so affectingly enthusiastic awaited Nelson from the officers of the fleet that he speaks of it as one of the sweetest sensations of his life.

It was at this very first meeting with them that he submitted the plan of battle which he had worked out, a design which he calls "the Nelson Touch," a plan which he afterwards supplemented by the detailed memorandum he issued on the 9th October.

* * * *

Instances of generosity of every kind are to be culled from the records of his career; but there is probably none that for gracious knightliness excels his conduct at this time towards Sir Robert Calder, one of the few men who had displayed hostility towards him since the day when, as Captain of the Fleet, he had drawn attention to Nelson's glorious disobedience at Saint Vincent, and had been snubbed for his pains.

Nelson came charged by the First Lord with the disagreeable task of conveying to Calder the Government's censure for his conduct of the July action against Villeneuve. Calder's inevitable answer was to ask for the court of inquiry, which in any case must have been ordered in view of public feeling.

Nelson wrote: "He is in adversity, and if he ever has been my enemy, he now feels the pang of it, and finds me one of his best friends." And again: "I have given him advice as to my dearest friend." That this magnanimity was not merely of words was proved when he was confronted by Calder's distress at the necessity of quitting his flagship under charges before the fleet. Considering Nelson's urgent needs for the approaching conflict, he was not in a position to part with a single ship. Yet so that he might spare humiliation to a man whom he had reason to believe had been his enemy, he allowed him to go home in his ninety-gun flagship. Thereby Nelson rendered himself liable to the just censure of the Admiralty. It was an action as indefensible as it was knightly, noble, and characteristic.

* * * *

The main body of the British fleet took up its station fifty miles west of Cadiz. A squadron of frigates was pushed forward close to the harbour, and between the two, so as to maintain communications, stood an advanced squadron of seventy-fours.

Thus Nelson waited. That the enemy must come forth was beyond doubt. So as to expedite matters, the British did what they could by tightening the blockade, rendering intolerable the strain upon Cadiz of maintaining such a body of men. What eventually brought them out, however, was the news that reached Villeneuve that another admiral was being sent by Bonaparte to supersede him.

* * * *

"The enemy are coming out of port."

So ran the signal from masthead to masthead on the morning of the 19th October.

So as to cut Villeneuve off from the Mediterranean, Nelson at once moved the fleet south-east, to station it off Cape Trafalgar, where it commanded the entrance to the Straits, and there the following daybreak was to find it.

Having given the order, he sat down to write his last letter to Lady Hamilton.

> My dearest beloved Emma, the dear friend of my bosom. The signal has been made that the enemy's combined fleet are coming out of Port. We have very little wind, so that I have no hopes of seeing them before to-morrow. May the God of Battles crown my endeavours with success; at all events I will take care that my name shall ever be most dear to you and Horatia, both of whom I love as much as my own life. And as my last writing before the battle will be to you, so I hope in God that I shall live to finish my letter after the battle. May Heaven bless you, prays your
>
> Nelson and Bronte.

He wrote also to Horatia:

> My dearest Angel, I was made happy by the pleasure of receiving your letter of September 19th, and I rejoice to hear that you are so very good a girl and love my dear Lady Hamilton, who most dearly loves you. Give her a kiss for me. The combined fleets of the enemy are now reported to be coming out of Cadiz; and therefore I answer your letter my dearest Horatia, to mark to you that you are ever uppermost in my thoughts. I shall be sure of your prayers for my safety, conquest, and speedy return to dear Merton and our dearest good Lady Hamilton. Be a good girl, mind what Miss Connor says to you. Receive, my dearest Horatia, the affectionate parental blessing of your Father,
>
> Nelson and Bronte.

As his letter to Lady Hamilton assumed would be the

case, the lack of wind postponed engagement. Villeneuve,
indeed, suspended his sallying movement until the morrow, when, with a fresh south-westerly wind, which
brought heavy rain, he came boldly forth.

The allied fleets consisted of four three-deckers of one
hundred to one hundred and thirty guns, all Spanish, including the *Santisima Trinidad,* still the largest vessel
afloat, six eighty-gun ships, twenty-two seventy-fours, and
one sixty-four. The whole was commanded by Villeneuve
as Commander-in-Chief, with the Spanish Admiral Gravina
subservient to him. There were in addition four junior
admirals in the fleet, two French and two Spanish.

Against this host Nelson went into action with seven
three-deckers of ninety-eight to a hundred guns, one
eighty-gun ship, sixteen seventy-fours, and three sixty-
fours.

In the afternoon of the 20th, the wind shifted west-
north-west, and the weather cleared. The fleets moved
about ten miles apart, out of sight of each other, the
frigates keeping touch. At midnight the wind fell to a
light westerly breeze, and was so to continue throughout
the 21st, but with a heavy swell from the west, announcing a gathering storm.

At dawn on the 21st the fleets, now first in view of each
other, were moving along parallel lines, the British heading north, the allies south.

Soon after daybreak Nelson was on deck, wearing his
Admiral's frock on the left breast of which sparkled the
stars of four different orders. Considering how conspicuous
these must make him to sharpshooters in the enemy's crosstrees when action should be joined, it was proposed that
Beatty, the surgeon of the *Victory,* should warn him against
this display. Circumstances, however, conspired to prevent

the utterance of a warning it was not likely would have been heeded.

Shortly after Nelson's appearance on deck, Captain Henry Blackwood of the frigate *Euryalus,* who had done valuable service in the last two days, came on board, and as a personal friend of Nelson's he was required together with Captain Hardy to witness a codicil which the Admiral had added to his will. In this, having enumerated the main services rendered to his knowledge, as he states, to king and country, by Emma Hamilton in Naples, he proceeds:

> Could I have rewarded these services I would not now call upon my country; but as that has not been in my power, I leave Emma Hamilton, therefore, a legacy to my King and country, that they will give her an ample provision to maintain her rank in life.
>
> I also leave to the beneficence of my country my adopted daughter Horatia Nelson Thompson, and I desire she will use in future the name of Nelson only.
>
> These are the only favours I ask of my King and country at this moment when I am going to fight their battle.

After that was done, Nelson kept Blackwood on board until they were under fire, so that the Captain might receive the Admiral's latest instructions for the conduct of the frigates, all of which were placed under his command.

At 7 A.M. Nelson made the signal "Prepare for Battle," following it a few minutes later with the signal "Bear up." At once the *Victory's* course was set for the enemy, leading a column of twelve ships. They went under full sail, even to studding sails spread at the sides, to catch the scanty breeze. A mile away, to the south, Collingwood in the *Royal Sovereign* took the lead of the other division.

Thus, in two columns, they advanced rectangularly upon the allies who sailed in a line of battle five miles long.

This form of attack was a departure, entailed by the respective stations of the two fleets and the conditions of wind, from the plan which Nelson had propounded.

Collingwood's division was aimed at the enemy's southern flank. Nelson steered to break the line north of the centre, so that the main part of the enemy's van would be temporarily cut off and left disengaged whilst a preponderance of force was thrown upon the points attacked, as Nelson's plan provided.

Perceiving this disposition of the British, and so that he might have Cadiz under his lee, Villeneuve signalled his fleet to wear together. As a result of this manœuvre, what had been the enemy rear, now became the van, and Gravina's ship, which had been leading the line, now became the rearmost.

Whilst the enemy, towards whom they were creeping with a feeble one-and-a-half-knot breeze, was still some three miles distant, Nelson left the quarter-deck, and went alone to his cabin. A little later the signal lieutenant, going to seek him, found him on his knees, writing. He was making in his diary the last entry, and this was in the form of a prayer:

> May the Great God, whom I worship, grant to my Country, and for the benefit of Europe in general, a great and glorious victory; and may no misconduct in anyone tarnish it; and may humanity after victory be the predominant feature in the British fleet. For myself, individually, I commit my life to Him who made me, and may His blessing light upon my endeavours for serving my country faithfully. To Him I resign myself and the just cause which is entrusted to me to defend. Amen. Amen. Amen.

When he returned to the quarter-deck, Blackwood would have had Nelson transfer his flag to the *Euryalus,* directing thence the operations. When Nelson would not do this, and as they were bearing down upon the enemy, he ventured to urge that one or two ships should precede the *Victory,* which was leading one of the two columns of attack. Nelson appeared to assent; but when the *Temeraire* came creeping alongside, he hailed her in his rather high-pitched, slightly nasal voice:

"I'll thank you, Captain Harvey, to keep to your proper station, which is astern of the *Victory.*"

After that, at a little before twelve o'clock, when they were almost within range, Nelson turned to Blackwood: "I will now amuse the fleet with a signal." He called up the signal officer, Lieutenant Pasco, and directed him to telegraph to the fleet: "Nelson confides that every man will do his duty." He urged him to make haste, since he had another signal for him.

In view of this, Pasco ventured to observe that the words "Nelson" and "Confides" were not in the code, and would have to be spelled out, which would take time. He suggested substituting the words "England" and "Expects."

"That will do, Pasco. Make it directly."

A ringing cheer rose from the British ships in acknowledgment of the signal. As it died down, the first gun of the battle spoke: fired by the *Fouguex* at the *Royal Sovereign.* For ten minutes, without a shot in answer, the *Royal Sovereign* stood on under fire for the point at which Collingwood meant to break the enemy line. When he reached it, at a few minutes after noon, the column led by the *Victory* was still a mile and a half from her objective.

Having ordered the signal for "Close Action" to be made, Nelson turned to Blackwood, who was still with him. "Now I can do no more. We must trust to the Great Disposer of all events and to the justice of our cause.

I thank God for this great opportunity of doing my duty."

It would be ten minutes later when Villeneuve's flagship, the *Bucentaure*, fired her first shot; it was followed by a second, and then by a third which passed over the *Victory*. Upon this, Nelson dismissed Blackwood to his frigate with his final orders. Blackwood took his hand, and expressed the hope that on his return he would find his lordship well and in possession of twenty prizes.

"God bless you, Blackwood," he was answered. "I shall never speak to you again."

He voiced that sense of doom which had been upon him ever since leaving Merton, a month ago. It had received other expressions, not all of them as light as that uttered at his London upholsterers where he stored the coffin Hallowell had given him, suggesting that he would probably require it on his return.

Blackwood went down the side as the fire was growing hotter. From that moment the *Victory* became ever increasingly a target for some seven or eight ships about the *Bucentaure*. It was endured with the same fortitude and the same reserving of fire that had been shown by Collingwood. But the ordeal was a much longer one. For forty minutes, at an ever-diminishing speed, in a measure as her sails were shot away and torn, she crawled forward in purposeful silence.

Nelson's secretary was killed by a round shot in Nelson's sight. At a quarter-mile from the *Bucentaure*, the *Victory's* mizzen topmast was shot away, and the hurricane of lead that swept her deck shattered the wheel, so that thereafter she had to be steered from below. When eight of the marines drawn up on the poop were killed by a single shot, Nelson ordered the survivors to disperse about the deck. Another shot across the quarter-deck passed between Nelson and Hardy, striking the fore-brace bitts, a splinter of which bruised Hardy's foot. It drew from Nelson the remark: "This is too warm work, Hardy, to last long."

They had fifty casualties by then, and still they had not fired a shot. Not until one o'clock when the bows of the *Victory* crossed under the stern of the *Bucentaure,* so close that the projecting yardarms scraped the enemy's rigging, did Nelson's guns reply. Then at last, at point-blank range, as they bore on, one after another the double-shotted guns of the *Victory* tore through the timbers of the French flagship.

The effect was terrific. Twenty of the *Bucentaure's* guns were at once dismounted, and the loss by a single discharge was estimated at four hundred Frenchmen. Leaving her in that state to the ships that followed, the *Victory* put up her helm, and lay in the heavy smoke of battle along the port side of the *Rédoutable.* Locked in a death struggle, the two vessels drifted to eastward, and whilst the *Victory's* guns were rending the Frenchman's sides, the Frenchman was punishing the *Victory* above decks with musketry fire. She had several marksmen aloft, a practice deprecated by Nelson, as being merely murderous without any definite influence on the issue.

Whilst this was doing, Nelson and Hardy paced the quarter-deck to and fro together on the port side, which was farthest from the *Rédoutable.* They were turning at the usual point when Nelson abruptly swung half-round, and Hardy saw him sink to his knees, putting out his single hand to save himself. The arm giving way, he fell on his left side. Raising him in concern, Hardy voiced the hope that he was not badly hurt.

"They have done for me at last," was the answer. "My backbone is shot through."

A bullet from one of the sharpshooters in the crosstrees of the *Rédoutable* had struck him on the left epaulette.

With characteristic selfless thought even in that extremity, he covered his face and the decorations on his breast as they were carrying him below, so that the ship's company might not be dismayed by identifying him in such a moment.

Thus, for the second time in his career, at the height of an action which he had planned and launched, he was borne into a mephitic, lantern-lighted cockpit, crowded with the wounded and the dying.

To the surgeon who hastened to succour him, he said: "You can do nothing for me, Beatty. I have but a short time to live."

Examination confirmed the opinion. The bullet had pierced the lung, severing a large artery, and had passed through the spine to lodge in the muscles of the back. It was impossible to do more than attempt to mitigate his sufferings. The chaplain and the purser of the *Victory* between them raised the bed under him, so that he was in the semi-recumbent position in which he found most ease. Thus, whilst they fanned him and gave him the lemonade which his intolerable thirst constantly demanded, he remained alert to what was passing and to the sounds on deck.

The issue, which admitted of little doubt from the moment Nelson's plan of breaking the line and enveloping a part of it had been carried into effect, was decided within the hour that followed upon his being shot down.

As he lay there in the depths of the lurching ship, with

the din of battle raging overhead, the roar of guns and occasional bursts of cheering, he asked for Hardy. It was some time before the Captain could quit the quarter-deck, where, virtually as commander of the fleet, he watched the coming into action of the ships for which the leading four, the *Victory* and the *Temeraire,* the *Royal Sovereign* and the *Belleisle,* acting as spearheads, had rent a way into the hostile flank. Entering through the breach made, those following ships gave a faithful fulfilment to the plan Nelson had conceived.

Hardy's absence began to fret the dying man. He feared that Hardy might be dead, and became more insistent in his demands for him. At long last, his captain and faithful friend, who had been with him ever since Saint Vincent, was bending over him, pressing his hand.

"How goes the battle, Hardy? How goes the day with us?"

"Very well, my lord," Hardy could report. "Some twelve or fourteen of their ships have struck, the *Bucentaure* amongst them."

"I hope none of our ships have struck, Hardy."

"No, my lord. There is no fear of that."

"I am a dead man, Hardy. I am going fast. It will be all over soon. Come nearer to me. Pray let my dear Lady Hamilton have my hair and all other things belonging to me."

Hardy protested his hopes that there might yet be a chance of life.

"Oh, no. It is impossible. My back is shot through. Beatty will tell you so."

Duty recalled Hardy to the quarter-deck. He was absent for an hour, and in that hour what remained to do was done. When at about four o'clock he came back to the chief whose life was now slipping fast away, he came to report a complete victory and to congratulate the expiring genius that had organized it. How many ships were captured he could not say for certain, but they were not less than fourteen or fifteen.

"That is well," said Nelson. "But I bargained for twenty."

Then, remembering that heavy swell, the forerunner of a storm, and remembering that before the engagement it had caused him to make signal that the ships should anchor after the battle, so as to avoid the dangers of the lee shore, he exclaimed: "Anchor, Hardy! Anchor!"

Perhaps embarrassed, Hardy answered that he supposed Admiral Collingwood would now assume command.

"Not while I live, I hope, Hardy." And again the injunction: "Do you anchor, Hardy."

"Shall we make the signal, sir?"

"Yes. For if I live I'll anchor."

Thus, still with the thought of duty in his mind, he faced his imminent end. Had that last injunction of his prescience been heeded, a deal of loss might have been avoided that was incurred through neglect of it.

Then he reverted to thoughts of himself. "Don't throw me overboard, Hardy. You know what to do." And upon this followed his last request to his faithful captain. "Take care of my dear Lady Hamilton, Hardy. Take care of poor Lady Hamilton. Kiss me, Hardy."

The Captain knelt and kissed his cheek.

"Now I am satisfied. Thank God, I have done my duty."

Hardy stood silently beside him for a moment, then knelt again, and kissed his brow.

"Who is that?" he asked.

"It is Hardy."

"God bless you, Hardy," was the Admiral's farewell, and so Hardy left him, to return on deck.

After that his breathing became difficult, and his voice grew faint. He begged the chaplain that it be remembered he left Lady Hamilton and his daughter Horatia as a legacy to his country.

A quarter of an hour after Hardy left him, he uttered his last audible words: "God and my country."

The surgeon found his pulse gone. But upon laying his hand on his forehead, Nelson opened his eyes, in only one of which there was sight, looked up, and then closed them for the last time.

It was half-past four. The battle was over, the victory complete. The shots being fired as he expired were the last. Of the great fleet of thirty-three sail upon which the British had borne down that day, eleven survived to retreat with Gravina upon Cadiz, and four escaped to sea.

*   *   *   *

When the news of that great victory, which finally frustrated Bonaparte's plans for the invasion of England, came at once to uplift English hearts in thankfulness and cast them down in sorrow, Lord Minto wrote:

> Great and important as the victory is, it is bought too dearly even for our interest by the death of Nelson . . . the navy is certainly full of the bravest men, but . . . brave as they all are, there was a sort of heroic cast about Nelson that I never saw in any other man and which seems wanting to the achievement of impossible things which became easy to him, and on which the maintenance of our superiority at sea seems to depend against the growing navy of the enemy.

The full truth, which Lord Minto missed here, but

which time was to reveal, was that when Nelson died he left a task fully accomplished. By heroic labours upon which Trafalgar set the crown he had definitely established British supremacy upon the seas; the inspiration of his glorious name was to maintain it.

The administrators of a grateful nation, whose reward of Nelson's inestimable services had been marked in his lifetime by a shabbiness that left him (in view of the claims upon him) almost pressed at times for money, showered wealth and honours lavishly at last, after his death, upon relatives of his who had done nothing to deserve them.

The governing impulse of this honourable attempt to discharge a debt should naturally be to discharge it in the manner in which the dead hero would wish it to be discharged. Yet the plain indication in the codicil of his will of wishes that were sacred—"the only favours that I ask of my King and country at this moment when I am going to fight their battle"—was ignored. Not a farthing went to his only child.

This is amongst the things that are not to be understood.

VI
THE LADY-IN-CHIEF
FLORENCE NIGHTINGALE

VI

THE LADY-IN-CHIEF

SOME of Florence Nightingale's most ardent admirers in her own day compared her with Joan of Arc.

It is no detraction from the merit of either of those heroines to say that no parallel exists.

On the one hand, we have a peasant girl acting upon an instinctive impulse, driven and guided by an inner voice which assumes to her simple mind an objective character, taking up a task that properly belongs to the other sex.

On the other hand, we have a lady, delicately nurtured and carefully educated, pursuing a reasoned course in a province entirely feminine.

In common they possess a selfless devotion to a cause and to the service of an ideal, so unstinting that it is not to be daunted by any personal sacrifice. They have it also in common that each was under the necessity of overcoming at the outset barriers of prejudice and opposition before which souls less altruistic would have fainted, and that each, in the sphere of her activity, left behind her, as all heroes leave, an inspiration to posterity.

Of the particular prejudices which Miss Nightingale was called upon to face, class prejudice was the first. In seeking a channel for her innate impulse to devote herself to the service of mankind—as a full and practical manner of serving God—she was drawn towards that which directly makes for the relief of human affliction. In the care of the sick she beheld not only the field in which woman could be most fruitfully active, but a field which in her day was not being cultivated as it should be. The profession of nursing was in disrepute. Recruits to it were drawn from the least desirable classes. Uneducated and perforce untrained, since scarcely any facilities for training them existed, these women remained the hospital drudges they were fitted to be, slatterns notorious for drunkenness and unchastity.

Coming from the class which produced her, it is readily understood with what repugnance Miss Nightingale's family and the society in which it had its place should have viewed her ardent wish to take up a life of such associations. Dissuasions, even a mildly exerted parental authority, were employed to restrain her, to bring her to what in her circle was regarded as reason.

Of the society to which she belonged and the distractions which it offers, she was conscious, as are all those in whom resides the impulse to justify existence by productive activity, only of the futility. She was equipped by education to find in intellectual pursuits an outlet for her superabundant energies. She possessed a good command of French and German; she had been well-schooled, too, in Latin and Greek; she was widely read; she had a critical appreciation of music and of art; of her literary ability there is evidence in the lucidity of the many essays and pamphlets which she was to give the world on the subject so dear to her heart. It remained, however, that the vocation she had discovered in herself, and the hunger to fulfil it, precluded satisfaction in any other pursuit.

And so, in her twenties, at Lea Hurst in Derbyshire, at Embley in Hampshire, or in London during the season, she passes listless and uninterested from one to another of those idle functions which her social position imposed upon her. The bars of prejudice confined her eager spirit in a cage of uselessness, until at the age of thirty, overwhelmed by a sense of the sterility to which she seems irrevocably doomed, having no interest in the amiable emptiness of the life available to her, and being denied access to the life of service on which the eyes of her desire are set, she exclaims: "Oh, God! What is to become of me?"

*   *   *   *

Her family had sought to provide her with distractions from an attitude of mind which it regarded as morbid, and to arouse in her interests more natural to the station of life into which she had been born. Foreign travel had been prescribed.

Her close friends Mr. and Mrs. Bracebridge—a couple destined in the future to be very closely associated with her—were going to spend the winter of 1847 in Italy, and she was urged to accompany them.

Italy was the land of Miss Nightingale's birth. The name of Florence, which in honour of her, conscious or unconscious, has been borne by so many women since (it was formerly a masculine name), was bestowed upon her because it was in Florence that she first saw the light, in 1820. In this her parents pursued a fancy, already indulged in the case of her elder sister, who, born in Naples, had, in the same spirit, been named Parthenope.

She agreed to the proposal, and that winter of 1847–48 was spent with the Bracebridges in Rome. If her lively æsthetic perceptions found there much to delight her, from the glories of the Sistine Chapel to the antiquities of Imperial days, she discovered matters even more absorbing in the beneficent work of the Roman Catholic Sisterhoods.

And this lady—a Unitarian by birth, but by inclination of too deep and sincere a Christianity to be limited by sectarianism of any kind—went to dwell for ten days in the Convent of the Sacred Heart, at the Trinità dei Monti, so that at close quarters, and without distractions, she might study the organization of that sisterhood, devoted to education and to the care of orphanages.

She was well aware too—for it may have supplied much of her own inspiration—of the work being done by nuns in the care of the sick. Whilst in England female nursing was in the crude state that has been mentioned, in Latin countries a very different condition of things prevailed. Among the orders of women, many of them of birth and culture, who had dedicated themselves to the religious life, some sisterhoods there were which for centuries had chosen to express the love of God by which they were actuated, in the service of those among God's creatures who stood most in need of service. In these sisterhoods of pure, good women, protected by their vows, as by an armour, against the onslaughts of vice, trained in the arts of nursing, and possessing such expertness in it as was then available, Miss Nightingale beheld some fulfilment of her own ideal. The notion was vaguely stirring in her mind to create in England some organization akin to these upon secular lines.

Already in Germany something of the kind was being done. At Kaiserswerth, Theodor Fliedner, a Protestant minister, had established an Institute for Deaconesses, which, amongst other things, was a training-ground for nurses. Miss Nightingale had studied its reports, and whilst in that institute she might find a more immediate model for what she dreamed of doing in England, yet she did not consider herself dispensed by that study from giving in Italy a close attention to the original pattern of which Pastor Fliedner had made an adaptation.

In Italy, too, in the course of this sojourn which was meant to divert her mind from its prepossessions, Destiny, never to be cheated, wove its strands into the warp of her life, in the meeting with Sidney Herbert.

This generous, gifted, attractive son of the Earl of Pembroke, who already in 1845 had been Secretary at War in Peel's Cabinet, was now a man of thirty-eight. With his wife he, too, was wintering in Rome; and the friendship that existed between the Herberts and the Bracebridges soon brought within its ambit the graceful, sincere, and cultured Florence Nightingale.

She was now in her twenty-eighth year, tall, slender, elegant, and very straight, her hair of a rich brown, her complexion delicate; her grey eyes are described as pensive, yet ready to light into mirth, and her smile as of the sweetest and most winning. The charm of her personality had not permitted her to reach the age of eight-and-twenty without opportunities of fulfilling the desire of her mother's heart by marrying and finding in the administration of a home an employment for her energies. Her vocation, however, seems to have left her insensible to the lure of matrimony. Friendships with men she formed in plenty; deep, close and lasting friendships; and later in life, expressing herself upon this, she manifested a contemptuous impatience of those who can conceive of no attachment between a man and a woman into which the thought of sex does not intrude.

Of all such ties that she ever formed, none was more intimate or more far-reaching in its consequences than this friendship formed in Rome with Sidney Herbert, in which Mrs. Herbert was included. It was cemented by the humanitarian impulses common to both.

*   *   *   *

By her family that winter sojourn in Italy must have been accounted a failure, since hospitals and other charitable institutions continued to engross Miss Nightingale after her return. Some comparatively unimportant work in connection with them which she contrived to do, far from satisfying, merely served to whet her appetite.

In the following year her friends the Bracebridges planned an Egyptian sojourn, and again invited her to join them. She went, and once more there was a rise in the mercury of the family hopes. What Rome had failed to do, Egypt might yet accomplish. There would be not merely an entirely new scene to engage her notice, but in Egyptology a fresh avenue of study would be presented to her inquiring mind.

All this she found, and in all this she delighted. But she found also, and delighted even more in the study of the work of the Sisters of Saint Vincent of Paul, in Alexandria. Similarly when, in the spring of 1850, she moved on with the Bracebridges from Egypt to Greece, whilst she considered the Parthenon the most beautiful object on earth, she sought the study of it less eagerly than that of the orphanage conducted in Athens by an American mission.

From Greece, at the end of June, the travellers came by way of Trieste and Dresden to Berlin; and at the end of July she experienced the greatest joy that she had yet found in foreign travel, when she reached at last the Mecca of her aspirations, Kaiserswerth.

At Pastor Fliedner's Institute, with which her acquaintance was already considerable from the reports which she had studied, she spent now a fortnight, verifying the impressions formed, and acquainting herself in the fullest detail with the rules observed and the methods practised. The result of these investigations she embodied in a booklet, afterwards published, under the title of *The Institution of Kaiserswerth on the Rhine for the Practical Training of Deaconesses &c.*, the first of a long series of works on nursing and sanitation which were to come from her pen in the course of fifty thoughtful, laborious years. The pamphlet was issued not merely to interest the curious, but as a piece of propaganda calculated to stimulate among the women of England an emulation of the Deaconesses of Kaiserswerth.

But since to be a pioneer is not merely to point the way, but actually to lead it, she came home more firmly resolved than ever upon the course which, despite prejudice and opposition, her life must take.

* * * *

The disappointment of her family must gradually have given place to resignation. For less than a year later, when a visit to Carlsbad was prescribed for her ailing sister Parthenope, we find her accompanying her mother and sister to Germany, so that she might spend at Kaiserswerth the time during which Parthenope would be detained by her cure at Carlsbad.

This opportunity to extend the practical knowledge, as yet merely superficial in her, which was to be gained in Pastor Fliedner's Institute, was eagerly and unsparingly embraced. For three months she lived the Spartan life, underwent the training and performed the tasks allotted to a deaconess, rising at five in the morning, sharing the frugal meals of the sisterhood, caring for the sick in hospital, and attending the lectures on nursing delivered by the Pastor.

In this life, of peculiar physical hardship and self-denial for one nurtured as delicately as Miss Nightingale and in the ease that always had surrounded her, she must have found a greater degree of happiness than she had yet known. For to the end of her days she expressed herself upon those three months at Kaiserswerth in terms which show the reverent sweetness of the memories they left with her. It was an experience glorified by the consciousness that at last she was gathering, in knowledge, the strength necessary for the noble task to which she was resolved to dedicate herself.

From Kaiserswerth, then, she returned confirmed in her determination and in her confidence of ability to fulfil it. Her father would no longer make difficulties. A man of broad views and clear perceptions, he had seen in the stedfastness of his daughter's pursuit of her ideal that which, by commanding his admiration, ultimately won his approval; so that he was willing to support her aims and to endow her to the extent necessary for their prosecution. Her mother and her elder sister, however, could not bring themselves to contemplate with anything but pain the idea of her abandoning all those things which to them made existence pleasant and desirable, so as to replace them by toil and discomfort and associations that were repellent. The loving reluctance to inflict this pain upon them may well have supplied fetters which still retarded her progress towards her goal.

In the meantime, in order to widen the knowledge and experience gained at Kaiserswerth, she obtained introductions and made arrangements enabling her to observe at close quarters the work of the French Sisters of Charity in Paris and to study the hospitals there. But it was only after considerable difficulty and delay that, at last, in the early part of 1853 she had her way in this; and not even then to the extent which she had hoped. Before entering the house of the Sisters of Charity to which she was recommended, she took full advantage of the facilities earned her by her introductions so as to devote some time to visiting the Paris hospitals, where all was laid open to her inspection, from the wards to the operating theatres. And then, abruptly, her visit to Paris was interrupted by a recall to England, due to the illness of her grandmother.

She returned, and at the bedside of the aged invalid she was given her first opportunity of seriously practising her vocation, and of applying something of all that she had learnt from observation, and had considered for herself, of the care of the sick.

When she had acquitted herself of this task, she was free to return to Paris. But before this happened another door was opened for her in London.

* * * *

There existed in Chandos Street, Cavendish Square, a philanthropic institution entitled *Establishment for Gentlewomen During Illness*. It was a nursing-home for governesses and other ladies of restricted means. Its affairs were managed by a committee of society ladies of charitable inclination, amongst whom Miss Nightingale counted some friends—particularly Mrs. Sidney Herbert—who were aware of her aims and appreciative of her obvious sincerity and competence.

There was a desire to find new and more suitable prem-

ises for the establishment and entirely to reorganize it.
Miss Nightingale was named as a suitable person, both by
social position and ability, to take charge of it; and if some
members of the committee took the view that the office
would include duties hardly becoming in a gentlewoman,
Miss Nightingale herself disposed of this objection.

She must have impressed the committee; for in appointing her superintendent of the establishment, she was given
—very possibly as a result of her own insistence—a free
hand in the choice of the new premises, the management
of the funds, and the selection of the personnel. Her ample
means permitted her to give her services gratuitously.

This matter being settled, she wisely chose to take advantage of the time until the new premises should be
found and equipped, so as to return to Paris and resume
her interrupted studies. This time she went straight to
the Sisters of Charity of the Maison de la Providence. But
again Fate thwarted her. At the end of three weeks of this
hospital work, she was laid low by an attack of measles;
and by the time her recovery was complete, she was required in London, to take up her new duties.

Even whilst abroad she had not neglected what these
duties involved, and her letters had indicated to the committee what would constitute suitable premises, and how
they should be fitted.

Her instructions guided the selection made of No. 1
Harley Street, a large house which she now came home to
furnish and equip. It was a laborious task, which she had
only ten days to accomplish. In addition, there were meetings of the committee to be attended, rules and regulations
to be considered, discussed, and framed. Nor did all go
smoothly. The committee would have excluded Catholic
patients from the establishment. Miss Nightingale, with

her wide humanity, which took no account of sects, insisted that if she were to be retained as superintendent the house must be open to Christian and Jew alike.

She won her way in this and in other matters concerned with the welfare of the patients. As shrewd and efficient as she was resolute, her rule at No. 1 Harley Street affords an instance of the advantage to any community, large or small, of government by a benevolent despot.

She lived on the premises, and in addition she had rooms of her own outside, which she used as opportunity offered. She had emancipated herself from home-ties, much in the spirit of the priest who, taking the whole world for his family, lays claim to no personal one.

She took her first holiday in August of 1854, after a year's service at Harley Street, and she went to spend it with her people at Lea Hurst. But an outbreak of cholera in London made her cut short her rest and come back to offer her services to the Middlesex Hospital. There she toiled unremittingly, nursing female patients until the epidemic was under control, when she returned to her post in Harley Street.

The superintendence of the Governesses' Sanatorium, whilst affording her a certain scope, was still far from satisfying her aspirations. Her real aim was the reformation and proper organization of nursing in England, raising it from the casual, perfunctory, incompetent business that it was into a skilled and dignified profession, for which women should be properly qualified, and which so should prove attractive to a better class of nurse. Kaiserswerth and the Catholic Sisterhoods were ever in her mind, as furnishing the basis upon which not merely to build, but to improve. She may have hoped that Harley Street would supply the occasion to make a beginning, and that of this nursing-home she could also make a training ground for nurses. When these hopes began to dwindle, she listened sympathetically to a proposal that she should assume the superintendence of the nurses of King's College Hospital, an office in which she more clearly perceived the desired opportunity.

Circumscribed though her field of action had been so far, her work was already attracting attention, and her fame was quietly beginning to be spread by the medical men who came in contact with her and had occasion to admire the thoroughness, initiative, and hygienic value of her dispositions.

A far wider horizon, however, than that of King's College Hospital was about to be opened out to her.

*   *   *   *

England was at war.

Between the 13th and the 18th September of that year 1854, an allied army, British, French, and Turkish, fifty thousand strong, under the joint command of Saint Arnaud and Raglan, had landed in the Crimea to march on Sebastopol. On the 20th, on the heights of the river Alma, they met the Russian army under Menshikov, and from the disposition of these allied forces it resulted that the British bore the brunt of the attack. Before them the ground rose like a glacis to the heights commanded by the Russians. But their steadiness under fire brought them victorious to the summit, and the Battle of Alma was won.

The achievement made a heroic tale to stir the pride of Britain. But in the wake of it came matter to arouse indignation. In terms that were bitter but deserved, the special correspondent of *The Times* denounced the shameful lack of proper provision for the care of the wounded.

"Not only," ran his article, "are there not sufficient surgeons; that, it might be urged, was unavoidable; not only are there no dressers and nurses; that might be a defect of system for which no one is to blame; but what will be said when it is known that there is not even linen to make bandages for the wounded?"

In summoning the Government to inquire into the conduct of those who had so grossly neglected their duty, the writer went on mercilessly to describe events: of wounded men left for a week without medical attention only to expire in agony at the end; of the lack of the commonest appliances of a workhouse sick-ward; of the utter uselessness as nurses and dressers of the old pensioners who had been sent out for the purpose. He went on to compare with this criminal lack of provision the excellent medical arrangements of the French, with their numerous surgeons and their regiments of Sisters of Charity to act as nurses.

The country was stirred to anger and to shame.

"Why have we no Sisters of Charity?" demanded a letter to *The Times,* answering the question with the assertion that we had no lack of devoted women who would willingly undertake the nursing of the wounded if they could be associated for this purpose. In that letter spoke the voice of public opinion, tearing down, under stress of necessity, the barriers of prejudice which hitherto had excluded female nurses from military hospitals.

Upon the eager mind of Miss Nightingale, who for years now had aimed at the service of the sick and the afflicted, who had contemplated the creation in England of the profession of nursing, and who had devoted herself to a study of every aspect of the subject, the events were as a summons at once to her vocation and her patriotism. When she was presently invited by the members composing it to take charge of a small private group of nurses, she perceived how the summons should be answered.

She interviewed Dr. Andrew Smith, of the Army Medical Board, who authorized her to give effect to her intentions, and was ready to furnish her with an introduction to the Chief Medical Officer at Scutari.

She wrote at once to her friend Mrs. Sidney Herbert, a member of the ladies' committee responsible for the Harley Street establishment, to express the hope that this committee would relieve her of her obligations by actually urging her to go out to Scutari with that group of nurses. And she sought at the same time the views of Sidney Herbert, who was again in office, as Secretary at War, in the hope that he, too, would assist her with advice and recommendations.

Sidney Herbert was prepared to do a great deal more, and this upon his own initiative. He had two spurs to action: one supplied by his official position, and the other by his natural inclination towards philanthropy.

The notion of sending female nurses to the Crimea had actually been weighed by the Government before the troops embarked; but it had been rejected on the ground that it would not be liked by the military authorities. Now, however, the existing scandal had removed all such considerations.

What was to be done, and done without delay, Sidney Herbert instantly perceived; and the thought of Miss Nightingale may have helped him to a perception in which it played a leading part.

The letter to his wife, in which Miss Nightingale sought his advice and assistance, actually crossed with a letter

from him to Miss Nightingale. It was a very long letter
in the course of which he dealt with the charges brought
against the Government, and showed how, in respect of
several of them, the grounds must already have disappeared. In the matter of nursing, however, he freely admitted that the accusations were well-founded. There were
no female nurses, none having ever been admitted to military hospitals. He took the view that it would be impossible to have a large staff of female nurses with the army
in the field. But in the hospital established at Scutari,
where the Turks had given us a large barrack for the purpose, there was no reason against their introduction.

He had already received applications from a number of
ladies to go out; but they were ladies who had no conception of what a hospital was, or of what would be the
duties that awaited them.

> There is [he continued] but one person in England that
> I know of who would be capable of organizing and super-
> intending such a scheme; and I have been several times on
> the point of asking you hypothetically if, supposing the at-
> tempt were made, you would undertake to direct it.
> The difficulty of finding women equal to a task, after
> all, full of horrors, and requiring, besides knowledge and
> goodwill, great energy and great courage, will be great. The
> task of ruling them and introducing system among them,
> great; and not the least will be the difficulty of making the
> whole work smoothly with the medical and military au-
> thorities out there. This it is which makes it so important
> that the experiment should be carried out by one with a
> capacity for administration and experience. A number of
> sentimental enthusiastic ladies turned loose into the Hos-
> pital at Scutari would probably, after a few days, be *mises
> à la porte* by those whose business they would interrupt and
> whose authority they would dispute.
> My question simply is: Would you listen to the request

to go and superintend the whole thing? You would of course
have plenary authority over all the nurses. . . . I think
upon your decision will depend the ultimate success or failure of the plan. Your own personal qualities, your knowledge and your power of administration, and among greater
things your rank and position in society give you advantages
in such a work which no other person possesses.

If this succeeds, an enormous amount of good will be
done now, and to persons deserving everything at our
hands; and a prejudice will have been broken through, and
a precedent established, which will multiply the good to all
time.

To such an appeal there could, of course, be only one
answer from a woman consumed with the desire to render
the service now asked of her. On the morrow she had an
interview with Sidney Herbert, and settled details, and
three days later she received from the Secretary at War
an official letter of appointment as Superintendent of the
Female Nursing Establishment in the English General
Hospitals in Turkey.

Her instructions were to proceed to Scutari and report
to the Chief Army Medical Officer there, under whose
orders she would carry out the duties of her appointment.

The distribution of nurses, their hours of attendance
and the particular duties allotted to them were placed in
her hands, subject to the approval of the Chief Medical
Officer.

The selection of the nurses in the first instance was
left entirely to her, and similarly the power to dismiss any
of them, as well as to determine their rate of pay.

Financial arrangements were made, and to those concerned—the Commander of the Forces, the Purveyor-
General, and the Chief Medical Officer—went instructions

to render Miss Nightingale every assistance in the execution of the arduous duties she had undertaken.

* * * *

Miss Nightingale received her letter of appointment on the 19th October, and two days later she set out from London with the group of nurses she had assembled.

Such promptitude was rendered possible only because for a week before receiving her instructions, and even before she had any notion of being given an official government appointment, she had been making her preparations to act upon the suggestion that she should take charge of a party of nurses for the East.

The number of nurses to accompany her was fixed by herself and Sidney Herbert at forty. But whilst applicants were numerous enough, they were in the main of so undesirable a class that the proportion it was possible to engage was very small. In the end she had to be content with thirty-eight; and to reach even this number, in the time at her disposal, ten Roman Catholic Sisters had to be included. The balance was composed of eight Anglican Sisters, fourteen nurses drawn from various hospitals, and six nurses from Saint John's House. An establishment known as the Protestant Institution for Nurses was approached; but the committee would not place nurses under the control of Miss Nightingale. Only if the committee remained in control of its own nurses would it supply them. The condition was, of course, an impossible one.

With her party of thirty-eight nurses, Miss Nightingale set out for Marseilles on Saturday the 21st October. In the party were included also her devoted friends Mr. and Mrs. Bracebridge, who willingly accompanied her, so that they might lend her their assistance and support.

In England the announcement of her appointment by the Government had brought her instant celebrity. The natural curiosity which sprang up concerning her elicited the facts that she was a gentlewoman, young, attractive, rich and popular, who abandoned the ease and luxury into which she had been born so as to render "the holiest of women's charities to the sick, the dying and the convalescent, without regard to the danger, toil, and horror she would have to confront." When this was realized, she became at once, and deservedly, a heroine in the public esteem. Blessings were showered upon her, donations were sent to her, aggregating considerable sums with which she supplemented the funds placed by the Government at her disposal.

At Boulogne, and again at Marseilles, the party of nurses was cheered on its way, and Miss Nightingale was the recipient of every attention that could smooth her path.

At home she had left her sister and Miss Mary Stanley to act as her agents, to receive gifts and donations intended for the troops, to interview the women who continued to offer themselves as nurses, to select from among these the few who might be suitable, but to send out no more until Miss Nightingale should ask for them.

Whilst on the one hand thus loyally supported and encouraged in her mission, and the subject of laudatory articles in the Press, on the other she was already the victim of detraction. And whilst her detractors might be contemptible in number and unimportant of station, yet the noise they made compelled attention. The religious Press, always helpful in these matters, threw fuel recklessly on the fires secretarianism had lighted. For the attempt to make trouble for a lady who self-sacrificingly had embraced this holiest of Christian duties was entirely secretarian.

On the 28th October, the day after Miss Nightingale had sailed from Marseilles for Scutari, the first shot was fired by *The Daily News* with a denunciation of the composition of her party. It was complained that she had recruited it from a High-Church establishment (the Anglican Sisters) and from a Roman Catholic one. In the scorn to which on this account she was held up by the fanatics, the Government came to be included. These circumstances revealed, it was claimed, the nature of the party-spirit at work in appointing Miss Nightingale to this important office, whilst rejecting the claims to it of another lady—the Lady Maria Forester. And the nation was summoned to rouse itself at once and to express its feelings (which it was hoped would be indignant) so that this calamity might be repaired before it was too late.

It is not to be supposed that these attacks remained unanswered. But the zealots continued vociferous and scathing even after reports had begun to reach England of the heroic work that this lady was doing in the Levant. Not until Queen Victoria gave her personal benediction by letter to Miss Nightingale, in the following December, were the ill-natured voices of these bigots silenced. Her Majesty desired Miss Nightingale to be made aware that her goodness and self-devotion in giving herself up to soothing attendance upon these wounded and sick soldiers had been observed by the Queen with sentiments of the highest approval and admiration.

It was a commendation that may well have added weight to Miss Nightingale's authority at a time when she required it so as to overcome difficulties less negligible than those created by pietistic criticism.

* * * *

The mind reels at the contemplation of the variety and comprehensiveness of the work accomplished by this lady immediately upon arrival at Scutari. We are lost in wonder of the vision and energy which so speedily resolved into some order the abominable chaos she discovered there. We realize how just was the later phrase of Sidney Herbert which describes her as a woman of genius. Had she been anything less, her spirit must have fainted at sight of the Augean Stable she was called upon to clean.

Those at home who sang the praises of her womanly devotion to the care of the sick would have been beggared of terms if they had conceived what her mission really came to comprise.

The scandal caused by the exposure in *The Times* of the muddle of official administration had resulted in the despatch to Scutari of a Commission of Inquiry, which arrived at about the same time as Miss Nightingale. This commission proceeded to investigate, so thoroughly that it spent four months in preparing its report. That report travelled home, there to be considered anew, and a few months later a Select Committee of the House of Commons, giving voice to its findings, pronounced the state of the hospitals to be disgraceful. Whilst all this was doing and these long months were passing, in the East men would daily have been perishing, victims of the ills with which the report was concerned.

What was required in this, as is required in any real emergency, was not a commission, but an individual vested with plenary powers, not merely to investigate, but immediately to correct the wrong upon the spot. It is scarcely an exaggeration to say that fortunately for the suffering soldiers the place of such an individual was spontaneously filled by Miss Nightingale. She took action upon the strength of such powers as had been entrusted to her, powers which she considerably widened by the exercise of infinite tact, patience, and forbearance, and with the help of moneys from *The Times* Fund—whose commissioner associated himself with her—of moneys sent to her by private benevolence, and of moneys from her own purse.

* * * *

The *Vectis,* in which Miss Nightingale had sailed from Marseilles, reached Constantinople on the 4th November, and that same afternoon she proceeded with her staff of nurses to the Barrack Hospital at Scutari. For ten days from that date, such were the labours awaiting her, she was never outside of hospital walls.

She arrived at a critical moment. Balaclava had been fought a week before, and the wreckage of the cavalry (some four hundred wounded) was being landed at almost the same moment that Miss Nightingale went ashore.

There were two British hospitals at Scutari: the Turkish Military Hospital, known as the General Hospital, which had been assigned to the British in May of that year. This had been handed over partially fitted, and by the efforts of a first-class staff surgeon it had been brought into fairly good order. It could accommodate a thousand patients. But the Battle of Alma had strained its capacity, whereupon the Semiliyeh Barracks had also been made over to the British so as to supplement it. This it was that had come to be known as the Barrack Hospital, and it was here that Miss Nightingale and her nurses were now established.

In the North-West Tower she appropriated a small room for herself and Mrs. Bracebridge; another room was given to Mr. Bracebridge, and the nurses occupied the rest; altogether an accommodation no greater than that appropriated by the Commandant. They were cramped, uncomfortable, insanitary quarters, infested with vermin, as, indeed, was the whole hospital. "The vermin might," she wrote, "if they had but unity of purpose, carry off the four miles of beds on their backs, and march with them into the War Office, Horse Guards, S.W."

That, however, was written later. At the moment there were no four miles of beds. There was a criminal shortage of beds, of bedsteads and of mattresses, and whilst this in itself may seem a terrible evil in a hospital into which the sick and wounded were now pouring, it was almost the least of the evils by which Miss Nightingale found herself confronted.

The vast Barrack Hospital, so imposing of exterior, was of an incredible, indescribable foulness within. "The sewers were of the worst possible construction, loaded with filth, mere cesspools in fact, through which the wind blew sewer air up the pipes of numerous open latrines into the corridors and wards where the sick were lying."

This state of the atmosphere, of a foulness so heavy as to seem almost palpable, was matched by the filth and disorder of the quarters through which it blew, quarters infested with rats, crawling with vermin of every description.

The medical staff had assumed that a coat of whitewash was all that it was necessary to supply in the interests of hygiene. There were not even the necessary appliances for producing and maintaining cleanliness, or the necessary utensils demanded by decency; whilst so destitute was the place of articles of furniture that empty bottles were doing duty as candlesticks.

When it came to the more personal requisites of the wounded, not only were medical appliances either insufficient or entirely lacking, but the absence of all proper supply of clothing and linen, imposed directly upon the body of the unfortunate sufferer the filth of his surroundings. There were no basins or towels, brooms or soap. The Purveyor-General had contracted for the washing of such bedding and linen as existed, but those he entrusted with the contract had proved so unequal to the task that what washing was being done at all was being done with cold water.

The dilapidation of some of the wards into which it was proposed to put the emaciated sufferers arriving from the Crimea was so terrible that they would have proved death-traps to sound, robust men.

No provision whatever had been made for cooking special diets, nor were the necessary elements present. A kitchen had been set up with thirteen large coppers at one end of the enormous building, whence, when the hospital came to be filled, it took three or four hours to serve out the dinners, with no facilities whatever for supplying anything at any other time.

In coming into the hospital that awaited them, the men merely passed from one battlefield to another, and this a battlefield of passive suffering where the death-rate was forty-two per cent.

Such was the state of things confronting Miss Nightingale.

It was not merely for her a question of realizing that before she could address herself to the task of nursing, she must shoulder the burdens of administration, since no one else was present to undertake the responsibility, but that she must combine the two offices.

Unhesitatingly she appears to have done so, and it is in this that she achieves real greatness. Little wonder that for ten days from the date of her arrival she was never outside hospital walls.

From the British Ambassador, Lord Stratford de Redcliffe, her reception was all that could be desired. Lord Raglan, the Commander of the Forces, welcomed her heartily in a letter which commended her devotion to those who had suffered.

But from some of those with whom the duties of her appointment brought her more immediately in contact there were jealousies of the authority vested in her, which seemed to encroach upon their own, and resentments of what was regarded as a supremely foolish innovation. So that whilst concern for her duty towards the wounded demanded a widespread activity, flowing far beyond the bounds of what was strictly her province, yet she walked delicately in exercising it, and with so much quiet tact and regard for the authority of others that she very soon succeeded in conquering prejudice and subduing opposition where she perceived it. This was more easily accomplished with those who were brought directly into contact with her than with those who remained at a distance. The former came under the spell of her winning personality, admired her obvious competence, and yielded to her gentle calm, scarcely aware of the underlying masterfulness.

Her first concern—if there can be a first where so many claimed her simultaneously—was to establish cleanliness. Scrubbers and sacking for washing floors were her earliest need, and to procure them she was assisted by Macdonald, the commissioner of *The Times* Fund, since to obtain them through the Purveyor-General would mean interminable delays in a matter that admitted of none.

To provide for the proper washing of clothes and linen —since the Purveyor's contractor had broken down—she took immediate steps, which apparently had not occurred to the Purveyor's official mind. She rented a house in Scutari, and equipped it with the necessary boilers. So as to act promptly and avoid the deadly delays of application to the Treasury, she met the expense partly out of her own purse and partly, again, with the assistance of *The Times* Fund.

But for her timely arrival in Scutari and her bold initiative, it is possible that the powerful beneficent weapon of this Fund would never have found employment. Macdonald had approached the British Ambassador for information as to the needs upon which he should lay out the moneys of which he had the dispensation. He was met by the reply that nothing was needed, and the suggestion that the Fund should be applied to the erection of an English Church at Pera.

That Lord Stratford could have returned such an answer at a time when the patients in hospital were destitute of the commonest necessaries may appear extraordinary until we realize that, from official information, he had every reason to suppose that all possible requirements were abundantly supplied. Their absence resulted from no government parsimony. Actually the supplies from the government at home were abundant. But the blundering of officialdom on the spot rendered these supplies unobtainable. Presently, and no doubt as a result of Miss Nightingale's representations to him, we find the Secretary at War, writing:

> . . . there has been evidently a want of co-operation between departments. . . . No expense has been spared at home, and immense stores are sent out, but they are not

forthcoming. Some are at Varna, and for some inexplicable reason are not brought down to Scutari. When stores are in the hospital, they are not issued without forms so cumbrous as to make the issue unavailing through delay.

The situation may be said to have been saved, and a terrible and criminal loss of life averted, by the prompt association of Miss Nightingale and Mr. Macdonald, and the application of funds, which Lord Stratford thought might worthily be employed to build a church, to the establishment of a store from which without loss of time it was possible to supply such essentials as the Purveyor might lack.

To the Ambassador, who had the power of drawing upon the Government for the uses of the sick and wounded, she reported the absence of linen, and requisitioned at once one hundred pairs of sheets and two hundred shirts. What sheets she had found were of canvas, so coarse that the wounded, emaciated men begged to be allowed to lie in their blankets. She requested at the same time a few American stoves upon which delicate food for the worst cases might be prepared, explaining that such cases required to be fed every two or three hours, and that many deaths were resulting from the fact that the existing arrangements did not admit of this. Going further in this particular matter, she set up two extra-diet kitchens in different parts of the building and three further appliances for the preparation of special foods.

With admirable foresight she had brought with her from Marseilles a considerable store of provisions, and it was out of this that she was now able promptly to supply delicacies requisitioned by the medical officers but unobtainable from the Purveyor, either because they did not exist, or because in the general disorder they were not to be discovered.

The Commission of Inquiry, in reporting upon this difficulty, stated that it was not to be assumed from the fact that requisitioned articles were not forthcoming that they were not in the stores. Goods, the commissioners added, had to their knowledge, been refused whilst lying in plenty in the store of the Purveyor, because the Purveyor was officially powerless to release them for use until they had been inspected by the Board of Survey, a Board which acted in its own good time. The Commissioners discovered a case of almost criminal delay from this cause in the matter of hospital rugs urgently needed in that cold December. Miss Nightingale employed insistence, and there is at least one instance of high-handed action on her part when shirts were urgently needed. She knew of a consignment from home of twenty-seven thousand, which had been landed and awaited the good pleasure of the Board of Survey. In flagrant defiance of the Board, and to the consternation of the Purveyor's officers, she ordered the bales to be opened.

Under her direction and superintendence, the engineering miracle was wrought of conquering the loathsome insanitary conditions, and presently, too, on her own responsibility and with the concurrence of the senior medical officer, she set about building operations, so as to restore the dilapidated wards and render them fit for occupation.

Since no one else would undertake the responsibility of an action that so flagrantly defied all rule and ventured in an emergency to ignore the leisurely official channels of routine, she was obliged to pay the builders out of her own resources. She was reimbursed, however, by a War Office that approved an action the advantages of which could not be concealed. It was not approved, however, by some of those upon the spot. The prejudice which she had to encounter peeps out of a letter from Colonel Anthony Sterling, who was in the Crimea with the Highland Division:

> Miss Nightingale coolly draws a cheque. Is this the way to manage the finances of a great nation? Vox populi! A divine afflatus. Priestess Miss Nightingale! Magnetic impetus drawing cash out of my pocket!

That her action should have had the result, not otherwise to be reached, of mitigating the sufferings of men wounded in the service of their country and of saving many of their lives, was not weighed by the Colonel in the balance against a procedure that violated the sacrosanctity of official forms.

* * * *

The variety of her activities fully justified her saying that whilst she had gone out expecting to be a Hospital Matron, she had never expected to be a Barrack Mistress. In fact, however, the Lady-in-Chief, as she soon came to be called, was both.

Whilst some of the medical officers might in those early days make sneering allusions to "the voice of the Nightingale" and superciliously speak of her as "the Bird," yet from the majority she earned respect, not only by her clear, unassuming ability, but also by her tact, by her sense of discipline, and by the discipline which she enforced upon her staff.

It may have helped this discipline that, departing from the free-and-easy ways that permitted a nurse to dress as she pleased, Miss Nightingale gave her nurses a distinctive uniform: grey tweed wrappers, worsted jackets, caps, short woollen capes, and a scarf of brown holland bearing in red the legend "Scutari Hospital." Their lives were governed by the Rules and Regulations which she drew up. Those few who were unable to accept the discipline and the privations of the life she at once sent home.

On arrival at Scutari, she appointed ten of her nurses to the General Hospital, in which there were at the time six hundred and fifty severely wounded cases, and twenty-eight to the Barrack Hospital, in which there were one thousand, seven hundred and fifteen sick and wounded, including one hundred and twenty cholera patients. She divided her own duties of superintendence between the two. Upon all her staff she had strictly enjoined that in every matter concerned with the care of a patient they were to take no action whatsoever save upon the instructions of the medical officer concerned.

Within a week, to the patients already on their hands were added over five hundred from the shambles of Balaclava, who arrived at short notice.

Feverishly, when this occurred, Miss Nightingale directed work, the difficulties of which were immeasurably increased by the shortage of furniture and appliances. In eight hours they had the mattresses stuffed, sewn up and laid down, upon matting on the floor, for lack of bedsteads, and the patients washed and put to bed, their wounds dressed.

The ships which might be called hospital ships took over a week on the three-hundred-mile voyage across the Black Sea, from the Crimea to Scutari. So ill-furnished were they for the service that the losses on the voyage exceeded seven per cent, and so bad were the landing arrangements that the survivors arrived in hospital in a state of agony, and many succumbed at once.

It was after those arrivals from Balaclava that the cases in the Barrack Hospital made up four miles of beds, laid in the corridors and wards, not eighteen inches apart, with just room for a single person to pass between the rows. Another shipload was arriving, and two more vessels were taking wounded aboard at the Crimea.

The operations were all performed in the wards. There was neither time to move the patient, nor a place to which to move him. Each submitted to the knife in his own bed, and in full view of his comrades, whose own courage was chilled by the ghastly spectacle. To a man awaiting amputation, the sight of a neighbour dying under the knife was in itself a shock that lowered his powers of resistance and lessened his own chances in the ordeal to come.

To remedy this barbarity Miss Nightingale proceeded almost at once to provide screens.

> One poor fellow, exhausted with hæmorrhage, has his leg amputated as a last hope, and dies ten minutes after the surgeon has left him. Almost before the breath has left his body, it is sewn up in its blanket, and carried away and buried the same day. We have no room for corpses in the wards. The surgeons pass on to the next, an excision of the shoulder-joint beautifully performed and going on well. . . . The next poor fellow has two stumps for arms, and the next has lost an arm and a leg. . . .

Thus Miss Nightingale, in a letter describing not singular cases, but conveying an idea of what lies in her daily work. "In all our corridors," she says, "I think we have not an average of three limbs per man."

And amongst those who survived operation the mortality from gangrene was terrible, for we are only upon the eve of Lister's discoveries and the introduction of antiseptic surgery.

Through these terrible scenes not only does Miss Nightingale steer her staff, and quicken its efficiency by precept, but also by example. A witness of her first steps commends her nerves as being equal to her good sense, and speaks of her being as cool at an amputation as if she were performing it herself.

Whilst she was stimulating those about her by her courage, her energy and her skill, she was herself being stimulated to still higher endeavours and greater sacrifice by the heroic fortitude of those to whom she was sent to minister.

"As I went my night-rounds," she writes, "among the newly wounded . . . there was not one murmur, not one groan, the strictest discipline—the most absolute silence and quiet prevailed—only the steps of the sentry . . ."

The respect and admiration those sufferers thus compelled from her was transmuted into that love for the British soldier to which she ever afterwards confessed, and which added to her natural vocation an inspiration to every self-sacrifice that might be demanded of her in his service.

* * * *

To the thirty-eight nurses Miss Nightingale took out with her, additions were made as time went on until by the end of the war the number under her control had risen to a hundred and twenty-five.

Not everything even in this connection went smoothly for her. She had scarcely been at Scutari a month, had scarcely brought the necessary order and discipline into the ranks of her staff, reduced by a few dismissals, when another forty-six came out in the charge of her friend Miss Mary Stanley. This was something in contravention of her clear stipulations and of her clear understanding with the Secretary at War that no further nurses should be sent out until she asked for them; and there was on her part some resentment of an action that threatened to increase her difficulties and weaken the authority obtained by so much prudence and firmness.

In the end, however, Miss Nightingale took over some of the newcomers, thereby increasing her staff to fifty. The remainder were sent, some to Balaclava, and some with Miss Stanley to Koulali.

Another lady who presented herself in Scutari to offer her services was the Lady Alicia Blackwood, who, with her husband, Dr. Blackwood, went out after Inkerman.

Miss Nightingale at the time was deeply exercised on the score of the soldiers' wives who had followed their husbands to the East, and who found themselves in a condition of utter wretchedness. She was glad enough to avail herself of Lady Alicia's services; and Lady Alicia chronicles the words in which Miss Nightingale bestowed the charge upon her:

> In this barrack are now located some two hundred poor women in the most abject misery. A great number have been sent down from Varna; they are in rags and covered with vermin. My heart bleeds for them; but my work is with the soldiers, not with their wives. Now will you undertake to look after them? If you will take them as your charge, I will send you an orderly, who will show you their haunts.

*   *   *   *

In January of 1855 the Government of Lord Aberdeen resigned, and was replaced by Lord Palmerston's.

Sidney Herbert, too, went out of office, and Lord Panmure became Secretary of State for War, amalgamating the two secretaryships into which this office had hitherto been divided. Not on that account, however, did Miss Nightingale lose Sidney Herbert's support. The influence that he wielded rendered him still a valuable channel for her representations. In addition to this there was the fact that she was by now well established in the public regard. In the two months that she had been at her post, she had given abundant proof of her very exceptional worth.

The sanitary reforms which she had so far carried out could not be regarded as more than palliatives for the terrible conditions that she had found. Something of a more radical nature was urgently needed. And not only did she press the need upon the attention of the Government, but, having moved for weeks in an exasperating atmosphere of shirked responsibilities, she stressed the fact that the mere issuing of orders was not enough. It was necessary to empower officials and to render them responsible for immediate action.

It resulted from this that in February of 1855, a Sanitary Commission, composed of two medical men and a civil engineer, was sent out with full powers to undertake work, and the injunction personally to see it carried out. As a consequence of activities which gave effect to Miss Nightingale's recommendations, the hospital death-rate, which had previously stood at the ghastly figure of forty-two per cent, fell rapidly to a shade over two per cent. From being a pest-house, the Barrack Hospital at Scutari was converted into an establishment the hygienic like of which had never been seen in military hospitals.

On the subject of the absence or inaccessibility of supplies as a result of maladministration, Miss Nightingale's recommendations were equally forcible and equally effective. Of the abundance of supplies being shipped from home, some were going on to the Crimea, to be lost there; others were being landed in Constantinople to fall into the hands of the customs authorities, when the ineptitude of Turkish officialdom would be added to that of British officialdom, and only with the utmost difficulty and after exasperating delays could delivery be obtained. It was left for Miss Nightingale to put her finger on these evils, and for her common-sense to suggest an easy remedy in the shape of a hulk, where British stores, from whatever ship, could be received at once.

The state of the troops arriving from the Crimea in that rigorous winter of 1854–55 exposed to her another scandalous lack, on the subject of which she wrote to Sidney Herbert:

> The state of troops who return here . . . is frost-bitten, demi-nude, starved, ragged. If the troops who work in the trenches are not supplied with warm clothing, Napoleon's Russian campaign will be repeated here.

The following letter to Sidney Herbert in January is invaluable as shedding a deal of light not only upon the condition of things with which she was wrestling, but also upon her valiant character:

> I feel that this is no time for compliments or false shame; and that you will never hear the whole truth, troublesome as it is, except from one independent of promotion. . . .
>
> I subjoin a rough estimate of what has been given out to me during *one month*—the whole at the requisition of the medical men—all of which I have by me (merely in order to substantiate the destitution of these hospitals).
>
> Since the 17th December we have received 3400 sick, and I have made no sum total yet of what has been done for

these newcomers by us—excepting for one corridor, which I enclose.

(1) Thus the Purveying is nil; that is the whole truth, beyond bedding, bread, meat, cold water, fuel.

Beyond the boiling *en masse* in the great coppers of the general kitchen, the meat is not cooked, the water is not boiled, except what is done in my subsidiary kitchens. My schedule will show what I have purveyed. . . .

(2) The extraordinary circumstance of a whole army having been ordered to abandon its kits, as was done when we landed our men before Alma, has been overlooked entirely in all our system. The fact is that I am now clothing the British Army. The sick were re-embarked at Balaclava for these hospitals, without resuming their kits, also half-naked besides. And when discharged from here, they carry off, small blame to them, even my knives and forks—shirts, of course, and hospital clothing also. The men who were sent to Abydos as convalescents were sent in their hospital dresses, or they must have gone naked. The consequence is that not one single hospital dress is now left in store, and I have substituted Turkish dressing-gowns from Stamboul (three bales in the passage are marked Hospital Gowns, but have not yet been "sat upon"). To purvey this hospital is like pouring water into a sieve; and will be until regimental stores have been sent out from England enough to clothe the naked and refill the kit.

I have requisitions for *uniform trousers,* for each and all of the articles of a kit, sent in to me.

We have not yet heard of boots being sent out. The men come into hospital half-shod.

In a time of such calamity, unparalleled in the history, I believe, of calamity, I have little compassion left even for the wretched Purveyor, swamped amid demands he never expected. But I have no compassion for men who would rather see hundreds of lives lost than waive one scruple of the official conscience.

She continues at length to tabulate defects and short-comings, and thereafter states what the requirements are that will mend the prevailing disorder: an effective staff of purveyors; a Head, someone with authority, to mash up the departments into uniform and rapid action; medical officers; three deputy inspectors-general to share the work now being done by only one; discharged non-commissioned officers as ward-masters, assistant ward-masters and stewards; she urges that the purveyor's office be divided up into three departments: one to provide food; another, hospital furniture and clothing; and a third to keep the daily routine going. She complains that this daily routine is not performed at all, saving in so far as she herself performs it by being cook, housekeeper, scavenger, washerwoman, general dealer, and storekeeper.

These and the further practical suggestions that she makes came a few months later to be embodied in a Royal Warrant for the better care of the sick and wounded.

It will be seen how just was her observation to Sidney Herbert that "nursing was the least important of the functions into which she had been forced."

Yet, notwithstanding all that she accomplished by her initiative, her courage, her common-sense, and her devotion to the task assumed, Sir John Hall, the Inspector-General of Hospitals in the Crimea, could write home to Dr. Andrew Smith, the Director-General of the Army Medical Department, in the following terms:

> When one reads such twaddling nonsense as that uttered by Mr. Bracebridge, and which was so much lauded in *The Times* because the garrulous old gentleman talked about Miss Nightingale putting hospitals, containing three or four thousand patients, in order in a couple of days by means of *The Times* funds, one cannot suppress a feeling of contempt for the man who indulges in such exaggerations, and pity for the ignorant multitude who are deluded by these fairy tales.

It is not difficult to understand the bitterness in which the Inspector-General thus deprecated commendation (quite possibly coloured by some exaggeration) of activities the occasion for which was a reflection upon his own capabilities.

*   *   *   *

Whilst nursing, in her own words, might be the least important of the functions into which she had been forced, yet it was upon her services as a nurse that her fame rested. Only the officials with whom she was brought into contact were aware—and not always with satisfaction—of her enormous constructive labours in every branch of hospital administration.

Of all this, neither the sick in hospital nor the great public at home saw more than the results. To them, and particularly to the former, she was the sweetly charitable tender woman, the "Ministering Angel" of Macdonald's phrase in *The Times*. For incredible though it may seem, the burden of administrative work which she had shouldered was never permitted to interfere with the functions of the nurse.

As well as an infinite capacity for taking pains, genius is also a capacity for swift accomplishment, following upon a clear and acute perception of the need. Within the twenty-four short hours of Miss Nightingale's day, she seems to have contrived to find time for everything, saving only perhaps a proper care of herself and the husbanding of her own physical resources. These she spent prodigally and recklessly in the service to which she had consecrated herself.

Her enormous correspondence, her letters to ministers at home, to officials in the East, to charitable subscribers of funds, to the bereaved relatives of soldiers who died on her hands, her accountancy and the rest of the clerical work that devolved upon her, was done in the North-East Tower of the Barrack Hospital—now called The Sisters' Tower—in the still hours of the night, and with the loyal help of Mr. and Mrs. Bracebridge, to whom she could delegate some portion of her labours, but whom she must still direct in them.

Of this, the sick and wounded to whom she ministered unceasingly and tirelessly in their waking hours can have had no suspicion.

She had been known to spend eight hours on her knees, dressing wounds and administering comforts. She had been known, upon an influx of patients, to stand for twenty hours at a stretch, superintending the accommodation of the wounded, directing her nurses and assisting in operations.

On the arrival of a ship with wounded, the insufficient surgeons were constrained by overwork to confine attention to the less desperate cases which there was a hope of saving. Those whose chances of recovery appeared slender were set aside as hopeless. There is an instance alike of her alertness and her devotion in a case of five so condemned, of whom she begged and obtained the charge. Assisted by one of her nurses, she spent the night in tending them, easing them, maintaining their strength by careful nourishment, with the result that in the morning they were found fit for operation.

To the risks of contagion she was as indifferent as to fatigue. During an epidemic of cholera and typhus, which carried off three of her nurses and seven doctors, she spent hours over men who hung between life and death. "The more awful to every sense, any particular case, especially if it was that of a dying man, the more certainly might her slight form be seen bending over him, administering to his ease by every means in her power, and seldom quitting his side till death released him."

It was her custom, late at night, or in the early hours of the morning, when her administrative and clerical labours were done, and before retiring to such rest as she allowed herself, to make a last tour of the wards, so as to bestow comfort or assistance in isolated cases that might be in urgent distress or need.

Down those long aisles, between the rows of beds, she would pass, camp-lamp in hand, a tall, slender figure in black merino trimmed with black velvet, from which the white of collar and cuffs and apron sharply detached, her rich brown hair covered by a white cap with a black handkerchief tied over it.

Slowly she proceeded on her solitary round of that seemingly endless succession of aisles that were now wrapped in silence, pausing ever and anon to set down her lamp and bend over a sufferer whose condition gave her more than ordinary concern.

To the men she had become an object of worship. They would kiss her shadow as it fell across their pillows, and lay down their heads again in content.

They spoke of her, too, as being full of life and fun, with a wonderful gift for cheering the despondent, and with a power over them which made them master themselves so that they might deserve her approval.

With all this, she still found time to take the last messages of the dying and to transmit them to many a bereaved wife, mother, or sister, and she not merely encouraged the sick to communicate with home, but actually would write their letters for them at their dictation.

Yet all this care, direct and indirect, for the wounded still left her leisure to realize the ills that beset the convalescents, and to devote herself to providing against them. She perceived that if they were to be drawn away from the canteen and kept out of the drunkenness that was regarded as natural to the British soldier, counter-attractions must be provided. She assumed that drunkenness was simply the result of leisure spent in the canteen, and this because the soldier had nowhere else to go. Lord Panmure's scorn was moved when he heard of the measures she proposed. To him they were simply proofs of her ignorance of the nature of the British soldier. But the result of these measures, when she had taken them, justified her faith and proved that the ignorance was in those who thought as did Lord Panmure.

She set up and organized reading-rooms for the convalescent, and they were well attended. Books, games, and amusements were provided, and the men were glad to take advantage of them. A little later she established in Scutari a coffee-house for soldiers, the Inkerman Café, and it found no lack of customers among those for whom formerly there had been only the canteen.

Decrease in drunkenness followed automatically, and to these means she added her own personal influence. She extracted promises from men that they would not drink; and what they promised the venerated Lady-in-Chief, they generally fulfilled.

* * * *

For the first six months of her sojourn in the East, Scutari was the scene of Miss Nightingale's labours. It remained, however, that her responsibilities extended over the female nursing staffs in the hospitals of the Crimea itself, which had remained hitherto under superintendents acting as her deputies.

In May of 1855, by when the stress of work in the hospitals at Scutari was easing, she resolved to take advantage of this so as to pay a visit to the Crimea, and to extend to its hospitals her measures for the promotion of sanitation and hygiene.

Accompanied by Mr. Bracebridge, four nurses, two cooks, and a boy, she sailed from Scutari on the 2nd May in the *Robert Lowe,* which was taking back to the Crimea a draught of convalescents, returning to their regiments. The vessel reached Balaclava on the 5th, and for lack of accommodation ashore, Miss Nightingale's cabin aboard remained her headquarters.

In the absence of Lord Raglan, who was not then at Balaclava, she was made welcome by the officers, and still more heartily by the men, who loudly cheered her as she passed.

A visit to the front lines helped her to understand the condition in which the wounded from the Crimea had arrived in Scutari during the terrible winter that was now over. She saw the trenches in which the men spent five nights out of the seven that made up the week, going often for forty-eight hours with raw salt pork sprinkled with sugar, and rum and biscuit for their only food; "nothing hot because the exhausted soldier could not collect his own fuel, as he was expected to do, to cook his own ration."

It was not, however, the trenches that she had come to see. Her concern lay in the inspection of hospitals, the organizing of the nursing system, the installing of kitchens for special diets, akin to those which she had set up at Scutari; and she devoted herself also to actual nursing, tending fever patients with her usual disregard of the danger of infection, but not with her usual immunity. Perhaps because her powers of resistance had been lowered by her unsparing dissipation of bodily energy, she succumbed at last, herself, to the fever through which she had nursed so many.

She became a patient in the Castle Hospital, an enclosure of huts on the Genoese Heights above Balaclava.

The attack was so severe that for a time, fortunately brief, a doubt arose of her recovery. Not until after three days, when, the crisis overpast, the doctors were now hopeful that all would go well, did Lord Raglan send home the news by telegraph. It seems to have been received almost as if it were the loss of a battle.

Blessings are never so keenly valued as when we are in peril of losing them. The news that Miss Nightingale was ill, her life in danger, struck not merely her family, but all England, with dismay; whilst in the hospitals of the Levant the concern was deeper than it could have been on behalf of any other person living at that moment. Bulletins were forwarded to the Queen, by her Majesty's request; and when at last, by the end of May, Miss Nightingale was reported to be progressing favourably, the Queen, in a letter to the Secretary of State for War, expressed her thankfulness "to learn that that excellent and valuable person, Miss Nightingale, is safe."

* * * *

She came out of that bout of fever with the loss of her beautiful brown hair, with her strength so impaired that it is doubtful if she was ever again quite the same woman, but with her high courage and eager devotion no whit diminished.

A voyage to England and a rest taken just then might completely have re-established her. But she rejected the suggestion. She would spend her convalescence where her work lay, so that she might the sooner resume it. In her exhausted state that convalescence was long. But by August, and in spite of all remonstrances, she had resumed her duties in Scutari, and pursued them with the same enthusiastic, unflagging zeal as of old.

The anxiety which the danger to her life had occasioned in England, and the jubilation following upon the news of her recovery, had the effect of elevating her in the public mind to the eminence of a national heroine. In a day when scarcely anyone is too unimportant to afford a subject for a biographer, we may be in danger of missing the inference from the fact that a brisk trade was being driven then in biographies of Miss Nightingale. She became the subject of rhymed broadsheets, adorned by portraits, not always authentic; and she was celebrated in song by poet and musician. Her name was given to ships, to streets, and even to a racehorse. Painters found inspiration in her, and her picture in every form, from woodcuts to portaits on china, was widely exhibited for sale.

That the enthusiasm which swept the country was shared by royalty is shown by the following letter from Queen Victoria:

DEAR MISS NIGHTINGALE—You are, I know, well aware of the high sense I entertain of the Christian devotion which you have displayed during this great and bloody war, and I need hardly repeat to you how warm my admiration is for your services, which are fully equal to those of my dear and brave soldiers, whose sufferings you have had the privilege of alleviating in so merciful a manner. I am, however, anxious of marking my feelings in a manner which I trust will be agreeable to you, and, therefore, send you with this letter a brooch, the form and emblems of which commemorate your great and blessed work, and which I hope you will wear as a mark of the high approbation of your Sovereign.

It will be a great satisfaction to me, when you return at last to these shores, to make the acquaintance of one who has set so bright an example to our sex. And with every prayer for the preservation of your valuable health, believe me, always, yours sincerely,

VICTORIA R.

The brooch bore the cross of Saint George in red enamel and the royal cipher surmounted by a crown in diamonds and encircled by the legend, "Blessed are the Merciful," and the word "Crimea."

If Miss Nightingale was touched by these evidences that England loved her, as her sister wrote, "with a passionate tenderness that goes to my heart," yet she was troubled by the thought that her enterprise might suffer from the expression of it.

I do not affect indifference to real sympathy, but I have felt painfully, the more painfully since I have had time to think of it, the *éclat* which has been given to this adventure. The small, still beginning, the simple hardship, the silent and gradual struggle upwards, these are the climate in which an enterprise really thrives and grows.

But, however she might deprecate it, the notion spread in England of marking in some significant manner the national appreciation of her self-sacrificing services. When approached as to the form which the testimonial should take, her reply was that she must decline any that was of a personal character. Respecting her wishes in this, and taking a line which it was felt would commend itself to her, a committee was assembled under the secretaryship of Sidney Herbert, to raise the Nightingale Fund, for the purpose of enabling her to establish and control an institute for the training, sustenance, and protection of nurses.

A crowded meeting was held at Willis's Rooms, "To give expression to the general feeling that the services of Miss Nightingale in the hospitals of the East demand the grateful recognition of the British people."

The Duke of Cambridge was in the chair, and among other speakers were Lord Stanley, Sidney Herbert, the Duke of Argyll, and Lord Lansdowne.

Miss Nightingale conveyed in a letter to Sidney Herbert how deeply touched she was by the expression of sympathy and confidence in their proposal, which she accepted on the understanding that there was great uncertainty—arising out of her present commitment—as to when it would be possible to carry it out.

Meetings in promotion of the Fund were held up and down the country, and of all that was uttered in acclamation of the object, no words are more memorable than those of Lord Stanley, in the course of a speech he made in Manchester:

> The best test of a nation's moral state is the kind of claim which it selects for honour. And with the exception of Howard, the prison reformer, I know no person, besides Miss Nightingale, who, within the last hundred years, within this island, or perhaps in Europe, has voluntarily encountered dangers so imminent, and undertaken offices so repulsive, working for a large and worthy object, in a pure spirit of duty towards God and compassion for man.

*　　*　　*　　*

Miss Nightingale's fears of harm to her enterprise from these displays of public favour were not entirely illusory. She was well aware of how it must sharpen the resentment already existing among those who, like Colonel Sutherland, looked askance upon this feminine intrusion upon a province which they regarded as peculiarly their own.

Whilst, when the notification of the establishment of the Nightingale Fund reached the East, the troops contributed the enormous sum of nine thousand pounds towards the subscriptions pouring in from all quarters, yet it afforded some a means of expressing their scorn of the movement. Thus we find a medical officer in Scutari writing to Sir John Hall, the Inspector-General of Hospitals in the Crimea:

> I hear that you have not (any more than myself) sub-scribed your day's pay to the Nightingale Fund. I certainly said, the moment it appeared in orders, I would not do so, and thereby countenance what I disapproved. Others may do as they please, but though Linton, Cruikshanks, and Lawson have all subscribed, I believe the subscriptions in the hospitals are not many or large.

Of the feelings to which this letter bears witness, Miss Nightingale had been conscious from the outset. She had not allowed it to wound her, or to deflect her in the least degree from the stedfast pursuit of what she accounted her duty. But she must have been at some pains, involving the exercise of infinite tact and forbearance, to avoid provoking it into manifestations which might have become embarrassing.

In the Crimea itself, at about this time (she was at Balaclava again in October and November of 1855), she was experiencing this official hostility. It was perceptible in various ways, and in none more deplorably than in the probably deliberate neglect of instructions left by her on the occasion of her former visit for the amelioration of conditions for the patients. It was necessary for her to become combative so as to prevail, and this very insistence which she was called upon to employ will have served further to sharpen the resentment.

"There is not," she wrote, "an official who would not burn me like Joan of Arc if he could, but they know that the War Office cannot turn me out because the country is with me."

Sir John Hall probably supplied the justification for that assertion. He had written angrily about "a system of detraction against our establishments, kept up by interested parties under the garb of philanthropy." When he spoke of "a system of detraction," he overstated grossly. There was no such system. There had been in *The Times* a frank exposure of the state of things for which Sir John was primarily responsible. This had stirred up a scandal which had led to Miss Nightingale's appointment, and this he regarded as a condemnation of his dispositions, without considering how condemnable they were. Sir John would seem to have been very human. He chose to ignore the control of the nurses vested in the Lady-in-Chief, and himself made transferences of nurses among the various hospitals in the Crimea. These arrangements did not meet with Miss Nightingale's approval, and friction resulted, which was in danger of completely undermining her authority with the nurses.

From Scutari, whither she returned at the end of November, in consequence of an outbreak there of cholera, she wrote stating her case to Sidney Herbert. Her letters, and perhaps more than her letters, the independent reports from Scutari at about that time made by Colonel Lefroy, soon produced the desired effect.

In this Colonel Lefroy the Lady-in-Chief found a new

and valuable ally. Sent out in October by Lord Panmure to report upon the hospitals, he formed and expressed of the work accomplished by Miss Nightingale so high an opinion that the Secretary of State for War had no hesitation in the action to be taken. Lefroy had frankly asserted that the medical men were jealous of her mission, and that Dr. Hall would gladly upset it; and he had invited Lord Panmure to define her position in a General Order.

When, at the end of the following March, Miss Nightingale returned to Balaclava, she found that her path had been considerably smoothed by the Secretary of State's adoption of Lefroy's suggestion. In a despatch to the Commander of the Forces, to be promulgated in General Orders, Lord Panmure had expressed himself as follows:

> It appears to me that the Medical Authorities of the Army do not correctly comprehend Miss Nightingale's position as it has been officially recognized by me. I therefore think it right to state to you briefly for their guidance, as well as for the information of the Army, what the position of that excellent lady is. Miss Nightingale is recognized by Her Majesty's Government as the General Superintendent of the Female Nursing Establishment of the military hospitals of the Army. No lady, or sister, or nurse, is to be transferred from one hospital to another, or introduced into any hospital, without consultation with her. Her instructions, however, require to have the approval of the Principal Medical Officer in the exercise of the responsibility thus vested in her. The Principal Medical Officer will communicate with Miss Nightingale upon all subjects connected with the Female Nursing Establishment, and will give his directions through that lady.

It came late, because the war was all but over. Peace was signed on the 30th of that month of March of 1856. But it was none the less effective for the hospital work that yet remained to be done, work which kept her in Balaclava until the beginning of July.

* * * *

Her labours during those her second and third visits to the Crimea, each of about two months' duration, were amongst the heaviest that she undertook, and this at a time when her health was no longer as robust as it had been before her attack of fever. There were four hospitals under her direction, and the distances separating them were considerable. She went her rounds in all weathers, chiefly on horseback and sometimes in a little hooded, springless cart, never sparing herself. Her work was in all respects similar to that which she had performed at Scutari; there was the same improvement of sanitation, the same establishment of special diet kitchens, the same care for the comfort and solace of the convalescents.

To sustain her now in all that she did, to give her strength to endure physical fatigue and courage to bear petty rancours, she had the consciousness of how completely her measures had succeeded, how justified had been her every endeavour. The facts were established statistically. During the first seven months of the Crimean campaign, the mortality amongst the troops from disease alone had been at the rate of sixty per cent per annum. During the last six months of that campaign, which was now ending, the mortality amongst the sick had been scarcely higher than the average among the healthy guards at home.

As time went on, and they entered the summer of 1856, her labours upon the aftermath of war grew ever lighter, and early in July she returned to Scutari, with little more to do than send home her nurses and wind up affairs.

Her situation at that moment could not be more beautifully expressed than it was by Lord Ellesmere in the House of Lords, in the course of moving the Address on the conclusion of peace:

> The angel of mercy still lingers to the last on the scene of her labours; but her mission is all but accomplished. Those long arcades of Scutari in which dying men sat up to catch the sound of her footstep or the flutter of her dress, and fell back content to have seen her shadow as it passed, are now comparatively deserted. She may probably be thinking how to escape as best she may, on her return, the demonstrations of a nation's appreciation of the deeds and motives of Florence Nightingale.

*   *   *   *

Lord Ellesmere had perfectly gauged her attitude towards the demonstrations that awaited her.

She was offered a battleship in which to return to England. She declined the offer, and travelled home overland from Marseilles. Threatened with a popular reception, which in her exhausted state she dreaded, she disguised an identity grown too famous for her comfort, under the name of Smith, and eluding bands, triumphal arches, military escorts, and other similar displays which were being held in readiness to give her welcome, she reached her Derbyshire home at Lea Hurst alone and unheralded on the 7th August, having quietly walked from the station.

*   *   *   *

The story of the Lady-in-Chief may be said to end here, with her return to England.

But this ending is also a beginning—a beginning of the building of the splendid edifice to which her Crimean mission laid the foundations and traced the lines.

Her health more or less permanently impaired by the unstinting manner in which she had spent herself in the East, she was nevertheless to live on for another half-century, a semi-invalid, often bedridden, yet indomitably devoting the undiminished energies of her mind to the beneficent application of the lessons her great experiment had taught.

Lord Stanley had indicated one aspect of this when he said:

> Mark what, by breaking through customs and prejudices, Miss Nightingale has effected for her sex. She has opened for them a new profession, a new sphere of usefulness. I do not suppose that in undertaking her mission, she thought much of the effect which it might have on the social position of women. Yet probably no one of those who made that question a special study has done half as much as she towards its settlement. A claim for more extended freedom of action, based on proved public usefulness in the highest sense of the word, with the whole nation to look on and bear witness, is one which must be listened to, and cannot easily be refused.

The life-task which she now made her own was of a two-fold nature. There was the application of that testimonial of the nation's gratitude, the Nightingale Fund, amounting to fifty thousand pounds. With this she founded the Nightingale Home for training nurses, at Saint Thomas's and King's College Hospitals. One of the most important of the many works and pamphlets that flowed from her pen during the years that were to follow was her *Notes on Nursing,* which may be regarded as the textbook of her training establishment. By these means she raised nursing, from a casual, slovenly, despised, and ill-recruited pursuit, into a dignified calling that demanded women of character, of education, and of intelligence to master its scientific qualifications.

The other and no less arduous branch of her labours was concerned with the improvement of the physical and moral conditions of the soldiers' life at home.

The urgent need for this was made more than plain by those Crimean statistics which showed that, once her hygienic and sanitary reforms had become effective at Scutari, the rate of mortality among the sick there was no higher than the rate among the healthy in the barracks in England. A further statistical investigation revealed that the death-rate in these barracks of vigorous men between the ages of twenty and thirty-five was nearly twice the death-rate between the same ages in civil life. There could be no more terrible indictment of the conditions prevailing in the British barracks. To combat these, Miss Nightingale applied herself with the same zeal and enthusiasm which had distinguished her in the Levant. It was a difficult task for a woman; it would have been impossible to any woman less accredited by accomplishment. To her it was rendered comparatively easy by the assistance of her friend Sidney Herbert, who shared her interest in the soldiers' welfare. It was the collaboration between them, in which she was the guiding spirit, he the speaking voice, which gradually overcame administrative inertia and brought about reform.

She gathered authority not only from the national faith in her, but also from the royal favour she enjoyed. Some marks of Queen Victoria's appreciation of her work she had received whilst abroad. There was a more direct and signal one to follow soon upon her return.

Sir James Clark, who was Queen Victoria's physician, was a friend of her father's, and one from whom she had received encouragement in the days when she was still battling against prejudice. He wrote to her when she had been home a fortnight, to invite her to Birk Hall, his place near Ballater, with which she was already acquainted. It would be good for her health, and the Queen, who was aware of the invitation, would shortly be at Balmoral, and would wish to see her.

She accepted, perhaps the more eagerly because she perceived here an opportunity to further the work she saw was still to do. She was at Birk Hall in mid-September, and was almost immediately presented by Sir James to the Queen and the Prince Consort at Balmoral. A few days later she was sought by the Queen at Birk Hall for a further protracted interview on the subject of her hopes and future endeavours for the soldiers' welfare.

It is recorded by the Prince Consort in his Diary:

> She put before us all the defects of our present military hospital system, and the reforms that are needed. We are much pleased with her. She is extremely modest.

On her side, she had every reason to consider the interviews satisfactory. The Queen opened a door for her, by retaining her at Ballater, to see Lord Panmure. To his lordship, meanwhile, her Majesty wrote:

> Lord Panmure will be much gratified and struck with Miss Nightingale—her powerful, clear head, and simple, modest manner.

Thus, under the royal ægis, she set about a beneficent work, at which, side by side with the direction of the Nightingale Home for nurses, she was to toil assiduously, and in the course of which she permitted no prejudices, no difficulties, no ministerial inertia to discourage her.

She was rightly regarded as the greatest living authority

on hospital administration, and in this capacity she was consulted down the years. Her fame grew to international proportions, and she was officially consulted by the Americans during the Civil War.

Ten years after the Crimea, the Secretary of the United States Christian Communion was writing to her:

> Everywhere throughout our broad country, during these years of inventive and earnest benevolence, in the constant endeavour to succour and sustain our heroic defenders, the name and work of Florence Nightingale have been an encouragement and inspiration.

She was consulted also by the French on the administration of military hospitals during the Franco-Prussian War.

In 1907, by when she was an old lady approaching ninety, King Edward VII bestowed upon her the Order of Merit, "in recognition of invaluable services to the country and to humanity," and in the following year the Freedom of the City of London was bestowed upon her. She was the second woman in history to receive the latter honour, and the first ever to receive the former. But by the time these honours reached her—three years before her death, at the age of ninety—her memory and her eyesight were fading, and it is doubtful if she fully apprehended their significance; doubtful, indeed, if, had she been fully apprehensive of them, they would have brought her a higher satisfaction than she had derived from the sense of having accomplished the work to which, with heroic self-abnegation, she had devoted her life.

THE END